Inefficient Markets

An Introduction to Behavioral Finance

ANDREI SHLEIFER

OXFORD

UNIVERSITY PRESS

OXFORD

UNIVERSITY PRESS

Great Clarendon Street, Oxford OX2 6DP

Oxford University Press is a department of the University of Oxford.
It furthers the University's objective of excellence in research, scholarship,
and education by publishing worldwide in

Oxford New York

Athens Auckland Bangkok Bogotá Buenos Aires Calcutta
Cape Town Chennai Dar es Salaam Delhi Florence Hong Kong Istanbul
Karachi Kuala Lumpur Madrid Melbourne Mexico City Mumbai
Nairobi Paris São Paulo Shanghai Singapore Taipei Tokyo Toronto Warsaw

with associated companies in Berlin Ibadan

Oxford is a registered trade mark of Oxford University Press
in the UK and in certain other countries

Published in the United States
by Oxford University Press Inc., New York

© Andrei Shleifer, 2000

The moral rights of the author have been asserted
Database right Oxford University Press (maker)

First published 2000

British Library Cataloguing in Publication Data

A catalogue record for this book is available from the British Library

Library of Congress Cataloging in Publication Data
Shleifer, Andrei.
Inefficient markets : an introduction to behavioral finance / Andrei Shleifer.
p. cm.—(Clarendon lectures in economics)
Includes bibliographical references and index.
1. Finance. 2. Investments. 3. Stocks—Prices. 4. Efficient market theory. I. Title.
II. Series.
HG4515.S54 1999 332.6—dc21 99–057647
ISBN 0–19–829228–7 (Hbk)
ISBN 0–19–829227–9 (Pbk)

5 7 9 10 8 6 4

Typeset by J&L Composition Ltd, Filey, North Yorkshire
Printed in Great Britain
on acid-free paper by Biddles Ltd
Guildford and King's Lynn

For Nancy

Contents

Acknowledgments

This book grows out of the Clarendon Lectures given at Oxford in the Spring of 1996. I appreciate the hospitality of Oxford University Press and its economics editor, Andrew Schuller.

I started working on the efficiency of financial markets as a graduate student in the mid-1980s. At the time, there were only a handful of academic papers in behavioral finance, written by people like Robert Shiller, Larry Summers, and Richard Thaler. The assessment by financial economists of this research was not especially generous. Nonetheless, the area seemed to me to be incredibly exciting. During graduate school, I wrote a paper on stock inclusions into the S&P 500 Index and started on a series of theoretical projects with Brad De Long, Larry Summers, and Robert Waldmann. Behavioral finance experienced an upsurge of research in the late 1980s. I had intended to write a book about it while visiting the Russell Sage Foundation in 1992, but that plan did not materialize. In some ways, this is fortunate, since much work has been done in this area since then. I am still very grateful to the Russell Sage Foundation for getting me started.

During the 1990s, I have worked on a number of projects with Josef Lakonishok and Robert Vishny, both of whom have greatly contributed to the material presented in this book. I also learned a lot about arbitrage from Gabe Sunshine and Nancy Zimmerman, who introduced me to some fascinating analytical issues which arise from a more practical understanding of markets. The invitation to give the Clarendon Lectures came at a perfect moment and allowed me to write this book. I am finally finishing it during a sabbatical year at the Massachusetts Institute of Technology, which both kindly hosted me and encouraged me to present some chapters as Independent Activities Period lectures.

Many of the chapters draw heavily on my joint research with a number of colleagues. Chapter 2 draws on 'Noise Trader Risk in Financial Markets,' written with Brad De Long, Lawrence

Summers, and Robert Waldmann and published in the *Journal of Political Economy* in 1990. Chapter 3 is based on 'Investor Sentiment and the Closed End Fund Puzzle,' written with Charles Lee and Richard Thaler and published in the *Journal of Finance* in 1991. Chapter 4 borrows heavily from 'The Limits of Arbitrage,' written with Robert Vishny and published in the *Journal of Finance* in 1997. Chapter 5 follows 'A Model of Investor Sentiment,' written with Nicholas Barberis and Robert Vishny and published in the *Journal of Financial Economics* in 1998. Chapter 6 uses material from 'Positive Feedback Investment Strategies and Destabilizing Rational Speculation,' written with Brad De Long, Lawrence Summers, and Robert Waldmann and published in the *Journal of Finance* in 1990. While I have borrowed liberally from these articles, I have equally liberally added and subtracted material. I am grateful to all my co-authors for years of collaboration.

I was fortunate to receive many extremely perceptive comments on this book from Nicholas Barberis, Olivier Blanchard, John Campbell, Edward Glaeser, Paul Gompers, Oliver Hart, Simon Johnson, Daniel Kahneman, David Laibson, Rafael La Porta, Florencio Lopez-de-Silanes, Andrew Metrick, Sendhil Mullainathan, Michael Rashes, Lawrence Summers, Richard Thaler, Daniel Wolfenzon, and Jeff Wurgler. Their comments had a significant impact on the final draft. Nicholas Barberis and David Laibson were particularly helpful. I am also very grateful to Clare MacLean, who worked tirelessly to get this book out the door, and to Malcolm Baker for preparing the index.

My two greatest debts, however, are to Larry Summers and Nancy Zimmerman. Larry got me started as an economist and introduced me to behavioral finance. He has been a shining example in many ways. Nancy's insight into financial markets is always inspiring. This book is dedicated to her.

1

Are Financial Markets Efficient?

THE efficient markets hypothesis (EMH) has been the central proposition of finance for nearly thirty years. In his classic statement of this hypothesis, Fama (1970) defined an efficient financial market as one in which security prices always fully reflect the available information. The efficient markets hypothesis then states that real-world financial markets, such as the U.S. bond or stock market, are actually efficient according to this definition. The power of this statement is dazzling. Perhaps most radically, the EMH 'rules out the possibility of trading systems based only on currently available information that have expected profits or returns in excess of equilibrium expected profit or return' (Fama 1970). In plain English, an average investor—whether an individual, a pension fund, or a mutual fund—cannot hope to consistently beat the market, and the vast resources that such investors dedicate to analyzing, picking, and trading securities are wasted. Better to passively hold the market portfolio, and to forget active money management altogether. If the EMH holds, the market truly knows best.

In the first decade after its conception in the 1960s, the EMH turned into an enormous theoretical and empirical success. Academics developed powerful theoretical reasons why the hypothesis should hold. More impressively, a vast array of empirical findings quickly emerged—nearly all of them supporting the hypothesis. Indeed, the field of academic finance in general, and security analysis in particular, was created on the basis of the EMH and its applications. The University of Chicago, where the EMH was invented, justly became the world's center of academic finance. In 1978, Michael Jensen—a Chicago graduate and one of the creators of the EMH—declared that 'there is no other proposition in economics which has more solid empirical evidence supporting it than the Efficient Markets Hypothesis' (Jensen 1978, p. 95).

Such strong statements portend reversals, and the EMH is no exception. In the last twenty years, both the theoretical foundations of the EMH and the empirical evidence purporting to support it have been challenged. The key forces by which markets are supposed to attain efficiency, such as arbitrage, are likely to be much weaker and more limited than the efficient markets theorists have supposed. Moreover, new studies of security prices have reversed some of the earlier evidence favoring the EMH. With the new theory and evidence, behavioral finance has emerged as an alternative view of financial markets. In this view, economic theory does not lead us to expect financial markets to be efficient. Rather, systematic and significant deviations from efficiency are expected to persist for long periods of time. Empirically, behavioral finance both explains the evidence that appears anomalous from the efficient markets perspective, and generates new predictions that have been confirmed in the data.

This book introduces the research in behavioral finance. In this opening chapter, we describe both the theoretical and the empirical foundations of the EMH, as well as some of the cracks that have emerged in these foundations.

The theoretical foundations of the EMH

The basic theoretical case for the EMH rests on three arguments which rely on progressively weaker assumptions. First, investors are assumed to be rational and hence to value securities rationally. Second, to the extent that some investors are not rational, their trades are random and therefore cancel each other out without affecting prices. Third, to the extent that investors are irrational in similar ways, they are met in the market by rational arbitrageurs who eliminate their influence on prices.

When investors are rational, they value each security for its fundamental value: the net present value of its future cash flows, discounted using their risk characteristics. When investors learn something about fundamental values of securities, they quickly respond to the new information by bidding up prices when the news is good and bidding them down when the news is bad. As a consequence, security prices incorporate all the available information almost immediately and prices adjust to new levels corresponding to the new net present values of cash flows. Samuelson (1965) and Mandelbrot (1966) proved some of the first theorems showing how, in competitive markets with rational risk-neutral investors, returns are unpredictable—security values and prices follow random walks. Since then, economists have characterized efficient securities prices for risk-averse investors, with both varying levels of risk over time and varying tolerances toward risk. In these more complicated models security prices are no longer predicted to follow random walks. Still, investor rationality implies the impossibility of earning superior risk-adjusted returns, just as Fama wrote in 1970. The EMH is thus first and foremost a consequence of equilibrium in competitive markets with fully rational investors.

But remarkably, the EMH does not live or die by investor rationality. In many scenarios where some investors are not fully rational, markets are still predicted to be efficient. In one commonly discussed case, the irrational investors in the market trade randomly. When there are large numbers of such investors, and when their trading strategies are uncorrelated, their trades are likely to cancel each other out. In such a market, there will be substantial trading volume as the irrational investors exchange securities with each other, but the prices are nonetheless close to fundamental values. This argument relies crucially on the lack of correlation in the strategies of the irrational investors, and, for that reason, is quite limited. The case for the EMH, however, can be made even in situations where the trading strategies of investors are correlated.

This case, as made by Milton Friedman (1953) and Fama (1965), is based on arbitrage. It is one of the most intuitively appealing and plausible arguments in all of economics. A textbook definition (Sharpe and Alexander 1990) defines arbitrage as 'the simultaneous purchase and sale of the same, or essentially similar, security in two different markets at advantageously different prices.' Suppose that some security, say a stock, becomes overpriced in a market relative to its fundamental value as a result of correlated purchases by unsophisticated, or irrational, investors. This security now represents a bad buy, since its price exceeds the properly risk adjusted net present value of its cash flows or dividends. Noting this overpricing, smart investors, or arbitrageurs, would sell or even sell short this expensive security and simultaneously purchase other, 'essentially similar,' securities to hedge their risks. If such substitute securities are available and arbitrageurs are able to trade them, they can earn a profit, since they are short expensive securities and long the same, or very similar, but cheaper securities. The effect of this selling by arbitrageurs is to bring the price of the overpriced security down to its fundamental value. In fact, if arbitrage is quick and effective enough because substitute securities are readily available and the arbitrageurs are competing with each other to earn profits, the price of a security can never get far away from its fundamental value, and indeed arbitrageurs themselves are unable to earn much of an abnormal return. A similar argument applies to an undervalued security. To earn a profit, arbitrageurs would buy underpriced securities and sell short essentially similar securities to hedge their risk, thereby preventing the underpricing from being either substantial or very long-lasting. The process of arbitrage brings security prices in line with their fundamental values even when some investors are not fully rational and their demands are correlated, as long as securities have close substitutes.

Arbitrage has a further implication. To the extent that the securities that the irrational investors are buying are overpriced and the securities they are getting rid of are underpriced, such investors earn lower returns than either passive investors or arbitrageurs. Relative to their peers, irrational investors lose money. As Friedman (1953) points out, they cannot lose money forever: they must become much less wealthy and eventually disappear from the market. If arbitrage does not eliminate their influence on asset prices instantaneously, market forces eliminate their wealth. In the long run, market efficiency prevails because of competitive selection and arbitrage.

It is difficult not to be impressed with the full range and power of the theoretical arguments for efficient markets. When people are rational, markets are efficient by definition. When some people are irrational, much or all of their trading is with each other, and hence has only a limited influence on prices even without countervailing trading by the rational investors. But such countervailing trading does exist and works to bring prices closer to fundamental values. Competition between arbitrageurs for superior returns ensures that the adjustment of prices to fundamental values is very quick. Finally, to the extent that the irrational investors do manage to transact at prices that are different from fundamental values, they only hurt themselves and bring about their own demise. Not only investor rationality, but market forces themselves bring about the efficiency of financial markets.

The empirical foundations of the EMH

Strong as the theoretical case for the EMH may seem, the empirical evidence that appeared in the 1960s and the 1970s was even more overwhelming. At the most general level, the empirical predictions of the EMH can be divided into two broad categories. First, when news about the value of a security hits the market, its price should react and incorporate this news both quickly and correctly. The 'quickly' part means that those who receive the news late—for instance by reading it in the newspapers or in company reports—should not be able to profit from this information. The 'correctly' part means that the price adjustment in response to the news should be accurate on average: the prices should neither underreact nor overreact to particular news announcements. There should be neither price trends nor price reversals following the initial impact of the news. Second, since a security's price must be equal to its value, prices should not move without any news about the value of the security. That is, prices should not react to changes in demand or supply of a security that are not accompanied by news about its fundamental value. The quick and accurate reaction of security prices to information, as well as the non-reaction to non-information, are the two broad predictions of the efficient markets hypothesis.

The principal hypothesis following from quick and accurate reaction of prices to new information is that stale information is of no value in making money, as Fama (1970) points out. To evaluate this hypothesis empirically, researchers needed to define 'stale information' and 'making money.' The first definition turns out to be relatively straightforward. Defining 'making money,' in contrast, is enormously controversial. The reason is that 'making money' in finance means making a superior return after an adjustment for risk. Showing that a particular strategy based on exploiting stale information on average earns a positive cash flow over some period of time is not, therefore, by itself evidence of market inefficiency. To earn this profit, an investor may have to bear risk and his profit may just be a fair market compensation for risk-bearing. The trouble is that measuring the risk of a particular investment strategy is both difficult and controversial, and requires a model of the fair relationship between risk and return. One widely-accepted model is the Capital Asset Pricing Model (Sharpe 1964), but it is not the only possibility. The dependence of most tests of market efficiency on a model of risk and expected return is Fama's (1970) deepest insight, which has pervaded the debates in empirical finance ever since. Whenever researchers have found a money-making opportunity resulting from trading on stale information, critics have been quick to suggest a model of risk—convincing or otherwise—that would reduce these profits to a fair compensation for risk-taking.

The definition of stale information is far less controversial. Fama distinguishes between three types of stale information, giving rise to three forms of the EMH. For the so-called *weak form* efficiency, the relevant stale information is past prices and returns. The weak form EMH posits that it is impossible to earn superior risk-adjusted profits based on the knowledge of past prices and returns. Under the assumption of risk neutrality, this version of the EMH reduces to the random walk hypothesis, the statement that stock returns are entirely unpredictable based on past returns (Fama 1965).

Past returns are not the only stale information that investors have. The *semi-strong form* of the EMH states that investors cannot earn superior risk-adjusted returns using *any* publicly available information. Put differently, as soon as information becomes public, it is immediately incorporated into prices, and hence an investor cannot gain by using this information to predict returns. A semi-strong form efficient market is obviously weak form efficient as well, since past prices and returns are a proper subset of the publicly available information about a security.

It is still possible that while an investor cannot profit from trading on publicly available information, he can still earn abnormal risk-adjusted profits by trading on information that is not yet known to market participants, sometimes described as inside information. The *strong form* of the EMH states that even these profits are impossible because the insiders' information quickly leaks out and is incorporated into prices. To be fair, most evaluations of the EMH have focused on weak and semi-strong form efficiency, and have not taken the extreme position that there is no such thing as profitable insider trading, as would be required if the strong form EMH were to hold. Indeed, the insider traders occupying minimum security prisons for making illegal profits themselves represent some evidence against the strong form EMH. But there is more systematic evidence as well that insiders earn some abnormal returns even when they trade completely legally (Seyhun 1998, Jeng *et al.* 1999).

When economists have set out to test these predictions, their evidence was broadly supportive of the EMH. With respect to weak form efficiency, Fama (1965) finds that stock prices indeed approximately follow random walks. He finds no systematic evidence of profitability of 'technical' trading strategies, such as buying stocks when their prices just went up or selling them when their prices just went down. On a given day, the price of a stock is as likely to rise after a previous day's increase as after a previous day's decline. Early tests of more complicated trading rules have yielded similar failures to earn profits on average by predicting returns based on past returns, consistent with the weak form EMH.

The initial tests corroborated semi-strong form efficiency as well. One testing strategy is to look at particular news events pertaining to individual companies and to ask whether prices adjusted to this news immediately or over a period of a few days. These so-called *event studies*, pioneered by Fama *et al.* (1969), became the principal methodology of empirical finance, as multitudes of important corporate news events, such as earnings and dividend announcements, takeovers and divestitures, share issues and repurchases, changes in management compensation, and so on, came to be evaluated empirically through the effects of these news events on share prices. As an illustration, consider the study by Keown and Pinkerton (1981) of returns to targets of takeover bids around the announcement of the bid. The results for returns of an average target, adjusted for market movements, are reproduced in Figure 1.1. They show that share prices of targets begin to rise prior to the announcement of the bid as the news of a possible bid is incorporated into prices, and then jump on the date of the public announcement to reflect the takeover premium offered to target firm shareholders. But the jump in share prices on the announcement is not followed by a continued trend up or a reversal down, indicating that prices of takeover targets adjust

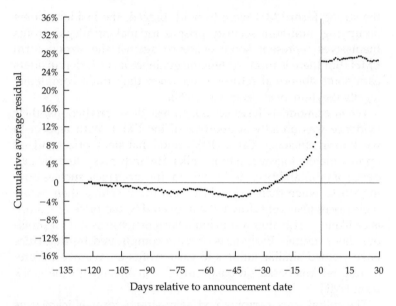

FIG. 1.1 Cumulative abnormal returns to shareholders of targets of takeover attempts around the announcement date.
Source: Keown and Pinkerton (1981).

to the public news of the bid instantaneously, consistent with the semi-strong form EMH.

Taken together, the early evidence on weak and semi-strong form market efficiency was almost entirely supportive. The same was also the case with the other implication of the EMH, namely that prices do not react to non-information. In the principal early empirical study of this proposition, Scholes (1972) uses the event study methodology to evaluate share price reactions to sales of large blocks of shares in individual companies by substantial stockholders. Scholes's work is particularly important because it deals directly with the issue central to the arbitrage arguments in the efficient markets theory: the availability of close substitutes for individual securities. An exact substitute for a given security is another security (or portfolio of securities) with identical cash flows in all states of the world. A close substitute is a security (or portfolio) with very similar cash flows in all states of the world, and therefore with similar risk characteristics to those of a given security. The availability of close substitutes for a given security, closely related to the assumption of complete markets, is essential for the working of arbitrage because it allows for more than one way to get a given pattern of cash flows in different states of the world.

Scholes reasons that when arbitrage is needed to make markets efficient, individual stocks must have close substitutes for such arbitrage to work well. When close substitutes are available, arbitrageurs can sell expensive securities and buy cheap close substitutes, thereby equalizing their relative prices and bringing markets to efficiency. When close substitutes are not available, arbitrageurs cannot make such trades. When stocks do have close substitutes, investors are indifferent as to which stocks with a given set of risk characteristics to hold. Sales of large blocks of shares—particularly if made by uninformed sellers—should not have a material impact on the stock price because that price is determined by the stock's value relative to that of its close substitutes rather than by supply. Scholes's argument, which he calls the substitution hypothesis, is virtually identical to the arbitrage argument for market efficiency. When a seller unloads a block of shares on the market, other investors would gladly increase their holdings of that stock a bit in exchange for only a trivial, if any, price concession, and perhaps reduce their holdings of close substitutes to keep the risk of their portfolio constant. Competition between these potential buyers assures that the price concession that an uninformed seller must give them is small.

In his study, Scholes finds relatively small share price reactions to block sales. He accounts for these reactions by the possible, but small, adverse news revealed by the decision of large blockholders to sell their shares. On Scholes's interpretation, this result is consistent with the substitution hypothesis, and therefore with the second crucial prediction of the EMH, namely that stock prices do not react to non-information. More importantly, the non-reaction of prices to non-information points to arbitrage in action: the willingness of investors to adjust their portfolios to absorb more shares without a large influence on the price.

As matters stood at the end of the 1970s, the EMH was indeed one of the great triumphs of twentieth-century economics. Standard economic theory—particularly the theory of arbitrage—predicted that financial markets were efficient. Mountains of empirical evidence based on some of the most extensive data available in economics, that on security prices, almost universally confirmed the predictions of the theory. Whenever researchers found small money-making opportunities, they could be easily explained away by a variety of arguments, the most pervasive of which was the failure to adjust properly for risk. At the time, Jensen's claim about the best established fact in economics was not all that outrageous.

Theoretical challenges to the EMH

Shortly after Jensen's pronouncement, the EMH was challenged on both theoretical and empirical grounds. Although the initial challenges were primarily empirical, it is easier to begin by reviewing some potential difficulties with the theoretical case for the EMH and then turn to the evidence. This chapter only highlights the principal challenges. They are developed in the rest of the book.

To begin, it is difficult to sustain the case that people in general, and investors in particular, are fully rational. At the superficial level, many investors react to irrelevant information in forming their demand for securities; as Fischer Black (1986) put it, they trade on noise rather than information. Investors follow the advice of financial gurus, fail to diversify, actively trade stocks and churn their portfolios, sell winning stocks and hold on to losing stocks thereby increasing their tax liabilities, buy and sell actively and expensively managed mutual funds, follow stock price patterns and other popular models. In short, investors hardly pursue the passive strategies expected of uninformed market participants by the efficient markets theory.

This evidence of what investors actually do is only the tip of the iceberg. Investors' deviations from the maxims of economic rationality turn out to be highly pervasive and systematic. As summarized by Kahneman and Riepe (1998), people deviate from the standard decision making model in a number of fundamental areas. We can group these areas, somewhat simplistically, into three broad categories: attitudes toward risk, non-Bayesian expectation formation, and sensitivity of decision making to the framing of problems.

First, individuals do not assess risky gambles following the precepts of von Neumann–Morgenstern rationality. Rather, in assessing such gambles, people look not at the levels of final wealth they can attain but at gains and losses relative to some reference point, which may vary from situation to situation, and display loss aversion—a loss function that is steeper than a gain function. Such preferences—first described and modeled by Kahneman and Tversky (1979) in their 'Prospect Theory'—are helpful for thinking about a number of problems in finance. One of them is the notorious reluctance of investors to sell stocks that lose value, which comes out of loss aversion (Odean 1998). Another is investors' aversion to holding stocks more generally, known as the equity premium puzzle (Mehra and Prescott 1985, Benartzi and Thaler 1995).

Second, individuals systematically violate Bayes rule and other maxims of probability theory in their predictions of uncertain outcomes (Kahneman and Tversky 1973). For example, people often predict future uncertain events by taking a short history of data and asking what broader picture this history is representative of. In focusing on such representativeness, they often do not pay enough attention to the possibility that the recent history is generated by chance rather than by the 'model' they are constructing. Such heuristics are useful in many life situations—they help people to identify patterns in the data as well as to save on computation—but they may lead investors seriously astray. For example, investors may extrapolate short past histories of rapid earnings growth of some companies too far into the future and therefore overprice these glamorous companies without a recognition that, statistically speaking, trees do not grow to the sky. Such overreaction lowers future returns as past growth rates fail to repeat themselves and prices adjust to more plausible valuations.

Perhaps most radically, individuals make different choices depending on how a given problem is presented to them, so that framing influences decisions. In choosing investments, for example, investors allocate more of their wealth to stocks rather than bonds when they see a very impressive history of *long-term* stock returns relative to those on bonds, than if they only see the volatile *short-term* stock returns (Benartzi and Thaler 1995).

A number of terms have been used to describe investors whose preferences and beliefs conform to the psychological evidence rather than the normative economic model. Beliefs based on heuristics rather than Bayesian rationality are sometimes called 'investor sentiment.' Less kindly, the investors whose conduct is not rational according to the normative model are described as 'unsophisticated' or, following Kyle (1985) and Black (1986), as 'noise traders.'

If the theory of efficient markets relied entirely on the rationality of individual investors, then the psychological evidence would by itself present an extremely serious, perhaps fatal, problem for the theory. But of course it does not. Recall that the second line of defense of the efficient markets theory is that the irrational investors, while they may exist, trade randomly, and hence their trades cancel each other out. It is this argument that the Kahneman and Tversky theories dispose of entirely. The psychological evidence shows precisely that people do not deviate from rationality randomly, but rather most deviate in the same way. To the extent that unsophisticated investors form their demands for securities based on their own beliefs, buying and selling would be highly correlated across investors. Investors would not trade randomly with each other, but rather many of them would try to buy the same securities or to sell the same securities at roughly the same time. This problem only becomes more severe when the noise traders behave socially and follow each others' mistakes by listening to rumors or imitating their neighbors (Shiller 1984). Investor sentiment reflects the common judgment errors made by a substantial number of investors, rather than uncorrelated random mistakes.

Individuals are not the only investors whose trading strategies are difficult to reconcile with rationality. Much of the money in financial markets is allocated by professional managers of pension and mutual funds on behalf of individual investors and corporations. Professional money managers are of course themselves people, and as such are subject to the same biases as individual investors. But they are also agents who manage other people's money, and this delegation introduces further distortions into their decisions relative to what fully-informed sponsors might wish (Lakonishok *et al.* 1992). For example, professional managers may choose portfolios that are excessively close to the benchmark that they are evaluated against, such as the S&P 500 Index, so as to minimize the risk of underperforming this benchmark. They may also herd and select stocks that other managers select, again to avoid falling behind and looking bad (Scharfstein and Stein 1990). They may artificially add to their portfolios stocks that have recently done well, and sell stocks that have recently done poorly, to look good to investors who are getting end-of-year reports on portfolio holdings. There indeed appears to be some evidence of such window-dressing by pension fund managers (Lakonishok *et al.* 1991). Consistent with the presence of costly investment distortions, pension and mutual fund managers on average underperform passive investment strategies (Ippolito 1989, Lakonishok *et al.* 1992). In some situations, they may be the relevant noise traders.

This brings us to the ultimate set of theoretical arguments for efficient markets, those based on arbitrage. Even if sentiment is correlated across unsophisticated investors, the arbitrageurs— who perhaps are not subject to psychological biases—should take the other side of unsophisticated demand and bring prices back to fundamental values. Ultimately, the theoretical case for efficient markets depends on the effectiveness of such arbitrage.

The central argument of behavioral finance states that, in contrast to the efficient markets theory, real-world arbitrage is risky and therefore limited. As we already noted, the effectiveness of arbitrage relies crucially on the availability of close substitutes for securities whose price is potentially affected by noise trading. To lay off their risks, arbitrageurs who sell or sell short overpriced securities must be able to buy 'the same or essentially similar' securities that are not overpriced. For some so-called derivative securities, such as futures and options, close substitutes are usually available, although arbitrage may still require considerable trading. For example, the S&P 500 Index futures typically sell at a price close to the value of the underlying basket of stocks, since if the future sells at a price different from the basket, an arbitrageur can always buy whichever is cheaper and sell whichever is more expensive against it, locking in a safe profit. Yet in many instances, securities do not have obvious substitutes. Thus arbitrage does not help to pin down price levels of, say, stocks and bonds as a whole (Figlewski 1979, Campbell and Kyle 1993). These broad classes of securities do not have substitute portfolios, and therefore if for some reason they are mispriced, there is no riskless hedge for the arbitrageur. An arbitrageur who thinks that stocks as a whole are overpriced cannot sell short stocks and buy a substitute portfolio, since such a portfolio does not exist. The arbitrageur can instead simply sell or reduce exposure to stocks in the hope of an above-market return, but this arbitrage is no longer even approximately risk-less, especially since the average expected return on stocks is high and positive (Siegel 1998). If the arbitrageur is risk-averse, his interest in such arbitrage will be limited. With a finite risk-bearing capacity of arbitrageurs as a group, their aggregate ability to bring prices of broad groups of securities into line is limited as well.

Even when individual securities have better substitutes than does the market as a whole, fundamental risk remains a significant deterrent to arbitrage. First, such substitutes may not be perfect, even for individual stocks. An arbitrageur taking bets on relative price movements then bears idiosyncratic risk that the news about the securities he is short will be surprisingly good, or the news about the securities he is long will be surprisingly bad. Suppose, for example, that the arbitrageur is convinced that the shares of Ford are expensive relative to those of General Motors and Chrysler. If he sells short Ford and loads up on some combination of GM and Chrysler, he may be able to lay off the general risk of the automobile industry, but he remains exposed to the possibility that Ford does surprisingly well and GM or Chrysler do surprisingly poorly, leading to arbitrage losses. With imperfect substitutes, arbitrage becomes risky. Such trading is commonly referred to as 'risk arbitrage,' because it focuses on the statistical likelihood, as opposed to the certainty, of convergence of relative prices.

There is a further important source of risk for an arbitrageur, which he faces even when securities do have perfect substitutes. This risk comes from the unpredictability of the future resale price or, put differently, from the possibility that mispricing becomes worse before it disappears. Even with two securities that are fundamentally identical, the expensive security may become even more expensive and the cheap security may become even cheaper. Even if the prices of the two securities ultimately converge with probability one, the trade may lead to temporary losses for an arbitrageur. If the arbitrageur can maintain his positions through such losses, he can still count on a positive return from his trade. But sometimes he cannot maintain his position through the losses. In the cases where arbitrageurs need to worry about financing and maintaining their position when price divergence can become worse before it gets better, arbitrage is again limited. This type of risk, which De Long *et al.* (1990*a*) dubbed 'noise trader risk,' shows that even an arbitrage that looks nearly perfect from the outside is in reality quite risky and therefore likely to be limited. As a consequence, the arbitrage-based theoretical case for efficient markets is limited as well—even for securities that do have fundamentally close substitutes.

An example may help illustrate the idea of risky and limited arbitrage. Consider the case of American stocks, particularly the large capitalization stocks, in the late 1990s. At the end of 1998, large American corporations were trading at some of their historically highest market values relative to most measures of their profitability. For example, the ratio of the market value of the S&P 500 basket of stocks to the aggregate earnings of the underlying companies stood at around 32, compared to the post-war average of 15. Both distinguished financial economists, such as Campbell and Shiller (1998) and leading policy makers such as Federal Reserve Chairman Alan Greenspan, called attention to these possibly excessive valuations of large capitalization American stocks as early as 1996. But their warnings are contradicted by the assessments of the new financial gurus, such as Abby Joseph Cohen of Goldman Sachs, who argue that large American companies are operating in a new world of faster growth and lower risk and hence rationally warrant higher valuations. In 1929, Irving Fisher similarly argued that 'stock prices have reached a new and higher plateau,' just before the market tanked and the economy plunged into the Great Depression.

But what is an arbitrageur to do? If he sold short the S&P 500 Index at the beginning of 1998, when the price earnings multiple on the Index was at an already high level of 24, he would have suffered a loss of 28.6 percent by year end. In fact, if he sold short early on when the experts got worried, at the beginning of 1997, he would have lost 33.4 percent that year before losing another 28.6 percent the next. If he followed a more sophisticated strategy of selling short the S&P 500 at the beginning of 1998 and buying the Russell 2000 Index of smaller companies as a hedge on the theory that their valuations by historical standards were not nearly as extreme, he would have lost 30.8 percent by the end of the year. Because the S&P 500 Index does not have good substitutes and relative prices of imperfect substitutes can move even further out of line, arbitrage of the Index is extremely risky. An arbitrageur who tried to exploit this apparent mispricing is unlikely still to be in business. Not surprisingly, very few arbitrageurs or even speculators have put on such trades. In the meantime, the puzzle of the overvaluation of large stocks as well as the market as a whole has only deepened.

Once it is recognized that arbitrage is risky, Friedman's selection arguments become questionable. When both noise traders and arbitrageurs are bearing risk, the expected returns of the different types depend on the amount of risk they bear and on the compensation for the risk that the market offers. Moreover, even if the average returns of the arbitrageurs exceed those of the noise traders, the former are not necessarily the ones more likely to get rich, and the latter impoverished, in the long run. Consider two illustrations. First, if the misjudgments of the noise traders cause them to take on more risk, and if risk taking is on average rewarded with higher average returns, then the noise traders may earn even higher average returns despite their portfolio selection errors. Second, there is an 'optimal' amount of risk taking for long-run survival. A risk-neutral investor, for example, may earn very high expected returns, but end up bankrupt with near certainty (Merton and Samuelson 1974). Some types of noise traders may have as good as or better chances of maintaining their wealth above a certain level in the long run as the arbitrageurs, simply because they bear the superior amount of risk from the perspective of survival. The point here is not to make descriptive statements, but rather to point out that the theoretical case for the irrelevance of irrationality for financial markets is far from watertight.

The bottom line of this work is that theory by itself does not inevitably lead a researcher to a presumption of market efficiency. At the very least, theory leaves a researcher with an open mind on the crucial issues.

Empirical challenges to the EMH

Chronologically, the empirical challenges to the EMH have preceded the theoretical ones. An early and historically important challenge is Shiller's (1981) work on stock market volatility, which showed that stock market prices are far more volatile than could be justified by a simple model in which these prices are equal to the expected net present value of future dividends. Shiller computed this net present value using a constant discount rate and some specific assumptions about the dividend process, and his work became a target of objections that he misspecified the fundamental value (e.g., Merton 1987b). Nonetheless, Shiller's work has pointed the way to a whole new area of research.

Consider first the weak form EMH: the proposition that an investor cannot make excess profits using past price information. De Bondt and Thaler (1985) compare the performance of two groups of companies: extreme losers and extreme winners. For each year since 1933, they form portfolios of the best and the worst performing stocks over the previous three years. They then compute the returns on these portfolios over the five years following portfolio formation. The results on the average performance of these loser and winner portfolios, presented in Figure 1.2, point to extremely high post-formation returns of extreme losers and relatively poor returns of extreme winners. This difference in returns is not explained by the greater riskiness of the extreme losers, at least using standard risk adjustments such as the Capital Asset Pricing Model. An alternative explanation of this evidence, advanced by De Bondt and Thaler, is that stock

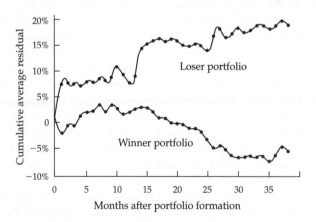

FIG. 1.2 Cumulative average residuals for winner and loser portfolios of 35 stocks (1–36 months into the test period).
Source: De Bondt and Thaler (1985).

prices overreact: the extreme losers have become too cheap and bounce back, on average, over the post-formation period, whereas the extreme winners have become too expensive and earn lower subsequent returns. This explanation fits well with psychological theory: the extreme losers are typically companies with several years of poor news, which investors are likely to extrapolate into the future, thereby undervaluing these firms, and the extreme winners are typically companies with several years of good news, inviting overvaluation.

Subsequent to De Bondt and Thaler's findings, researchers have identified more ways to successfully predict security returns, particularly those of stocks, based on past returns. Among these findings, perhaps the most important is that of momentum (Jegadeesh and Titman 1993), which shows that movements in individual stock prices over the period of six to twelve months tend to predict future movements in the same direction. That is, unlike the long-term trends identified by De Bondt and Thaler, which tend to reverse themselves, relatively short-term trends continue. Some of these results are discussed in Chapter 5, but for now suffice it to say that even the weak form efficient markets hypothesis has faced significant empirical challenges in recent years. Even Fama (1991) admits that stock returns are predictable from past returns and that this represents a departure from the conclusions reached in the earlier studies.

The semi-strong form efficient markets hypothesis has not fared better. Perhaps the best known deviation is that, historically, small stocks have earned higher returns than large stocks. Between 1926 and 1996, for example, the compounded annual return on the largest decile of the New York Stock Exchange stocks has been 9.84 percent, compared to 13.83 percent on the smallest decile of stocks (Siegel 1998, p. 93). Moreover, the superior return to small stocks has been concentrated in January of each year, when the portfolio of the smallest decile of stocks outperformed that of the largest decile by an average of 4.8 percent. There is no evidence that, using standard measures of risk, small stocks are that much riskier in January. Since both a company's size and the coming of the month of January is information known to the market, this evidence points to excess returns based on stale information, in contrast to semi-strong form market efficiency. Interestingly for the purposes of this book, both the small firm effect and the January effect seem to have disappeared in the last 15 years.

More recent research uncovered other variables that predict future returns. Suppose that an investor selects his portfolio using the ratio of the market value of a company's equity to the accounting book value of its assets. The market to book ratio can be loosely thought of as a measure of the cheapness of a stock. Companies with the highest market to book ratios are relatively the most expensive 'growth' firms, whereas those with the lowest ratios are relatively the cheapest 'value' firms. For this reason, investing in low market to book companies is sometimes called value investing. Following De Bondt and Thaler's logic, the high market to book ratios may reflect the excessive market optimism about the future profitability of companies resulting from overreaction to past good news. Consistent with overreaction, De Bondt and Thaler (1987), Fama and French (1992), and Lakonishok *et al.* (1994) find that, historically, portfolios of companies with high market to book ratios have earned sharply lower returns than those with low ratios. Moreover, high market to book portfolios appear to have higher market risk than do low market to book portfolios, and perform particularly poorly in extreme down markets and in recessions (Lakonishok *et al.* 1994).

The size and market to book evidence, on the face of it, presents a serious challenge to the EMH, because stale information obviously helps predict returns, and the superior returns on value strategies are not due to higher risk as conventionally measured. Yet this evidence again has been subjected to a radical version of the Fama critique. Fama and French (1993, 1996) ingeniously interpret both a company's market capitalization and its market to book ratio as measures of fundamental riskiness of a stock in a so-called three-factor model. According to this model, stocks of smaller firms or of firms with low market to book ratios must earn higher average returns precisely because they are fundamentally riskier as measured by their higher exposure to size and market to book 'factors.' Conversely, large stocks earn lower returns because they are safer, and growth stocks with high market to book ratios also earn lower average returns because they represent hedges against this market to book risk.

It is not entirely obvious from the Fama and French analysis how either size or the market to book ratio, whose economic interpretations are rather dubious in the first place, have emerged as heretofore unnoticed but critical indicators of fundamental risk, more important than the market risk itself. Fama and French speculate that perhaps the low size and market to book ratio proxy for different aspects of the 'distress risk,' but up to now there has been no direct evidence in support of this interpretation, and indeed Lakonishok *et al.* (1994) find no evidence of poor performance of value strategies in extremely bad times. The fact that the small firm effect has disappeared in the last 15 years, and before that was concentrated in January, also presents a problem for the risk interpretation. And even Fama and French do not offer a risk interpretation of the momentum evidence. Chapter 5 revisits some of this evidence and related controversies, and offers a behavioral analysis.

Finally, what about the basic proposition that stock prices do not react to non-information? Here again there has been much work, but three types of findings stand out. Perhaps the most salient piece of evidence bearing on this prediction is the crash of 1987. On Monday, October 19, the Dow Jones Industrial Average fell by 22.6 percent—the largest one day percentage drop in history—without any apparent news. Although the event caused an aggressive search for the news that may have caused it, no persuasive culprit could be identified. In fact, many sharp moves in stock prices do not appear to accompany significant news. Cutler *et al.* (1991) examine the 50 largest one day stock price movements in the United States after World War II, and find that many of them came on days of no major announcements. This evidence is, of course, broadly consistent with Shiller's earlier finding of excess volatility of stock returns. More than news seems to move stock prices.

A similar conclusion has been reached in two striking studies by Richard Roll (1984, 1988). In the first, Roll (1984) examines the influence of news about weather on the price of orange juice futures. Roll argues that because the production of oranges for juice in the United States is extremely geographically concentrated and tastes for orange juice are very stable, news about weather should account for most of the variation in futures prices. He finds that, although news about weather help determine futures price movements, they account for a relatively small share of these movements. Roll (1988) extends this idea to individual stocks. He calculates the share of variation in the returns of large stocks explained by aggregate economic influences, the contemporaneous returns on other stocks in the same industry, and public firm-specific news events. He finds the average adjusted R^2s to be only .35 with monthly data and .2 with daily data, suggesting that movements in prices of individual stocks are largely unaccounted for by public news or by movements in potential substitutes. In both of Roll's studies, shocks other than news appear to move security prices, in contrast to the efficient markets analysis.

Roll's second study is also important because, at least in principle, his R^2s are good indicators of the closeness of available substitute portfolios for a given stock. If a stock had perfect substitutes, which presumably are other stocks in the same industry, Roll's R^2s should be close to one, especially after he controls for firm-specific news events. In reality, the R^2s he finds are far below one, no matter how hard he works to raise them. The natural interpretation of this evidence is that the available substitutes are far from perfect.

Other, seemingly unrelated, results that show that prices react to uninformed demand shifts are those on inclusion of stocks into the Standard and Poor's 500 Index. The S&P 500 Index consists of 500 large U.S. companies, and is designed in part to include the largest firms, but also to be representative of the American economy. Every year, a few stocks are withdrawn from the Index, most often because these companies are taken over. These stocks are then replaced by the Standard and Poor's Corporation with other stocks, largely with the goal of maintaining the representativeness of the Index. Inclusion into the Index is an interesting event to study because it is unlikely to convey any information about the company, but at the same time entails substantial buying of shares. When a company is included in the Index, a significant number of its shares is acquired by so-called index funds, which hold passive portfolios replicating the Index, as well as by other professional money managers whose portfolios are supposedly kept close to the Index. The inclusion thus generates a substantial uninformed demand for the shares of the company.

Inclusion in the S&P 500 is a good way to revisit Scholes's logic and result. According to Scholes's theory, inclusion should not be accompanied by significant share price reactions in response to

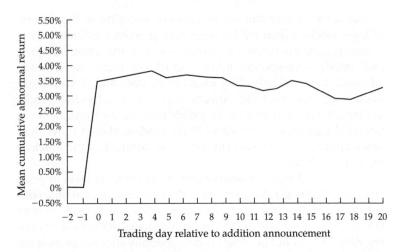

FIG. 1.3 Mean cumulative abnormal returns for stocks added to the S&P 500.

The sample includes 236 stocks that were added to the S&P 500 between September 22, 1976 and May 21, 1996 and were not the subject of contemporaneously reported news. Cumulative abnormal returns are calculated by summing returns in excess of CRSP value-weighted market returns. The standard error of the series is approximately 0.20 percent at day 0 and 0.45 percent at day +20.
Source: Wurgler and Zhuravskaya (1999).

new demand because the initial holders of included stocks should be pleased to sell and to move into substitutes. According to the view that securities do not have perfect substitutes, in contrast, the buying following the inclusion should be accompanied by share price increases since buyers need to get the shares from inframarginal sellers. Harris and Gurel (1986) and Shleifer (1986) examine this experiment. As Figure 1.3 taken from a recent study by Wurgler and Zhuravskaya (1999) illustrates, inclusion between 1976 and 1996 is actually accompanied by average share price increases of 3.5 percent. These increases are relatively permanent and have become larger as the relative share of the market held in index funds has increased (see Chapter 2). In December 1998, America Online—one of the glamourous Internet stocks of the late 1990s—rose 18 per cent on the news of its inclusion in the Index. This evidence casts doubt on a basic implication of the EMH: the non-reaction of prices to non-information. Moreover, it is consistent with Roll's analysis in suggesting that demand shifts move security prices, and that arbitrage does not eliminate the influence of these shifts on prices because securities do not have good substitutes.

Many of the results described here have been challenged on a variety of grounds, including data snooping, trading costs, sample selection biases, and most centrally improper risk adjustment. Nonetheless, it is difficult to deny that the thrust of this evidence is very different from what researchers found in the 1960s and the 1970s, and is much less favorable to the EMH. An interesting question is why have researchers failed to report much evidence challenging market efficiency until 1980? One possible explanation is the professional dominance of the EMH supporters, and the difficulty of publishing rejections of the EMH in academic journals. This explanation is not entirely satisfactory, since there are many competing journals in finance and economics aiming to publish novel findings. A more plausible, and scientifically more satisfactory, account of the failure to find contradictory evidence is provided by Summers (1986). Summers argues that many tests of market efficiency have low power in discriminating against plausible forms of inefficiency. He illustrates this observation by showing that it is often difficult to tell empirically whether some time series, such as the value of a stock index, follows a random walk or alternatively a mean-reverting process that might come from a persistent fad. It takes a lot of data, and perhaps a better theoretical idea of what to look for, before researchers can find persuasive evidence. Whatever the reason why it took so long in practice, the cumulative impact of both the theory and the evidence has been to undermine the hegemony of the EMH and to create a new area of research—behavioral finance. This book describes some of the theoretical and empirical foundations of this research.

Organization of the book

At the most general level, behavioral finance is the study of human fallibility in competitive markets. It does not simply deal with an observation that some people are stupid, confused, or biased. This observation is uncontroversial, although understanding the precise nature of biases and confusions is an enormously difficult task. Behavioral finance goes beyond this uncontroversial observation by placing the biased, the stupid, and the confused into competitive financial markets, in which at least some arbitrageurs are fully rational. It then examines what happens to prices and other dimensions of market performance when the different types of investors trade with each other. The answer is that many interesting things do happen. In particular, financial markets in most scenarios are not expected to be efficient. Market efficiency only emerges as an extreme special case, unlikely to hold under plausible circumstances.

As a study of human fallibility in competitive markets, behavioral finance theory rests on two major foundations. The first is limited arbitrage. This set of arguments suggests that arbitrage in real-world securities markets is far from perfect. Many securities do not have perfect or even good substitutes, making arbitrage fundamentally risky and, even when good substitutes are available, arbitrage remains risky and limited because prices do not converge to fundamental values instantaneously. The fact that arbitrage is limited helps explain why prices do not necessarily react to information by the right amount and why prices may react to non-information expressed in uninformed changes in demand. Limited arbitrage thus explains why markets may remain inefficient when perturbed by noise trader demands, but it does not tell us much about the exact form that inefficiency might take. For that, we need the second foundation of behavioral finance, namely investor sentiment: the theory of how real-world investors actually form their beliefs and valuations, and more generally their demands for securities. Combined with limited arbitrage, a theory of investor sentiment may help generate precise predictions about the behavior of security prices and returns.

Both of these elements of behavioral theory are necessary. If arbitrage is unlimited, then arbitrageurs accommodate the uninformed shifts in demand as well as make sure that news is incorporated into prices quickly and correctly. Markets then remain efficient even when many investors are irrational. Without investor sentiment, there are no disturbances to efficient prices in the first place, and so prices do not deviate from efficiency. A behavioral theory thus requires both an irrational disturbance and limited arbitrage which does not counter it.

Both the theory of limited arbitrage and the theory of investor sentiment allow researchers to make predictions about security prices. Some of these predictions can be made from the recognition of limited arbitrage alone: an exact model of investor sentiment is not required (Chapter 3). But the finer predictions tend to require a specification of how investors form beliefs, that is, a model of investor sentiment (Chapter 5).

As this book is being written, our state of understanding of the two ingredient theories of behavioral finance is very different. We understand a lot more about the limits of arbitrage than we do about investor sentiment. Part of the reason for that is that the theory of limited arbitrage is based on the behavior of rational actors, namely arbitrageurs, and economics is better at modeling and understanding such behavior. Another part of the reason is that psychological evidence on judgment errors has not been developed with an eye toward the interests of financial economists. There is a lot of psychology that might be relevant for the formation of investor sentiment, and no obvious way of deciding which psychological biases are the most important. As a consequence, the research on investor sentiment has been more tentative.

The goal of this book is to present some of the central ideas of behavioral finance, organized around the themes of limited arbitrage and investor sentiment. At various points, the book touches on many findings and results in behavioral finance. But it is not a survey. Rather, it is a presentation of a set of themes—and a selective presentation at that since all the main chapters originate in articles which the author of this book participated in writing. One further clarification is in order. There is no single unifying model in behavioral finance. Each theoretical chapter presented here contains its own model, suited for the points the chapter is trying to make. This state of affairs is not as satisfactory as a unified model, but it is quite similar to that prevailing in other fields of economics that develop theoretical models attempting to capture reality. Thus modern macroeconomics, trade theory, development theory, theory of industrial organization, and theory of corporate finance—to name a few—are all organized around a number of small models each focusing on a potentially important economic mechanism.

As a central organizing principle, the next three chapters of this book deal with limited arbitrage and its consequences and the following two focus on investor sentiment. Chapter 2 develops the concept of noise trader risk and examines how it limits arbitrage. This chapter also discusses in more detail the research related to the availability of close substitutes for stocks. Chapter 3 examines a particularly famous and important example of limited arbitrage, the closed end fund puzzle. This puzzle refers to the fact that closed end mutual funds—the funds that hold portfolios of other securities and have a fixed number of shares that are themselves traded in the market—often sell at prices different from the market values of the portfolios they hold. Chapter 3 shows that the closed end fund puzzle can be fruitfully analyzed in terms of the model of noise trader risk presented in Chapter 2. Chapter 4 considers noise trader risk in the agency context of arbitrage activity. When arbitrage is conducted by specialists using other people's money, arbitrageurs are affected by the inability of their investors to separate luck from skill. Because such arbitrage is even more limited and unstable than when arbitrageurs invest their own money, as they do in Chapter 2, Chapter 4 sheds further doubt on the effectiveness of arbitrage in achieving market efficiency. Chapter 4 also briefly discusses the turbulence of financial markets in the summer of 1998, which vividly illustrated the limits of arbitrage.

Chapters 2 through 4 reach two crucial conclusions. First, plausible theories of arbitrage do not lead to the prediction that markets are efficient—quite the opposite. Second, the recognition that arbitrage is limited, even without specific assumptions about investor sentiment, generates new empirically testable predictions, some of which have been confirmed in the data.

The two subsequent chapters focus on investor sentiment. Chapter 5 begins with an overview of some of the empirical violations of weak and semi-strong form market efficiency that recent models of investor sentiment try to address. It then presents one such model motivated by the idea that, in forecasting future earnings, investors interpret the data on recent past earnings using the representativeness heuristic. The simple model is consistent with both psychological evidence and the evidence from security prices. Chapter 6 presents another approach of overreaction based on the idea that some investors extrapolate past trends in prices. This chapter also describes the interaction of noise traders and arbitrageurs and shows that in cases where arbitrageurs trade in anticipation of noise trader demand they move prices away from rather than toward fundamental values. In addition to perhaps shedding further light on overreaction of security prices, this chapter continues and expands the themes of Chapters 2 and 4 by showing that rational arbitrage not only may be limited in bringing about market efficiency, but may actually in some circumstances move prices away from fundamentals and make markets less efficient. Chapters 5 and 6 reveal the benefits of modeling investor sentiment explicitly and of considering the interactions of noise traders and arbitrageurs in the same market.

The field of behavioral finance is still in its infancy. Yet it has presented financial economics with a new body of theory, a new set of explanations of empirical regularities, as well as a new set of predictions. The concluding chapter summarizes some of the successes of behavioral finance, and shows how this field can inform the analysis of broader questions in economics, including the study of real consequences of financial markets and of public policies toward them. In addition, Chapter 7 discusses some of the many problems that remain open.

2

Noise Trader Risk in Financial Markets

ONE of the fundamental concepts in finance is arbitrage, defined as 'the simultaneous purchase and sale of the same, or essentially similar, security in two different markets for advantageously different prices' (Sharpe and Alexander 1990). Theoretically speaking, such arbitrage requires no capital and entails no risk. When an arbitrageur buys a cheaper security and sells a more expensive one, his net future cash flows are zero for sure and he gets his profits up front. Arbitrage plays a critical role in the analysis of securities markets, because its effect is to bring prices to fundamental values and to keep markets efficient. For this reason, it is important to understand how well this textbook description of arbitrage approximates reality. This chapter argues that the textbook description does not describe realistic arbitrage trades. Moreover, we can gain a deeper understanding of market efficiency by focusing explicitly on some of the deviations of real-world arbitrage from the textbook model.

In this chapter, we explore some of the basic risks associated with arbitraging two fundamentally identical assets—the near textbook case. We thus abstract away from the additional risks arising from arbitrage of nearly, but not completely, perfect substitutes as well as from transaction costs, both of which would limit arbitrage even further. The risk we focus on is that of mispricing deepening in the short run. Such risk is extremely important for relatively short horizon investors engaged in arbitrage against noise traders: the risk that noise traders' beliefs become even more extreme before they revert to the mean.

If noise traders today are pessimistic about an asset and have driven down its price, an arbitrageur buying this asset must recognize that in the near future noise traders might become even more pessimistic and drive the price down even further. If the arbitrageur has to liquidate before the price recovers, he suffers a loss. Fear of this loss should limit his original arbitrage position. Conversely, an arbitrageur selling an asset short when bullish noise traders have driven its price up must remember that noise traders might become even more bullish tomorrow, and so must take a position that accounts for the risk of a further price rise when he has to buy back the asset. This risk of a further change of noise traders' opinion away from its mean—which we refer to as 'noise trader risk'—must be borne by any arbitrageur with a short time horizon and must limit his willingness to bet against noise traders.

The assumption that arbitrageurs have short horizons is essential to limit arbitrage in the case where securities have perfect substitutes. This assumption can be justified in a number of ways. Most arbitrageurs do not manage their own money, but are agents for investors. Investors evaluate arbitrageurs at regular, relatively short intervals and pay them according to performance. Mispricings that take longer than the evaluation horizon to correct do not increase arbitrageurs' pay, and the deepening of such mispricings actually reduces it. Moreover, many arbitrageurs borrow money and securities from intermediaries to put on their trades. They have to pay interest on this money, but also face the risk of liquidation by the lenders if prices move against them and the value of collateral falls. This risk also reduces the arbitrageurs' tolerance toward noise trader risk. In Chapter 4, we consider the agency problem between arbitrageurs and investors explicitly, but here simply begin with the plausible assumption that arbitrageurs' horizons are short. When securities do not have perfect substitutes, arbitrage is limited even with infinite horizon arbitrageurs, and more limited with finite horizon arbitrageurs than indicated here.

Economists have a strong intuition that fundamentally identical assets must sell at identical prices because of the workings of arbitrage. But this is not always the case, and noise trader risk appears to be a good explanation of price divergences between fundamentally identical securities. Perhaps the best known examples of such divergence of prices of identical securities are the so-called 'twin-securities,' such as the common shares of Royal Dutch and Shell (Rosenthal and Young 1990, Froot and Dabora 1998). According to Froot and Dabora (1998):

> Royal Dutch and Shell are independently incorporated in the Netherlands and England, respectively. The structure has

grown out of 1907 alliance between Royal Dutch and Shell
Transport by which the two companies agreed to merge their
interests on a 60:40 basis while remaining separate and distinct
entities. All sets of cash flows, adjusting for corporate tax considerations and control rights, are effectively split in these proportions. Information clarifying the linkages between the two
companies is widely available. Royal Dutch and Shell trade on
nine exchanges in Europe and the U.S., but Royal Dutch trades
primarily in the U.S. and the Netherlands (it is in the S&P 500
and virtually every index of Dutch shares), and Shell trades
predominantly in the UK (it is in the Financial Times Allshare
Index, or FTSE). In sum, if the market values of securities were
equal to the net present values of future cash flows, the value
of Royal Dutch equity should be equal to 1.5 times the value of
Shell equity. This, however, is far from the case.

Figure 2.1 presents the percentage deviation from the 60:40
ratio in the market values of equity of Royal Dutch and Shell
between September 1980 and September 1995. It shows enormous
deviations from parity, ranging from the relative underpricing of
Royal Dutch by 35 percent to relative overpricing by 10 percent.
There is no structural explanation of these deviations that we are

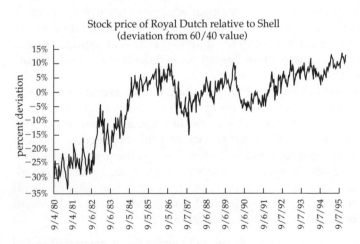

FIG. 2.1 Log deviations from Royal Dutch/Shell parity.
Source: Froot and Dabora (1998).

aware of, and indeed one might be especially difficult to find in light of the fact that sometimes one of the securities trades at a discount, and sometimes the other. Such deviations cannot exist in a market where arbitrageurs have infinite time horizon and face no transaction (including short-selling) costs, for an arbitrageur can simply buy the cheap shares, sell the same number of expensive shares, put the net proceeds in his pocket, and hold the hedged position forever.[1]

This evidence presents a deep challenge to the efficient markets hypothesis. This is not a case of high returns on a particular class of securities, where one can debate whether these returns are anomalous or simply a compensation for risk. Rather, here two fundamentally identical securities sell at different prices—a most basic contradiction to the claim that price equals value. There is no story in which the cash flows of one stock are subjected to a different fundamental risk than the cash flows of the other. The Fama critique is irrelevant. Moreover, the Royal Dutch/Shell example is not unique. There are other companies for which similar differences are observed. There are cases where ADRs (American Depositary Receipts) trade at different prices in the United States than identical shares sell at in local markets. Similar mispricings are common in the bond market. But perhaps the most celebrated illustration of the related phenomenon is closed end funds, which trade in the United States and elsewhere at market prices different from the market values of portfolios they hold. Although in the case of closed end funds there are alternative 'structural' explanations of the observed valuations, we show in Chapter 3 that the arguments presented in this chapter shed considerable light on the closed end fund puzzle as well.

An examination of Figure 2.1 points to a crucial cost of arbitrage in Royal Dutch and Shell: the risk that mispricing becomes more extreme. An arbitrageur who bought the relatively cheap Royal Dutch shares, and sold the corresponding number of the relatively expensive Shell shares in mid 1983, when the discount was 10 percent, experienced a severe deterioration of his position

---

[1] Actually, the optimal arbitrage strategy is not obviously to buy and sell the same amount of cheap and expensive shares, respectively. Rashes (1998b) works out the optimal arbitrage strategy, and applies it to a number of examples, including Royal Dutch/Shell arbitrage.

as the discount widened to nearly 25 percent six months later. If this arbitrageur was leveraged or if he had to explain his losses to investors (see Chapter 4), he might have failed to survive through these losses, and might have been forced to liquidate this position. To him, noise trader risk is very important.

Equally interesting, Figure 2.1 reveals that it takes about four years for the 30 percent mispricing of Royal Dutch and Shell prevalent in September of 1980 to go away. In return for bearing this noise trader risk, the arbitrageur earns about 7 percent per year. Note that this 7 percent comes from a period where we know ex post that the mispricing has corrected; it could of course have widened and led to a loss. In principle, the arbitrageur could have leveraged his position to earn a higher average return, but then he had to take into account the costs of leverage, as well as the possible risk of unfavorable liquidation as the mispricing widens. These calculations suggest that perhaps the arbitrage of Royal Dutch versus Shell was not ex ante especially attractive in September of 1980, when the mispricing was 30 percent, and these are fundamentally identical securities! The converse point is that, when mispricing can take a while to correct, enormous inefficiencies can be sustained without aggressive arbitrage activity coming in to correct them. From the point of view of the EMH, this observation is crucial, for it shows that—even for securities with perfect substitutes—large deviations of prices from fundamental values can be explained by somewhat risky arbitrage that takes time to correct.

In this chapter, we present a theory of arbitrage limited by noise trader risk, just as in the case of Royal Dutch and Shell. We study financial markets in which the mere unpredictability of investor sentiment—of future noise trader demand for assets—becomes an important source of risk and a deterrent to arbitrage. We derive equilibrium security prices, and show that—because arbitrage is risky and limited—financial markets are not efficient. We then examine Friedman's evolutionary argument in such a market and find that the conclusion that the unsophisticated investors earn lower average returns than the arbitrageurs is unwarranted. Finally, we discuss the costs of arbitrage activity more generally than we do in the formal model. In particular, we focus on a number of costs that the model does not include, as well as on the important case where mispriced securities do not have perfect substitutes.

2.1 Noise trading as a source of risk

A model

The model contains noise traders and arbitrageurs. Noise traders form erroneous beliefs about the future distribution of returns on a risky asset. In this chapter, it does not matter exactly why noise traders form erroneous beliefs. They may be subject to one of the behavioral biases in processing information and forecasting returns. Alternatively, they may incorrectly perceive the riskiness of returns, perhaps because they are overconfident. Noise traders select their portfolios on the basis of such incorrect beliefs. In response, it is optimal for arbitrageurs to exploit noise traders' misperceptions. Their investment strategies push prices toward fundamentals, but not all the way.

The basic model is a stripped-down overlapping generations model with two-period-lived agents (Samuelson 1958). For simplicity, there is no first-period consumption, no labor supply decision, and no bequest. As a result, the resources agents have to invest are exogenous. The only decision agents make is to choose a portfolio when young.

The economy contains two assets that pay identical dividends. One of the assets, the safe asset s, pays a fixed real dividend r per period. Asset s is in perfectly elastic supply: a unit of it can be created out of, and a unit of it turned back into, a unit of the consumption good in any period. With consumption each period taken as numeraire, the price of the safe asset is always fixed at one. The dividend r paid on asset s is thus the riskless rate. The other asset, the unsafe asset u, always pays the same fixed real dividend r as asset s. But u is not in elastic supply: it is in fixed and unchangeable quantity, normalized at one unit. The price of u in period t is denoted p_t. If the price of each asset were equal to the net present value of its future dividends, then assets u and s would be perfect substitutes and would sell for the same price of one in all periods. But this is not how the price of u is determined in the presence of noise traders.

The analysis below relies on a limited risk bearing capacity of arbitrageurs as a whole. There are two ways to justify this assumption. First, we can assume that noise trader risk is market-wide rather than idiosyncratic. For example, it can be a risk affecting the stock market as a whole, or a large group of stocks. In the Royal Dutch and Shell example, Froot and Dabora (1998) document that Royal Dutch shares comove with the Dutch market, whereas Shell shares comove with the British market—exposing an arbitrageur to price movements in both markets. Alternatively, we can assume as we do in Chapter 4 that the market in question requires specialized arbitrage resources, and that such resources dedicated to that market are limited. For example, arbitrage trades in emerging markets are often limited by the fact that access to these markets is restricted, and therefore only a few experts who set up specialized operations can engage in arbitrage. Still another way to proceed is to assume that there is a cost of learning about the valuation of a particular security or class of securities, which limits the entry of arbitrageurs (Merton 1987*a*).

Without one of these assumptions, there are too many possibilities for arbitrageurs to diversify, and hence their trading is more aggressive. For example, if noise traders' misperceptions of the returns to individual assets are uncorrelated and if each asset is small relative to the market, a large number of tiny arbitrageurs eliminate any possible mispricing for the same reasons that idiosyncratic risk is not priced in the standard capital asset pricing model. Such Ross-style arbitrage (Ross 1976) by a huge number of diversified arbitrageurs is what drives market efficiency in standard finance models, but it does not work when sentiment is correlated across investors or when markets are segmented. The model here is that of correlated sentiment and of the limited risk-bearing capacity of the arbitrageurs.

There are two types of agents: arbitrageurs (denoted *a*) who have rational expectations and noise traders (denoted *n*). We assume that noise traders are present in the model in measure μ, that arbitrageurs are present in measure $1-\mu$, and that all agents of a given type are identical. Both types of agents choose their portfolios when young to maximize perceived expected utility given their own beliefs about the ex ante mean of the distribution of the price of *u* at *t* + 1. The representative arbitrageur young in period *t* accurately perceives the distribution of returns from holding the risky asset, and so maximizes expected utility given that distribution. The representative noise trader young in period *t* misperceives the expected price of the risky asset by an independent and identically distributed normal random variable ρ_t:

$$\rho_t \sim N(\rho^*, \sigma_\rho^2). \tag{2.1}$$

The mean misperception ρ^* is a measure of the average 'bullishness' of the noise traders, and σ_ρ^2 is the variance of noise traders' misperceptions of the expected return per unit of the risky asset.[2] The results we derive below depend critically on the unpredictability of future investor sentiment; the exact form of this sentiment is not essential for our findings. Noise traders thus maximize their own expectation of utility given the next-period dividend, the one-period variance of p_{t+1}, and their false belief that the distribution of the price of u next period has mean ρ_t above its true value. Each agent's utility is a constant absolute risk aversion function of wealth when old:

$$U = -e^{-(2\gamma)w}, \tag{2.2}$$

where γ is the coefficient of absolute risk aversion and w is wealth when old. Given their beliefs, all young agents divide their portfolios between u and s. When old, agents convert their holdings of s into the consumption good, sell their holdings of u for price p_{t+1} to the new young, and consume all their wealth.

With normally distributed returns to holding a unit of the risky asset, maximizing the expected value of (2.2) generates demands for the risky asset proportional to perceived expected returns and inversely proportional to the perceived variance of returns. Denote by λ_t^a the amount of the risky asset u held by an arbitrageur, by λ_t^n amount held by a noise trader, and define $_t p_{t+1}$ to be the rationally expected at time t price of u at time $t + 1$, and

$$_t\sigma_{p_{t+1}}^2 = E_t\{[p_{t+1} - E_t(p_{t+1})]^2\} \tag{2.3}$$

to be the one-period-ahead variance of p_{t+1}. The quantities λ_t^n and λ_t^a of the risky asset purchased are functions of its current price p_t, its expected price and its variance, and of noise traders' misperception ρ_t. The exact demands are given by:

---

[2] The assumption that noise traders misperceive the expected price hides the fact that the expected price is itself a function of the parameters ρ^* and σ_ρ^2. Thus we are implicitly assuming that noise traders know how to factor the effect of future price volatility into their calculations of values. This assumption is made for simplicity.

$$\lambda_t^a = \frac{r + {}_t p_{t+1} - (1+r)p_t}{2\gamma({}_t\sigma_{p_{t+1}}^2)}, \qquad (2.4)$$

$$\lambda_t^n = \frac{r + {}_t p_{t+1} - (1+r)\, p_t}{2\gamma({}_t\sigma_{p_{t+1}}^2)} + \frac{\rho_t}{2\gamma({}_t\sigma_{p_{t+1}}^2)}. \qquad (2.5)$$

We allow noise traders' and arbitrageurs' demands to be negative; they can take short positions at will. Even if investors hold only positive amounts of both assets, the fact that returns are unbounded allows each investor to have negative final wealth. We use a standard specification of returns at the cost of allowing consumption to be negative with positive probability.[3]

The demands for the risky asset are proportional to its perceived excess return and inversely proportional to its perceived variance. The additional term in the demand function of noise traders comes from their misperception of the expected return. When noise traders overestimate expected returns, they demand more of the risky asset than arbitrageurs; when they underestimate the expected return, they demand less. Arbitrageurs exert a stabilizing influence in this model since they offset the volatile positions of the noise traders.

The variance of prices appearing in the denominators of the demand functions is derived solely from noise trader risk. Both noise traders and arbitrageurs limit their demand for asset u because the price at which they can sell it when old depends on the uncertain beliefs of the next period's young noise traders. This uncertainty about the price for which asset u can be sold afflicts all investors, no matter what their beliefs about expected returns and so limits the extent to which they are willing to bet against each other. If the price next period were certain, then noise traders and arbitrageurs would hold different beliefs about expected returns with certainty; they would therefore try to take infinite bets against each other. An equilibrium would not exist. Noise trader risk limits all investors' positions and in particular keeps arbitrageurs from driving prices all the way to fundamental values.

---

[3] An appendix of De Long *et al.* (1987) presents an example in which asset prices and consumption are always positive.

The pricing function

To calculate equilibrium prices, observe that the old sell their holdings and so the demands of the young must sum to one in equilibrium. Equations (2.4) and (2.5) imply that

$$p_t = \frac{1}{1 + r} [r + {}_t p_{t+1} - 2\gamma({}_t\sigma^2_{p_{t+1}}) + \mu\rho_t].$$ (2.6)

Equation (2.6) expresses the risky asset's price in period t as a function of period t's misperception by noise traders (ρ_t), of the technological (r) and behavioral (γ) parameters of the model, and of the moments of the one-period-ahead distribution of p_{t+1}. We consider only steady-state equilibria by imposing the requirement that the unconditional distribution of p_{t+1} be identical to the distribution of p_t. The endogenous one-period-ahead distribution of the price of asset u can then be eliminated from (2.6) by solving recursively:

$$p_t = 1 + \frac{\mu(\rho_t - \rho^*)}{1 + r} + \frac{\mu\rho^*}{r} - \frac{2\gamma}{r} ({}_t\sigma^2_{p_{t+1}}).$$ (2.7)

Inspection of (2.7) reveals that only the second term is variable, for γ, ρ^*, and r are all constants, and the one-step-ahead variance of p_t is a simple unchanging function of the constant variance of a generation of noise traders' misperception ρ_t.

$$_t\sigma^2_{p_{t+1}} = \sigma^2_{p_{t+1}} = \frac{\mu^2\sigma^2_\rho}{(1 + r)^2}.$$ (2.8)

The final form of the price of u, which depends only on exogenous parameters of the model and on public information about present and future misperception by noise traders, is

$$p_t = 1 + \frac{\mu(\rho_t - \rho^*)}{1 + r} + \frac{\mu\rho^*}{r} - (2\gamma)\frac{\mu^2\sigma^2_\rho}{r(1 + r)^2}.$$ (2.9)

Interpretation

The last three terms that appear in (2.9) show the impact of noise traders on the price of asset u. As the distribution of ρ_t converges to a point mass at zero, the equilibrium pricing function (2.9) converges to its fundamental value of one.

The second term in (2.9) captures the fluctuations in the price of the risky asset u due to the variation of noise traders' misperceptions. Even though asset u is not subject to any fundamental uncertainty and is known to be so by a large class of investors, its price varies substantially as noise traders' opinions shift. When a generation of noise traders is more bullish than the average generation, they bid up the price of u. When they are more bearish than average, they bid down the price. When they hold their average misperception—when $\rho_t = \rho^*$—the term is zero. As one would expect, the more numerous noise traders are relative to arbitrageurs, the more volatile are asset prices.

The third term in (2.9) captures the deviations of p_t from its fundamental value due to the fact that the average misperception by noise traders is not zero. If noise traders are bullish on average, this 'price pressure' effect makes the price of the risky asset higher than it would otherwise be. Optimistic noise traders bear a greater than average share of price risk. Since arbitrageurs bear a smaller share of price risk when ρ^* is higher, they require a lower expected excess return and so are willing to pay a higher price for asset u.

The final term in (2.9) is the heart of the model. Arbitrageurs would not hold the risky asset unless compensated for bearing the risk that noise traders become bearish and the price of the risky asset falls. Both noise traders and sophisticated investors present in period t believe that asset u is mispriced, but because p_{t+1} is uncertain, neither group is willing to bet too much on this mispricing. At the margin, the return from enlarging one's position in an asset that everyone agrees is mispriced (but different investors think is mispriced in different directions) is offset by the additional price risk that must be borne. Noise traders thus 'create their own space': the uncertainty over what next period's noise traders will believe makes the otherwise riskless asset u risky and drives its price down and its return up. This is so despite the fact that both arbitrageurs and noise traders always hold portfolios that possess the same amount of fundamental risk: zero. For the economy as a whole, there is no risk to be borne.

These results depend on three fundamental assumptions of the model: the overlapping generations structure, the fixed supply of the unsafe asset, and the systematic nature of noise trader risk. All three assumptions have significant economic content, and warrant some discussion.

The overlapping generations structure of the model plays two roles. In the model, equilibrium exists as long as the returns to holding the risky asset are always uncertain. In the overlapping generations structure, this is assured by the absence of a last period. For if there is a last period in which the risky asset pays a nonstochastic dividend and is liquidated, then both noise traders and arbitrageurs will seek to exploit what they see as riskless arbitrage. If, say, the liquidation value of the risky asset is $1 + r$, previous-period arbitrageurs will try to trade arbitrarily large amounts of asset u at any price other than one, and noise traders will try to trade arbitrarily large amounts at any price other than

$$p_t = 1 + \frac{\rho_t}{1 + r} \cdot \qquad (2.10)$$

The excess demand function for the risky asset will be undefined. But in a model with fundamental dividend risk on asset u, the assumption that there is no last period is not necessary because u and s are no longer perfect substitutes (Campbell and Kyle 1993). In this case, no agent is ever subjectively certain what the return on the risky asset will be, and so the qualitative properties of equilibrium are preserved even with a known terminal date. The overlapping generations structure is not needed when the two assets are not perfect substitutes.

The overlapping generations structure plays another function: it assures that each agent's horizon is short. No agent has any opportunity to wait until the price of the risky asset recovers before selling. Such a structure may be a fruitful way of modeling the effects on prices of a number of institutional features, such as frequent evaluations of money managers' performance, that may lead rational, long-lived market participants to care about short-term rather than long-term performance (see Chapter 4).

In our model, the horizons of arbitrageurs are important. If their horizons are long relative to the duration of noise traders' optimism or pessimism toward risky assets, then they can buy low, confident of being able to sell high when prices revert to the mean. Noise trader risk is an important deterrent to arbitrage only when the duration of noise traders' misperceptions is of the same order of magnitude as or longer than the horizon of the arbitrageurs.

In general, the longer the horizons of the arbitrageurs, the more aggressively they trade, and the more efficient are the markets. Although arbitrage is not riskless for long but finite-lived agents, their asset demands are more responsive to price movements than those of two-period-lived agents. There are two reasons for this. First, even if an $n > 2$ period-lived arbitrageur can liquidate his position in asset u only in the last period of his life, he bears the same amount of resale price risk as his two-period-lived counterpart, but gets some insurance from dividends. If, for example, he buys an undervalued asset u, he receives a high dividend yield for several periods before he sells. Because as the horizon expands so does the share of dividends in expected returns, agents with longer horizons buy more at the start. Second, a long-lived arbitrageur has many periods to liquidate his position. Since he makes money on arbitrage if the price reverts to the mean at any time before his death, having several opportunities to liquidate reduces his risk. For these two reasons, raising arbitrageurs' horizons makes them more aggressive and brings the price of u closer to fundamentals.

The assumption of the fixed supply of the unsafe asset prevents arbitrageurs from pursuing other money making strategies, such as the conversion of the safe asset into unsafe asset when the latter is overpriced, and vice versa when it is underpriced. If this assumption were completely removed, the opportunities for arbitrage would expand so as to restore market efficiency. In many instances, this assumption is completely realistic: the Royal Dutch and Shell shares indeed exist in fixed proportions and an arbitrageur could not convert the relatively cheap Royal Dutch shares into the relatively expensive Shell shares in the 1980s. In other instances, arbitrageurs may actually increase the supply of the expensive unsafe asset. Thus arbitrageurs create companies in overpriced industries and take them public, whether these are companies in hot industries such as biotechnology companies in the 1980s (Lerner 1994) or the Internet stocks in the late 1990s, or closed end mutual funds in the 1920s, 1960s, and 1980s (De Long and Shleifer 1991 and Chapter 3). Increases in the supply of securities during price bubbles have also been extremely important historically (see Kindleberger 1978 and Chapter 6).

Companies themselves can and do issue securities when they believe that these securities are overpriced. Such creation of

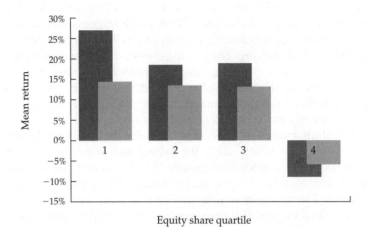

FIG. 2.2 Mean equity returns by prior-year equity share in new issues, 1928-1997.
Mean annual returns on the CRSP value-weighted (hatched) and equal-weighted (solid) indexes by quartile of the prior-year share of equity issues in total equity and debt issues. Real returns are created using the consumer price index from Ibbotson Associates.
Source: Baker and Wurgler (2000).

perfect or close substitutes in response to an overpricing of (a group of) unsafe assets is exactly what arbitrageurs would want to do in our model if they could. Baker and Wurgler (2000) show that the aggregate share of stock issues in total stock and bond issues is especially high in bull markets. Moreover, as Figure 2.2 taken from their paper shows, a high share is a good predictor of low future aggregate stock returns, and even of negative future returns when the share is in the top quartile of its distribution. This evidence suggests that companies issue stock when equities as a whole are overpriced. Such increases in supply are at least somewhat costly, and hence this arbitrage has its limits. Not everyone can start an Internet company, issue new overpriced stock, or package liquid securities into a closed end fund. The activity is profitable while it lasts. Consistent with this point and with our model, new issues of equity by both new and seasoned companies are notoriously overpriced (Stigler 1964, Ritter 1991, Loughran and Ritter 1995,

Brav and Gompers 1997, and Brav, *et al.* 1999), and earn low returns subsequent to issuance.[4] Just as arbitrageurs take advantage of noise traders and earn profits by selling short expensive securities and buying cheap substitutes, firms and entrepreneurs make money by issuing overpriced securities to new buyers. As we discuss in Chapter 7, it remains an open question whether taking advantage of overpricing is a minor or a major driving force behind security issues.

The third major assumption we make is that noise trader risk is systematic: it affects either the market as a whole or a significant segment of traded securities. If noise trader risk on each asset were purely idiosyncratic, it would not be priced in equilibrium. The necessity of noise trader risk being systematic for it to be priced implies that the securities influenced by noise trader sentiment must have correlated returns. This would be the case even if these securities were fundamentally uncorrelated, and the only common influence on their prices was noise trader demand. This observation generates a very sharp prediction: fundamentally unrelated securities subject to the same noise trader sentiment must observably move together. In the next chapter, we apply this observation to the study of closed end funds.

The converse implication of systematic noise trader risk is also important. Authors such as Fama and French (1993) have interpreted the evidence that particular groups of securities move together as pointing to a common *fundamental* risk to which their holders are exposed. The analysis in this chapter suggests that comovement may indeed be evidence of a common risk exposure, but shows that such risk does not have to be fundamental. Noise trader risk not only can, but *must* be systematic to be priced in equilibrium and hence the comovement of different securities can be pointing to their exposure to common noise trader risk rather than fundamental risk. In fact, the comovement of securities which can be shown to be fundamentally unrelated can be taken as strong evidence of the influence of investor sentiment on security prices.

---

[4] We come back to the various interpretations of these low returns in Chapters 5 and 7.

2.2 Relative returns of noise traders and arbitrageurs

We have demonstrated that noise traders can affect prices even though there is no uncertainty about fundamentals. Friedman (1953) and Fama (1965) argue that noise traders who affect prices earn lower returns than the arbitrageurs they trade with, and so economic selection works to weed them out. In our model, it need not be the case that noise traders earn lower returns. Noise traders' collective shifts of opinion increase the riskiness of returns to assets. If noise traders' portfolios are concentrated in assets subject to noise trader risk, noise traders can earn a higher average rate of return on their portfolios than the arbitrageurs.

The conditions under which noise traders earn higher expected returns than arbitrageurs are easily laid out. All agents earn a certain net return of r on their investments in asset s. The difference between noise traders' and arbitrageurs' total returns, given equal initial wealth, is the difference in their holdings of the risky asset u times the excess return paid by a unit of that asset. Call this difference in returns to the two types of agents:

$$\Delta R_{n-a} = (\lambda_t^n - \lambda_t^a)[r + p_{t+1} - p_t(1 + r)]. \tag{2.11}$$

Some calculations show that the expected value of this difference is given by:

$$E(\Delta R_{n-a}) = \rho^* - \frac{(1 + r)^2(\rho^*)^2 + (1 + r)^2\sigma_\rho^2}{(2\gamma)\mu\sigma_\rho^2}. \tag{2.12}$$

Equation (2.12) makes obvious the requirement that for noise traders to earn higher expected returns, the mean misperception ρ^* of returns on the risky asset must be positive. The first ρ^* on the right-hand side of (2.12) increases noise traders' expected returns through what might be called the 'hold more' effect. Noise traders' expected returns relative to those of arbitrageurs are increased when noise traders on average hold more of the risky asset and earn a larger share of the rewards of risk bearing. When ρ^* is negative, noise traders' changing misperceptions still make the fundamentally riskless asset u risky and still push up the expected return on asset u, but the rewards to risk bearing accrue disproportionately to arbitrageurs, who on average hold more of the risky asset than the noise traders do. Interestingly, the case of a positive ρ^* corresponds to excessive noise trader optimism, which Kahneman and Riepe (1998) describe as a common bias in judgment. As interestingly, if noise traders are overconfident—another common bias—they will also overinvest in the unsafe asset u.

The first term in the numerator in (2.12) incorporates the 'price pressure' effect. As noise traders become more bullish, they demand more of the risky asset on average and drive up its price. They thus reduce the return to risk bearing and, hence, the differential between their returns and those of arbitrageurs.

The second term in the numerator incorporates the buy high-sell low or 'Friedman' effect. Because noise traders' misperceptions are stochastic, they have the worst possible market timing. They buy the most of the risky asset u just when other noise traders are buying it, which is when they are most likely to suffer a capital loss. The more variable noise traders' beliefs are, the more damage their poor market timing does to their returns.

The denominator incorporates the 'create space' effect central to this model. As the variability of noise traders' beliefs increases, so does price risk. To take advantage of noise traders' misperceptions, arbitrageurs must bear this greater risk. Since arbitrageurs are risk averse, they reduce the extent to which they bet against noise traders' in response to this increased risk. If the 'create space' effect is large, then the 'price pressure' and 'buy high-sell low' effects inflict less damage on noise traders' average returns relative to arbitrageurs' returns.

Two effects—'hold more' and 'create space'—tend to raise noise traders' relative expected returns. Two effects—'Friedman' and 'price pressure'—tend to lower noise traders' relative expected returns. Neither pair clearly dominates. Noise traders cannot earn higher average returns if they are on average bearish, for if ρ^* does not exceed zero, there is no hold more effect and (2.12) must be negative. Nor can noise traders earn higher average returns if they are too bullish, for as ρ^* gets large the price pressure effect, which increases with $(\rho^*)^2$, dominates. For intermediate degrees of average bullishness, noise traders earn higher expected returns. And it is clear from (2.12) that the larger γ is, that is, the more risk-averse agents are, the larger is the range of ρ^* over which noise traders earn higher average returns.

The fact that bullish noise traders can earn higher returns in the market than arbitrageurs implies that Friedman's simple 'market selection' argument is incomplete. The key difference from Friedman's (1953) model is that here the demand curve of arbitrageurs shifts in response to the addition of noise traders and the resulting increase in risk. Because of this shift, arbitrageurs' expected returns may fall relative to the returns of the noise traders even though their expected utility rises relative to that of the noise traders. Since noise traders' wealth can increase faster than arbitrageurs', it is not possible to make any blanket statement that noise traders lose money and eventually become unimportant.

One should not overinterpret our result, however, for two reasons. First, although they may earn a higher average return, noise traders always receive a lower average utility. Still, wealth rather than utility is relevant for financial influence, so the noise traders might well be influential in the market, though not so happy, on average, because of the volatility of returns.

Second, and much more important, expected returns are not the same as long run survival. The greater variance of noise traders' returns might give them in the long run a high probability of having low wealth and a low probability of having very high wealth. Market selection might work against such traders even if their expected value of wealth is high since they would be almost surely poor. A more appropriate selection criterion would take this into account. This turns out to be difficult, since it requires modeling long-lived agents.

A preliminary effort to deal with some of the relevant issues was made by De Long *et al.* (1991), who show in a model where noise traders have no effect on prices that they might, in some circumstances, have higher survival chances. As shown by Merton and Samuelson (1974), long run survival in financial markets relies on a delicate tradeoff of risk and expected return. Among rational investors with different utility functions, those with logarithmic preferences over wealth have the highest probability of keeping their wealth above a given level in the long run. From this perspective, some types of noise traders might end up with more attractive portfolios than the arbitrageurs who simply have preferences that are not best suited for survival. For example, if both noise traders and arbitrageurs have preferences that are more risk-averse than logarithmic, and noise traders are overconfident, they may choose portfolios closer to those of rational investors with logarithmic preferences. As a consequence, they would have better long run survival chances than the rational, but more risk-averse, arbitrageurs (De Long *et al.* 1991).

Many other issues enter the survival arguments. If noise traders are on average bullish, they might under some conditions consume less and save more, thereby enhancing their long run wealth. This effect is not present in this model, but that does not mean that it is empirically unimportant. Moreover, when there is a variety of noise traders, some of them might get lucky and do well, thereby attracting imitators at least over some period of time. Such recruitment will also increase noise traders' influence on prices. And even if noise traders lose wealth, they may keep coming back into the market because they keep earning investable labor income themselves, and, besides, there is a noise trader born every minute (period). In the relatively long run, these surely are extremely important factors. In sum, while the empirical relevance of these various effects is hard to assess, any blanket statements that irrationality will be driven out of the market are surely false.

2.3 Further aspects of limited arbitrage

Perhaps the most immediate implication of the model is that even when securities are *fundamentally* perfect substitutes, i.e. pay identical dividends in all states of the world, they need not be perfect substitutes from the point of view of an arbitrageur who cannot literally convert one security into another. An arbitrageur taking a bet against the relative mispricing of the two securities bears the risk that mispricing widens, and that he might have to liquidate his position at that time. When an arbitrageur is risk-averse, his willingness to bet against the mispricing of fundamentally identical securities is limited and hence their prices can diverge from each other. The example of Royal Dutch and Shell at the beginning of this chapter is a striking illustration of this phenomenon.

For several reasons, the view of the effectiveness of arbitrage

presented in this chapter is in all likelihood excessively optimistic, even for fundamentally identical securities. First, in real
markets, an extremely important potential cost of this type of
arbitrage has to do with the mechanics of short selling. To sell
short a security, an arbitrageur must borrow it from a broker or
some other intermediary and then sell it on the market. In many
markets, short selling is prohibited, or at least restricted, by law.
Even when it is not, it is often difficult for arbitrageurs to find
securities that they can borrow and sell. And even in the
extremely developed markets where a security can be borrowed
and sold short, such loans are only good as long as the broker
retains a long position in the security in its own or a customer's
account. If the customer chooses to sell the security or with-
draws it from the brokerage account, the broker recalls the loan
and the arbitrageur must immediately buy back the security he
is short in the market 'to cover his short.' If the market for a
security is not perfectly liquid or if there are large holders of this
security who try to 'squeeze' the short-sellers, the premium that
an arbitrageur might have to pay to buy back the security can
be very large. This would be a further cost of arbitrage, which
can prevent the short-selling of overpriced securities and,
indirectly—to the extent that arbitrageurs wish to lay off fundamental risk—the buying of underpriced securities as well. In
many emerging markets, this fear of short squeezes is a crucial
deterrent of arbitrage activity.

Second, the arbitrageur here knows the model for investor sentiment and is only uncertain about the stochastic realization of
noise trader beliefs. Often, arbitrageurs, like the economists who
study security prices, are far less certain about the form of
investor sentiment. As Black (1986) and Summers (1986) make
clear, we know very little about noise. In this situation,
arbitrageurs are likely to be less effective in leaning against noise
trading than they are in our model, even when the securities they
trade are fundamentally identical.

Third, arbitrageurs here face no transaction costs. Some of these
costs, such as the trading costs per se, are probably not terribly
large *in liquid markets*, although the price impact of trades can
become very large in less than perfectly liquid markets. Other
transaction costs, such as the costs associated with the possible
need to cover a short position in an illiquid market discussed

above, can be substantial and hence can significantly limit arbitrage.

The above discussion explains why the prices of fundamentally identical securities can diverge from each other. Of course, when securities only have fundamentally *close* rather than fundamentally *perfect* substitutes, arbitrage becomes that much more risky because the relative prices of close substitutes can diverge for fundamental and not just for reasons of sentiment. This point might explain the anomalous S&P 500 inclusion evidence described in Chapter 1. When a stock is included in the Index and indexers and quasi-indexers begin buying the shares, arbitrageurs do not have a riskless trade. If they sell or sell short the stock and buy the substitute portfolio, they run the risks that (1) the included stock keeps going up in price relative to the substitute portfolio because the indexers keep buying it (noise trader risk), and (2) the substitute portfolio is an imperfect substitute, and hence its price deteriorates relative to that of the included stock for purely fundamental reasons. In light of these two sources of risk, it is not surprising that arbitrage of the S&P anomaly is limited, and the inclusion is accompanied by a share price increase without any fundamental good news about the company.

In a recent paper, Wurgler and Zhuravskaya (1999) explicitly examine the determinants of the reaction of share prices to inclusion into the S&P 500 Index. They measure the size of the demand shock by looking at the weight of each company in the Index, and considering the fraction of a company's equity likely to be acquired by index funds. They measure the availability of substitutes explicitly by asking, in the spirit of Roll (1988), how much of a past return on an included stock can be replicated by a potential substitute portfolio. Their paper presents a number of interesting findings. First, as Table 2.1 shows, stock price increases on the news of the inclusion in the Index have grown sharply over time as index funds grew, reaching an average announcement day appreciation of nearly 5 percent. Moreover, as Figure 2.3 shows, stocks that experience larger demand shocks as a consequence of inclusion also experience larger returns on the announcement, inconsistent with perfect arbitrage. Second, like Roll (1988), the paper shows that, even using historical data, it is difficult to construct portfolios that share more than 25 percent of the variance with a given included stock. If the comovement between that

Table 2.1 Announcement day returns for stocks added to the S&P 500 Index

Period	Number of clean additions	Mean announcement day abnormal return (%)	Percent of abnormal returns > 0 (%)
1976 - 1980	42	2.32	85
1981 - 1985	76	2.70	91
1986 - 1990	84	4.25	99
1991 - 1996	34	4.87	100

The sample includes 236 stocks that were added to the S&P 500 Composite Index between September 22, 1976 and May 21, 1996 and were not the subject of contemporaneously reported news. Abnormal returns are calculated as the excess over the CRSP value-weighted market return.
Source: Wurgler and Zhuravskaya (1999).

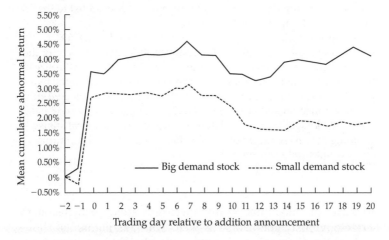

Trading day relative to addition announcement

FIG. 2.3 Mean Cumulative Abnormal Returns for Stocks added to the S&P 500, by size of index fund demand shock.
The sample includes 191 stocks that were added to the S&P 500 between September 22, 1976 and September 30, 1989 and were not the subject of contemporaneously reported news. To control for the level of imperfect arbitrage risk, we exclude stocks in the extreme two quartiles of the risk distribution (market index is the only hedge asset). We split the remaining 96 stocks into above-median and below-median dollar shock size groups. Cumulative abnormal returns are calculated by summing returns in excess of CRSP value-weighted market returns.
Source: Wurgler and Zhuravskaya (1999).

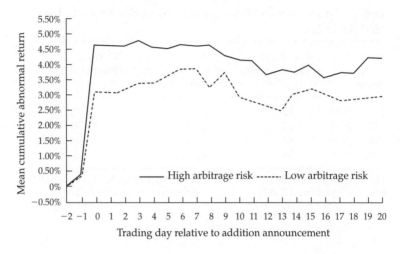

FIG. 2.4 Mean cumulative abnormal returns for stocks added to the S&P 500, by level of imperfect arbitrage risk.
The sample includes 191 stocks that were added to the S&P 500 between September 22, 1976 and September 30, 1989 and were not the subject of contemporaneously reported news. To control for the size of the index fund demand shock, we exclude stocks in the extreme two quartiles of the shock size distribution. We split the remaining 96 stocks into above-median and below-median risk groups, using market index as the only hedge asset. Cumulative abnormal returns are calculated by summing returns in excess of CRSP value-weighted market returns. *Source*: Wurgler and Zhuravskaya (1999).

stock and the substitute portfolio weakens after the inclusion, the hedge obviously gets worse as well. Third, as Figure 2.4 shows, stocks whose returns are harder to replicate experience larger returns on the announcement, suggesting that stock prices actually respond to uninformed demand shifts, and indeed more so when the substitutes are less perfect. These results provide striking evidence that stocks generally do not have perfect substitutes, arbitrage is limited, and for those reasons prices react to uninformed shifts in demand.

One crucial point in this regard is that, in many situations, whether or not two securities are perfect substitutes from the cash flow perspective is far from certain. Consider an example of sovereign debt, where it sometimes happens that two debt issues of the *same* sovereign in different currencies but with identical cash flows once the exchange rate risk is laid off, trade at different prices. The arbitrage opportunity here is nearly perfect, but the arbitrageur still needs to answer some questions. First, can there be a selective default on one debt issue without a default on the other, in which case of course the two debt issues are not perfect substitutes? Second, how good are the currency hedges and in particular might the counterparties default? While there are many legal rules that evidently protect investors from selective defaults, the Russian domestic debt default of August 1998 has shown both that such defaults are possible and that currency hedges are themselves subject to counterparty default.

This discussion shows that arbitrage of fundamentally identical securities is risky, and that when securities do not have perfect substitutes, it may be riskier still. Of course, when we get into the realm of quasi-arbitrage, where the relative prices of broad groups of securities seem to be out of whack, the risks become even more substantial. As an illustration, consider the anomalies discussed in Chapter 1, such as the superior average returns of stocks with poor past performance or of stocks with low ratios of market values to book values. Why doesn't 'arbitrage' eliminate such potential mispricing? An arbitrageur buying value stocks and hedging them with any other portfolio (an index fund or growth stocks), bears not only the risk that mispricing deepens, but also the risk that value continues to underperform because of bad fundamental news. Overall, noise trader risk is only the beginning of the long story of the costs of what traditional finance has come to call 'arbitrage.'

2.4 Conclusion

Risk created by the unpredictability of investor sentiment significantly reduces the attractiveness of arbitrage. As long as arbitrageurs have short horizons and so must worry about liquidating their investment in a mispriced asset, their aggressiveness will be limited even in the absence of fundamental risk. In this case noise trading can lead to a large divergence between market prices and fundamental values. Moreover, noise traders may be compensated for bearing the risk that they themselves create and so earn higher returns than arbitrageurs even though they distort prices. This result calls for a closer scrutiny of the standard argument that noise traders will not persist in the market.

The essential assumption behind these results is that the opinions of noise traders are to some extent unpredictable and arbitrage requires bearing the risk that their misperceptions become even more extreme tomorrow than they are today. Since 'unpredictability' seems to be a general property of the behavior of irrational investors, our conclusions are not simply a consequence of a particular parameterization of noise trader actions. Indeed, this chapter demonstrates that something can be learned about financial markets simply by looking at the effect of unpredictability of investor sentiment on the opportunities available to arbitrageurs.

Crucial for the argument in this book, this chapter has shown that arbitrage is extremely limited even in an environment that is very close to a textbook model. In more complicated environments, it is more limited still. The theoretical presumption for market efficiency based on arbitrage simply does not exist once the realities of real-world arbitrage begin to be modeled seriously. In some ways, the model of this chapter and even the discussion of the results underestimate the potential costs of arbitrage. In Chapter 4, we return to these costs and examine the constraints imposed by the agency relationship in which arbitrageurs function.

3

The Closed End Fund Puzzle

Few problems in finance are as perplexing as the closed end fund puzzle. A closed end fund, like the more popular open end fund, is a mutual fund which typically holds other publicly traded securities. Unlike an open end fund, however, a closed end fund issues a fixed number of shares that are traded on the stock market. To liquidate a holding in a fund, investors must sell their shares to other investors rather than redeem them with the fund itself for the net asset value (NAV) per share as they would with an open end fund. The closed end fund puzzle is the empirical finding that closed end fund shares typically sell at prices not equal to the per share market value of assets the fund holds. Although funds sometimes sell at premia to their net asset values, in recent years discounts of 10 to 20 percent have been the norm.

Several studies have attempted to solve the puzzle by pointing out that the methods used to value the securities in the portfolio might overstate the true value of the assets. Three factors are often cited as potential explanations: agency costs, tax liabilities, and illiquidity of assets. The agency costs theory states that management expenses incurred in running the fund are too high and/or the potential for subpar managerial performance reduces asset value. The tax explanation argues that capital gains tax liabilities on unrealized appreciations (at the fund level) are not captured by the standard calculation of NAV. Finally, because some funds hold restricted or letter securities which have trading restrictions, the argument has been made that such assets are overvalued in the calculation of NAV. While each of these explanations is logical and may explain some portion of the observed discounts, we show below that even collectively these factors fail to account for much of the existing evidence.

This chapter evaluates empirically an alternative explanation for the closed end fund puzzle suggested by the analysis in Chapter 2 and by Zweig (1973). Zweig (1973) suggests that discounts on closed end funds reflect expectations of individual investors. The model in Chapter 2 can be reinterpreted in this light, by thinking of the safe asset *s* as the portfolio of a closed end fund, and the unsafe asset *u* as the fund itself. On this interpretation, we can think of a closed end fund as subject to fluctuating investor sentiment about its future returns and derive implications about its equilibrium pricing. We show that this model is consistent with the available empirical evidence on closed end funds, but also yields new testable implications, which are examined and confirmed below. In this respect, this chapter addresses not only the closed end fund puzzle, but also a broad and invalid criticism of behavioral finance research in general, namely that it does not generate testable empirical predictions. In this chapter, we show that it does and actually do the tests.

Before the various explanations of closed end fund pricing can be evaluated, it is important to provide a more complete description of the facts. There are four important pieces to the puzzle which together characterize the life cycle of a closed end fund:

1 Closed end funds start out at a premium of almost 10 percent when organizers raise money from new investors and use it to purchase securities (Weiss 1989 and Peavy 1990). Most of this premium derives from the underwriting and start-up costs which are removed from the proceeds, thus reducing the NAV relative to the stock price. The reason that investors pay a premium for new funds when existing funds trade at a discount is the first part of the puzzle to be explained.

2 Although they start at a premium, closed end funds move to an average discount of over 10 percent within 120 days from the beginning of trading (Weiss 1989).[1] Thereafter, discounts are the norm. For illustrative purposes, Figure 3.1 shows the year-end discounts on the Tricontinental Corporation (TRI-CON) fund during 1960–86. Tricontinental is the largest closed end stock fund trading on U.S. exchanges, with net assets of over $1.3 billion as of December, 1986. Although there are some periods during which the fund sells at a premium relative to the NAV, most of the time it sells at a discount, which frequently hovers around 20 percent of the NAV.

---

[1] The sample of the Weiss study is closed end funds started during 1985–87. The average discount figure cited relates to stock funds investing in U.S. companies.

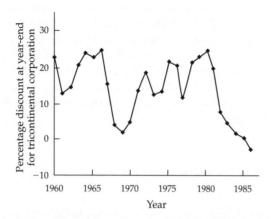

FIG. 3.1 Percentage discount or premium of Tricontinental Corporation at the end of each year during 1960-86.
The percentage discount is computed as $100 \times (NAV - SP)/NAV$; where NAV is the per share net asset value and SP is the share price of the fund. The mean (median) of the percentage discount or premium is 14.43 (15.0). The maximum (minimum) value is 25.0 (- 2.5) and the standard deviation is 8.56·

3 As Figure 3.1 illustrates for TRICON, discounts on closed end funds are subject to wide fluctuations over time. During 1960–86, year-end discounts for TRICON ranged from 25 percent to a premium of 2.5 percent. It is by no means the case that the discount is a constant fraction of net asset value (or a constant dollar amount). The fluctuations in the discounts appear to be mean reverting (Sharpe and Sosin 1975). Thompson (1978), Richards *et al.* (1980), Herzfeld (1980), Anderson (1986), and Brauer (1988) all document significant positive abnormal returns from assuming long positions on funds with large discounts.

4 When closed end funds are terminated through either a liquidation or an open ending, fund share prices rise and discounts shrink (Brauer 1984, Brickley and Schallheim 1985). Most of the positive returns to shareholders accrue when discounts narrow around the announcement of termination. A small discount persists, however, until final termination or open ending.

Our purpose is to understand this four-piece puzzle. We first argue that standard explanations of the puzzle cannot, separately or together, explain all four pieces of the puzzle. We then present an explanation of the puzzle based on the model in Chapter 2, discuss some implications of this explanation, and finally test them using data on U.S. closed end funds. The data are largely supportive of the investor sentiment explanation of the closed end fund puzzles.

3.1 Standard explanation of the closed end fund puzzle

Agency costs, illiquidity of assets, and tax liabilities have all been proposed as potential explanations of closed end fund discounts. These arguments, even when considered together, do not explain all four pieces of the closed end fund puzzle. This section explains why.

Agency costs

Agency costs could create discounts for closed end funds if management fees are too high or if future portfolio management is expected to be subpar (Boudreaux 1973). There are several problems with agency costs as a theory of closed end fund pricing. First, neither current nor future agency costs can account for the wide fluctuations in the discounts. Management fees are typically a fixed percentage of NAV and certainly do not fluctuate as much as do discounts. The present value of future management fees can in principle fluctuate with interest rates. Changes in discounts, however, are not significantly correlated with interest rate changes. Second, agency costs cannot explain why rational investors buy into closed end funds initially at a premium, since they should expect the funds to sell at a discount eventually. Third, agency costs do not seem to explain much of the cross-sectional variation in discounts (Malkiel 1977).

Illiquidity of assets

Two other theories posit that the NAV published by the funds exaggerates the true asset value. The first theory, the restricted stock hypothesis, says that funds hold substantial amounts of let-ter stock, the market value of which is lower than its unrestricted counterpart, and that such holdings are overvalued in the calcu-lation of NAV.[2] This idea can be ruled out immediately as a gen-eral explanation of discounts since many of the largest funds that trade at discounts hold only liquid publicly traded securities. For example, TRICON does not have any significant restricted hold-ings. An examination of the annual financial statements of TRI-CON reveals that for the years during the period studied, the assets which either required Board of Directors' valuation or were marked as 'unidentified' common stocks are always less than 0.5 percent of the total NAV of the fund.

The effect of holding restricted stocks is also mitigated by regulation, which requires the funds to discount such securities in computing NAV to an amount which their Boards of Directors have determined (and publicly attest) is a fair market value equivalent. Nevertheless, there is a small but significant relation-ship in the cross section between the level of restricted holdings and the level of discounts (Malkiel 1977). Apparently, the market does not believe the funds have adequately discounted these securities. Restricted stock holdings can thus explain a portion of the discount on certain specialized funds, but offer no explana-tion for the substantial discounts of large, diversified funds.

Another version of the illiquidity argument, the *block discount hypothesis*, is based on the observation that reported NAVs are computed using the trading price of a marginal share. Since closed end funds sometimes hold substantial blocks of individual securities, the realizable proceeds from a liquidation could be lower than the reported NAV especially if demand curves for stocks have significant downward slopes (Chapter 2). Like the restricted stock hypothesis, this argument runs obviously counter to the evidence that large abnormal positive returns are realized when closed end funds are open ended (Brauer 1984, Brickley

---

[2] Letter, or restricted, stock refers to securities of a corporation which may not be publicly traded without registration under the Securities Act of 1933 because they have not been previously registered. A fund acquires these securities through private placement and agrees to a 'letter' contract restricting their resale to the public within a specified time period. These securities can be resold privately with the letter attached.

and Schallheim 1985). Also, neither theory makes any contribution to explaining the other parts of the puzzle.

Capital gains tax liabilities

The reported NAV of a closed end fund does not reflect the capital gains tax that must be paid by the fund if the assets in the fund are sold.[3] The tax liability associated with assets which have appreciated in value would reduce the liquidation value of the fund's assets. This theory runs into a serious problem with the already mentioned evidence that, on open ending, closed end fund prices move up to net asset values rather than the net asset values falling down to the fund share prices, as would be the case if the measured net asset values were too high. Also, Malkiel (1977) demonstrates that, under fairly generous assumptions, the tax liabilities can account for a discount of no more than 6 percent.[4] Finally, the tax theory suggests that discounts should widen when the market rises (since unrealized appreciation tends to increase in a bull market), contrary to the evidence presented below.

To summarize, standard explanations have been marginally successful (for some funds) in explaining part two of the four-part puzzle—the existence of discounts. However, the existing theories do not provide satisfactory explanations for the other parts of the puzzle: why funds get started, why the discounts fluctuate over time, and why large positive abnormal returns are realized when the fund is open ended. Perhaps most important,

---

[3] The fund has a choice of retaining or distributing its net realized capital gains. If the fund distributes these gains, owners of the fund's shares must pay tax on the distributions according to their own personal tax status. If the fund retains a portion of its net realized capital gains, it is required to pay taxes in accordance with the highest marginal personal tax rate. A tax receipt is then issued to the shareholders which is deductible from personal income taxes.

[4] The key assumptions in this calculation are the percentage of unrealized appreciation in the assets, the period of time before the asset is sold by the fund, and the holding period of the investor after the sale. Malkiel (1977) assumed the unrealized appreciation was 25 percent of the fund's assets and, in the worst case the asset was sold immediately by the fund and the shares were sold immediately thereafter by the investor (which would maximize his tax liability) to arrive at the 6 percent amount. A more probable estimate, given the 25 percent unrealized appreciation, would be around 2 percent.

each of these explanations deals with the puzzle of closed end funds selling at discounts and fails to explain why funds sometimes sell at premia, particularly when they are started. Even taken collectively, these explanations cannot account for all the evidence.

3.2 Investor sentiment

The model applied to closed end funds

Consider the model in Chapter 2, and assume that the safe asset *s* is the portfolio of a closed end fund, and the unsafe asset *u* is the fund itself. This modeling assumption is particularly appropriate because the crucial feature of a closed end fund is that the supply of shares is fixed, as of course is the supply of the unsafe asset in the model in Chapter 2. Suppose further that noise traders' beliefs about the return on *u* relative to the return on *s* are subject to fluctuating sentiment. Some of the time noise traders are optimistic about returns on closed end funds and drive up their prices relative to fundamental values; other times they are pessimistic and drive down the price of *u* relative to that of *s*. For securities where fundamental values are hard to observe, the effects of this fluctuating sentiment will be hard to identify. But in the case of closed end funds, investor optimism will result in funds selling at premia or at smaller discounts, whereas their pessimism will result in wider discounts. In this way, stochastic changes in demand for closed end funds by investors with unpredictably changing expectations of returns cause stochastic fluctuations in the discounts.

In this model, the risk from holding a closed end fund (and any other security subject to the same stochastic sentiment) consists of two parts: the risk of holding the fund's portfolio and the risk that noise trader sentiment about the funds changes. In particular, any investor holding a closed end fund bears the risk that the discount widens in the future if noise traders become relatively more pessimistic about closed end funds. If this risk from the unpredictability of future investor sentiment affects many securities at the same time, it will be priced in equilibrium, just like the noise trader risk in Chapter 2's model.

What is this differential sentiment that might affect the prices of closed end funds relative to those of their underlying portfolios? In this chapter, we conjecture that the discount movements reflect the differential sentiment of *individual* investors, since in the United States these investors hold and trade a preponderance of closed end fund shares but are not as important an ownership group in the assets of the funds' investment portfolios.

There is ample evidence that in the United States closed end funds are owned and traded primarily by individual investors.[5] For example, Weiss (1989) found that three calendar quarters after the initial offering of new closed end funds, institutions held less than 5 percent of the shares in comparison to 23 percent of the shares of a control sample of Initial Public Offerings (IPOs) for operating companies. Similarly, the average institutional ownership in the closed end funds in this chapter's sample (Appendix I) at the beginning of 1988 is just 6.6 percent (median 6.2 percent). For the sake of comparison, at that point in time, average institutional ownership for a random sample of the smallest 10 percent of NYSE stocks is 26.5 percent (median 23.9 percent) and 52.1 percent (median 54.0 percent) for the largest 10 percent of NYSE stocks. Intraday trading data show that, in 1987, 64 percent of the trades in closed end funds were smaller than $10,000. This number is 79 percent for the smallest 10 percent of NYSE stocks and only 28 percent for the largest 10 percent of NYSE stocks.[6] Collectively, the evidence strongly indicates that closed end funds are both held and traded primarily by individual investors.

---

[5] This is not true everywhere in the world. For example, in the United Kingdom, closed end funds are primarily held by institutions, and so we would not predict that small investor sentiment matters for closed end fund pricing in the UK.

[6] Decile membership is based on total market capitalization at the beginning of each year. Firms are sorted by CUSIP, and every third firm is selected to form the random sample. Inclusion in the final sample is subject to availability of data. There were 44–48 firms in each decile portfolio of the final sample. Percentage institutional ownership is based on the first issue of the Standard and Poor's Stock Report in each year after adjusting for known closely-held shares and block holdings. That is, the values reported are percentages of institutional holdings, divided by (100 percent of closely-held or block shares). The intraday trading data is from the Institute for the Study of Security Markets (ISSM) based at Memphis State University.

This evidence suggests a conjecture that the sentiment that affects closed end fund discounts should also affect other securities that are held and traded predominantly by individual investors. As the evidence above shows, one set of such securities is small firms. If smaller capitalization stocks are subject to the same individual investor sentiment as closed end funds, then fluctuations in the discounts on closed end funds should be correlated with the returns on smaller stocks. When enough stocks in addition to closed end funds are affected by the same investor sentiment, risk from this sentiment cannot be diversified and is therefore priced.

The noise trader approach to the closed end fund puzzle explains why fund mispricing relative to its portfolio is not eliminated by arbitrage. The hedge in which an arbitrageur buys an underpriced closed end fund, and sells short its underlying portfolio, even if feasible and costless, is not a pure arbitrage opportunity unless the arbitrageurs have an infinite time horizon and are never forced to liquidate their positions. If, in contrast, an arbitrageur might need to liquidate at some finite time, then he faces the risk that the discount widens since the time the arbitrage trade was put on. If the discount widens, the arbitrage trade obviously results in a loss. Arbitrageurs would never need to liquidate their positions if they received the full proceeds from the initial short sales, since the initial investment would have been negative, and all future cash flows would be zero. But, since arbitrageurs do not get full proceeds, they might need to liquidate to obtain funds. In such cases, bearing noise trader risk is unavoidable. As long as arbitrageurs do not have infinite horizons, arbitrage against noise traders is not riskless because the discount can widen. Because of this risk, arbitrageurs take only limited positions, and mispricing can persist. Mispricing is thus the logical consequence of arbitrage limited by noise trader risk.

Although the risk of widening discounts is the essential building block of this model, there are other costs that in reality also limit arbitrage and thus allow mispricing to persist. These include, for example, the risk resulting from the difficulty of exactly replicating the closed end fund portfolio in an arbitrage trade and the interest that needs to be paid on borrowed securities. Pontiff (1996) presents evidence that, in a cross-section of closed end funds, higher levels of these costs are generally associated with greater mispricing of closed end funds relative to their portfolios. Finally, a possible alternative to the 'buy and hold' arbitrage is a takeover of a closed end fund, followed by a sell-off of its assets to realize the net asset value. The theoretical impediment to such takeovers has been identified by Grossman and Hart (1980), who show that free-riding fund shareholders would not tender their shares to the bidder unless they receive full net asset value. Because making a bid is costly, the bidder who pays full NAV cannot himself profit from the bid and so no bids will take place. In practice, managerial resistance and regulatory restrictions represent formidable hurdles for the would-be bidder. For example, by 1980 the Tricontinental and Lehman funds had each defeated four attempts at reorganization (Herzfeld 1980). If acquirers' profits from closed end fund takeovers are meager after transaction costs, then it is not surprising that such takeovers have not been more common.

Investor sentiment and the four-part puzzle

Changing investor sentiment has a number of empirical implications for the pricing of closed end funds. Most importantly, because holding the fund is riskier than holding its portfolio directly, and because this risk is systematic, the required rate of return on assets held as fund shares must, on average, be higher than the required return on the same assets purchased directly. This means that the fund must, on average, sell at a discount to its NAV to induce investors to hold the fund's shares. This implication is just the consequence of equation (2.9) in Chapter 2, and the 'create space' effect, applied to closed end funds. To get this result we do not need to assume that noise traders are, on average, pessimistic about funds: the average underpricing of closed end funds comes solely from the fact that holding the fund is riskier than holding its portfolio. This theory is consistent with the main closed end fund puzzle: they sell at a discount.

The theory is also consistent with the other three pieces of the puzzle. First, it implies that when noise traders are particularly optimistic about closed end funds (and other assets subject to the same movements in investor sentiment), entrepreneurs can profit by putting assets together into closed end funds and selling them to the noise traders. In this model, rational investors do not buy closed end funds at the beginning. On the contrary, if they could borrow the shares they would sell the funds short.[7] It seems necessary to introduce some type of irrational investor to be able to explain why anyone buys the fund shares at the start when the expected return over the next few months is negative. Noise traders, who are sometimes far too optimistic about the true expected return on the fund shares, serve that purpose in the model. In this theory, then, there is no 'efficiency' reason for the existence of closed end funds: they are a device by which smart entrepreneurs take advantage of a less sophisticated public.

Second, the theory implies that discounts on closed end funds fluctuate with changes in investor sentiment about future returns (on closed end funds and other securities). In fact, this theory *requires* that discounts vary stochastically since it is precisely the fluctuations in the discounts that make holding the fund risky and therefore account for average underpricing. If the discounts were constant, then the arbitrage trade of buying the fund and selling short its portfolio would be riskless even for a short horizon investor, and discounts would disappear.

Third, the theory explains why funds' share prices rise on the announcement of open ending and why discounts are reduced and then eliminated at the time open ending or liquidation actually occurs. When it is known that a fund will be open ended or liquidated (or even when the probability of open ending increases appreciably), noise trader risk is eliminated (or reduced), and so is the discount. This risk is largely eliminated when open ending or liquidation is announced, since at that time any investor can buy the fund and sell short its portfolio knowing that upon open ending his arbitrage position can be profitably closed for sure. The risk of having to sell when the discount is even wider no longer exists. The small discount that remains after the announcement of open ending or liquidation can only be explained by the actual transactions costs of arbitrage (the inability to receive short-sale proceeds or the unobservability of the fund's portfolio) or the effect of some of the standard explanations mentioned earlier. The investor sentiment theory thus predicts that the discounts which remain after

---

[7] Peavy (1990) shows that underwriters of closed end funds buy shares in the aftermarket to support the price. Short selling of closed end fund IPOs is extremely difficult.

the announcement of open ending or liquidation should become small or disappear eventually.

Additional implications

The investor sentiment explanation of discounts on closed end funds has a number of additional implications which have not been derived or tested in the context of other theories of discounts. As with the implications discussed above, the new implications are derived from the idea that discounts on closed end funds reflect widespread changes in investor sentiment rather than idiosyncratic changes in each fund's management or operations.

The first implication is that levels of and changes in discounts should be highly correlated across funds. Since the same sentiment drives discounts on all funds as well as on other securities, changes in this sentiment should determine changes in discounts.

Second, the observation that funds can get started when noise traders are optimistic about their returns can be taken further. Specifically, to the extent that closed end funds are substitutes, the model predicts that new funds should get started when investors favor seasoned funds as well, i.e. when old funds sell at a premium or at a small discount. This effect might be obscured by short-selling constraints on new funds and the fact that new funds are not perceived as perfect substitutes for seasoned funds. Nevertheless, we test this implication by examining the behavior of the discounts on seasoned funds when new funds are started.

The third implication of the theory is perhaps the most interesting and surprising. The theory requires that for investor sentiment to affect closed end fund prices, despite the workings of arbitrage, the risk created by changes in investor sentiment must be widespread. The same investor sentiment that affects discounts on closed end funds must affect other assets as well which have nothing to do with closed end funds. For example, returns on some portfolios of stocks might be correlated with changes in the average discount on closed end funds, controlling for market returns. Portfolios affected by the same sentiment as closed end funds should do well when discounts narrow and poorly when discounts widen. The theory itself does not specify which securities will be influenced by the same sentiment as closed end funds.

As we argued above, however, in the United States, smaller capitalization stocks, as well as other stocks held and traded predominantly by individual investors, are likely to be influenced by the same sentiment.

The last implication is, conceptually, the most important as well as the most general one. The reason is that it suggests that, contrary to be basic notion of efficient markets, there will be a *comovement* in the prices of securities that are fundamentally unrelated to each other solely because they are traded by similar investors and therefore influenced by similar sentiment. The prediction of such comovement is essential because it can, in principle, be detected in the data. The detection of such comovement contradicts the basic principle of efficient markets that security prices should not move when there is no news, since comovement represents a response to demand changes that are unlikely to be related to fundamental news for fundamentally unrelated securities. Methodologically, this is a crucial implication of noise trader theory.

Other models of closed end fund discounts are either silent about these three new predictions, or else they yield the opposite results. The evidence we present below, then, is either orthogonal to alternative theories, or else enables us to differentiate between them and the investor sentiment explanation of discounts.

3.3. Data and variable description for the basic analysis[8]

Closed end fund data were collected from two main sources. Information on annual discounts and net asset values, as well as background information on each fund, was obtained from the 1960–87 editions of Wiesenberger's Investment Companies Services annual survey of mutual funds. We were also able to obtain the year that each fund started from these sources. A total of 87 funds were initially identified through this source, of which 68 were selected for monthly analysis because they were known

---

[8] The empirical work described in this chapter was initially reported in Lee *et al.* (1991), and has not been updated. Recent research on the closed end funds is surveyed by Dimson and Minio-Kozerski (1998).

to have CUSIP identifiers. For these funds, we collected the weekly net asset value per share, stock price, and discount per share as reported by the *Wall Street Journal* (*WSJ*) between July, 1956 and December, 1985 (inclusive). Each week, generally on Monday, the *WSJ* reports the previous Friday's closing prices, NAVs, and discounts. To convert the data into a monthly series, the Friday which was closest to each month end was taken, so each observation is within three days of the last day of the month.[9] The NAV per share information from the *WSJ* and the number of shares outstanding at the end of each month, obtained from the monthly master tape of the Center for Research of Security Prices (CRSP), were used to arrive at the total net asset value for each fund.

For several of the tests which follow we constructed a value-weighted index of discounts (VWD) both at the annual and monthly levels as follows:

$$VWD_t = \sum_{i=1}^{n_t} W_i \, DISC_{it}$$

where

$$W_i = \frac{NAV_{it}}{\sum_{i=1}^{n_t} NAV_{it}},$$

$$DISC_{it} = \frac{NAV_{it} - SP_{it}}{NAV_{it}} \times 100,$$

NAV_{it} = net asset value of fund i at end of period t,

SP_{it} = stock price of fund i at end of period t,

n_t = the number of funds with available $DISC_{it}$.

---

[9] The use of a monthly interval allows for comparison with other macroeconomic variables. Various validity checks were employed both during the data collection and later analysis to ensure the integrity of this data. The inputting of a NAV and stock price, for example, generated an automatic discount calculation on the input screen which was checked against the figure reported in the *WSJ*. After input, univariate statistics were computed on all large funds to check for outliers, and unusual observations were traced back to the *WSJ*. Occasional inaccuracies in the *WSJ* figures were corrected through appeal to numbers reported in adjacent weeks. There were two weeks for which the *WSJ* did not appear to have reported this data. In constructing the monthly series the next closest Friday's close was used.

We also computed changes in the value-weighted index of discounts (ΔVWD). For this measure, we computed VWD in a similar fashion, except we required that each fund included in the index must have the $DISC$ and NAV data available for months t and $t - 1$, so that monthly changes in the index are computed over the same asset base. In other words, we require common membership in adjacent months. We then defined ΔVWD to be:

$$\Delta VWD_t = VWD_t - VWD_{t-1}$$

The change in the value-weighted index of discounts (ΔVWD) was computed with both annual and monthly data. For the monthly series, we computed this variable several ways. In the first case we excluded funds which specialize in foreign securities, specifically the American South African (ASA) Fund and the Japan Fund. In the second case we excluded bond funds (funds which invest primarily in debt securities). The results were similar irrespective of the ΔVWD measure used. The reported findings are based on ΔVWD computed using both foreign and domestic stock funds (i.e. excluding bond funds but including both the ASA Fund and the Japan Fund). This time series spanned 246 months (7/65 to 12/85).

Of the original sample of 68 funds, 18 were either missing data from the *WSJ* or did not have shares information available on CRSP and 30 others were bond funds, leaving a total of 20 stock funds participating in the monthly ΔVWD series (see Appendix I). Of these 20 funds, some had relatively short life spans, and others may occasionally have missing data points, so the actual number of funds included in computing VWD and ΔVWD varies from month to month. The stock fund ΔVWD series had monthly memberships ranging from 7 funds to 18 funds. In the vast majority of months, at least 10 funds were in the index. The key findings in this chapter are relatively insensitive to the choice of funds included in the value-weighted index.

3.4 Evidence

Comovements in discounts of different funds

The investor sentiment model predicts that both the levels and the changes in the discounts on closed end funds should be correlated. Figure 3.2 shows the levels of discounts for all closed end stock funds at the end of each year during 1960–86. The clear impression is that discounts on individual funds are highly correlated. In fact, the average pairwise correlation of year-end discounts for domestic funds is 0.497 (0.607 for diversified domestic funds). Individual pairwise correlations range from insignificant with specialized funds to above 0.8 for some diversified domestic funds. The average pairwise correlation of annual changes in discounts among domestic stock funds is 0.389.

The same conclusion emerges from an examination of monthly pairwise correlations. Tables 3.1 and 3.2 present the monthly correlations of both levels and changes in discounts for several major

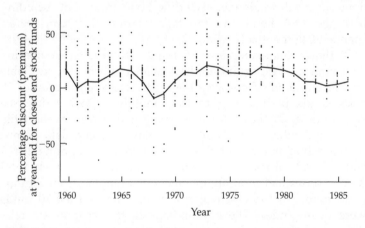

Fɪɢ. 3.2. Percentage discount or premium at the end of the year for all closed end stock funds during 1960-86.
The percentage discount is computed as $100 \times (\text{NAV} - \text{SP})/\text{NAV}$; where NAV is the per share net asset value and SP is the share price of the fund. The sample includes all 46 stock funds reported in the Wiesenberger Investment Companies Services Annual survey during this period. The discount on a value-weighted portfolio of these funds is represented by the solid line.

Table 3.1 Correlation of monthly discounts of individual funds

	AdExp	ASA	CentSec	GenAm	Japan	Lehman	Niag	Petr	TRICON	VWD
AdExp	—									
ASA	0.266 0.0001	—								
CentSec	0.654 0.0001	−0.286 0.0003	—							
GenAm	0.737 0.0001	0.065 0.3279	0.596 0.0001	—						
Japan	0.430 0.0001	0.235 0.0004	0.512 0.0001	0.395 0.0001	—					
Lehman	0.830 0.0001	0.303 0.0001	0.693 0.0001	0.785 0.0001	0.643 0.0001	—				
Niag	0.596 0.0001	0.106 0.1104	0.266 0.0007	0.633 0.0001	0.533 0.0001	0.753 0.0001	—			
Petr	0.378 0.0001	0.165 0.0129	0.159 0.0447	0.254 0.0001	−0.084 0.1947	0.230 0.0002	0.198 0.0019	—		

Table 3.1 Cont.

	AdExp	ASA	CentSec	GenAm	Japan	Lehman	Niag	Petr	TRICON	VWD
TRICON	0.651	0.075	0.651	0.459	0.533	0.666	0.671	0.279	—	
	0.0001	0.2630	0.0001	0.0001	0.0001	0.0001	0.0001	0.0001		
VWD	0.810	0.427	0.539	0.711	0.651	0.893	0.767	0.281	0.805	—
	0.0001	0.0001	0.0001	0.0001	0.0001	0.0001	0.0001	0.0001	0.0001	
NYVAL	-0.019	0.477	-0.860	-0.254	-0.053	-0.046	-0.084	-0.016	-0.316	-0.056
	0.7721	0.0001	0.0001	0.0001	0.4130	0.4714	0.1891	0.7976	0.0001	0.2787

Correlation between levels of discounts at month end for nine individual funds, the discount on a value-weighted portfolio of all closed end stock funds (VWD) and the total value of all New York Stock Exchange firms, NYVAL (7/65 to 12/85). The pairwise Pearson product–moment correlation and p-value for a two-tailed test of the null hypothesis of zero correlation are shown.

Table 3.2 Correlation of changes in monthly discounts of individual funds

	AdExp	ASA	CentSec	GenAm	Japan	Lehman	Niag	Petr	TRICON	ΔVWD
AdExp	—									
ASA	-0.054 0.3687	—								
CentSec	0.424 0.0001	0.037 0.6530	—							
GenAm	0.301 0.0068	-0.622 0.3687	0.063 0.4374	—						
Japan	-0.028 0.6732	0.0189 0.7870	-0.0311 0.7030	0.0181 0.7831	—					
Lehman	0.304 0.0001	0.061 0.3808	0.339 0.0001	0.406 0.0001	0.037 0.6700	—				
Niag	0.173 0.0075	0.082 0.236	0.178 0.028	0.188 0.0034	0.118 0.0719	0.263 0.0001	—			
Petr	0.269 0.0001	0.051 0.4650	0.056 0.4884	0.247 0.0001	0.173 0.0081	0.173 0.0077	0.249 0.0001	—		

Table 3.2 Cont.

	AdExp	ASA	CentSec	GenAm	Japan	Lehman	Niag	Petr	TRICON	ΔVWD
TRICON	0.358	−0.171	0.238	0.242	0.053	0.309	0.247	0.201	—	
	0.0001	0.0133	0.0033	0.0002	0.4187	0.0011	0.0001	0.0018		
ΔVWD	0.419	0.384	0.300	0.435	0.165	0.629	0.413	0.381	0.561	—
	0.0001	0.0001	0.0001	0.0001	0.0109	0.0001	0.0001	0.0001	0.0001	
VWNY	0.159	−0.143	0.199	0.059	−0.241	0.1061	0.225	−0.027	0.120	0.013
	0.0138	0.037	0.0131	0.3638	0.0002	0.3229	0.0004	0.6760	0.0629	0.8446

Correlation of changes in the monthly discounts between nine individual funds, a value-weighted portfolio of all closed end stock funds (ΔVWD) and the monthly return on a value-weighted portfolio of all New York Stock Exchange firms, VWNY (7/65 to 12/85). The pairwise Pearson product–moment correlation and p-value for a two-tailed test of the null hypothesis of zero correlation are shown.

funds. The ten funds in these tables have the highest number of available observations over the study period. With the notable exceptions of ASA Fund and the Japan Fund (two foreign funds), and perhaps Petroleum Resources (a fund specializing in oil and gas stocks), the levels of discounts on different funds show a high level of correlation. The average pairwise correlation of month-end discounts for domestic funds is 0.530 (0.643 for diversified domestic funds). The average pairwise correlation of monthly changes in discounts among domestic stock funds is 0.248 (0.267 for diversified domestic funds). That this comovement is captured by the *VWD* variable is seen in the strong correlation of this variable to the discounts of each individual fund. This is true even for the two foreign funds.

It seems clear from Tables 3.1 and 3.2 that discounts of different domestic funds tend to move together. In fact, these high correlations between discounts justify the construction of the value-weighted discount. The positive correlations are consistent with the hypothesis that discounts on different funds are driven by the same investor sentiment. Tables 3.1 and 3.2 also illustrate the point that neither the levels nor the changes in discounts on closed end funds are related very strongly to levels of stock prices or stock returns. The correlation between the returns on the value-weighted market index (VWNY) and the changes in the value-weighted discount index (ΔVWD) is not significantly different from zero. A similar result was obtained by Sharpe and Sosin (1975). Thus, if discounts are driven by movements in investor sentiment, this sentiment is not strongly correlated with the aggregate stock market returns. As we argued above, these movements in the United States reflect the differential sentiment of individual investors.

When do funds get started?

The investor sentiment model predicts that new funds get started when old funds sell at premiums or at small discounts. Testing this hypothesis presents several problems. First, over most of the period we examine, very few funds get started. Although this fact makes sense given that funds almost always trade at a discount during this period, it makes testing more difficult. Second, it takes time to organize and register a fund, which means that funds may start trading long after the time they are conceived. These delays also raise the possibility that fund offerings are withdrawn when market conditions change, creating a bias in the time series of fund starts. Third, new funds tend to be brought to market with features which distinguish them from existing funds. In the early 1970s, the funds which got started were primarily bond funds and funds specializing in restricted securities, types that had not previously existed. In the bull market of 1985–87, numerous foreign funds and so called 'celebrity funds' (funds managed by well-known money managers) came to market. The former offered easy access to markets in specific foreign countries, and the latter offered an opportunity to cash in on the expertise of famous managers. To the extent seasoned funds and existing funds are not seen as perfect substitutes, new funds could get started even when seasoned funds sell at discounts.

Figure 3.3 plots the number of stock funds started each year

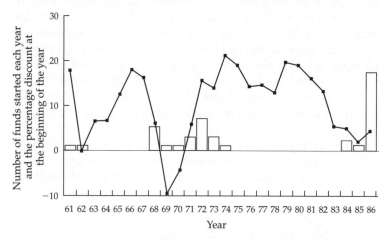

FIG. 3.3 The number of closed end stock funds started and the discount on stock funds at the beginning of the year.
This graph shows the number of closed end stock funds started during the year and the percentage discount on a value-weighted portfolio of closed end stock funds at the beginning of each year during 1961–86. The line graph represents the percentage discount at the beginning of the year. The bar graph represents the number of stock funds started during the year.

against the *VWD* at the beginning of the year. Fund starts tend to be clustered through time. Periods when many funds start roughly coincide with periods when discounts are relatively low. We can compare the value-weighted discounts on seasoned funds in years when one or more new stock funds begin trading and in years where no stock funds begin trading. Between 1961 and 1986, there are 12 years in which one or more stock funds get started and 14 years in which no stock funds start.

The average beginning-of-year discount in the former subset of years is 6.40 percent, and the average beginning-of-year discount in the latter subset of years is 13.64 percent. The difference between the average discounts in the two subsamples of years is significant at the 1 percent level. This result lends some support to the argument that new funds get started when discounts on old funds are lower, though the discounts are nontrivial even in the years with new start-ups. Given the caveats discussed above, the evidence on start-up of new funds is at least consistent with the investor sentiment hypothesis.

Discount movements and returns on small firms

In this subsection, we present evidence on perhaps the least obvious prediction of the theory, namely that changes in the discounts on closed end funds should be correlated with returns on baskets of stocks *that may have nothing to do with the funds themselves*. In particular, we look at portfolios of firms with different capitalizations, under the theory that the individual investors are significant holders and traders of smaller stocks, and so changes in their sentiment should affect both closed end funds and smaller stocks. Since we have established that discounts on different funds move together, we use the change in the value weighted discount (ΔVWD) as a proxy for discount changes. Our measure of market returns are returns on the value weighted index of NYSE stocks. Finally, the portfolios of stocks we consider are ten size-ranked portfolios. The first portfolio (Decile 1) are the 10 percent of all stocks that have the smallest equity value on NYSE, and the tenth portfolio (Decile 10) are the 10 percent with the largest equity value.[10]

Table 3.3 presents the results of time series regressions of returns of decile portfolios on market returns and on changes in *VWD*. As in previous studies, we find that all portfolios have market betas in the neighborhood of 1, with the smallest firms having a beta of 1.3 and largest firms having a beta of 0.93. Beta estimates are almost identical when these regressions are run without the *VWD* variable. For all portfolios, we also find evidence of a correlation between returns and changes in the *VWD* holding market returns constant. For Decile 10, the largest firms, we find that stock prices do poorly when discounts narrow. For the other nine portfolios, stocks do well when discounts shrink. As predicted, when individual investors become optimistic about closed end funds and smaller stocks, these stocks do well and discounts narrow. When individual investors become pessimistic about closed end funds and smaller stocks, smaller stocks do badly and discounts widen.[11]

For Decile 1, a drop of 1 percent in the monthly value weighted discount index is accompanied by an extra return of 0.67 percent

---

[10] The portfolio rebalancing algorithm used to compute decile portfolio returns follows Chen *et al.* (1986). Membership of each decile was determined at the beginning of each year and kept constant for the rest of the year. The returns of each firm in the decile were weighted by its beginning-of-month market capitalization. In case of missing returns, a firm was excluded from the portfolio for the current and following month. Since discounts are reported as of each Friday's close, the use of full monthly returns introduces a potential timing problem. We correct for this by computing the monthly market returns and the returns of the decile portfolios using the exact dates on which the discounts are computed. Slightly weaker results than those of Table 3.3 obtain if full monthly returns are used, although the coefficient on ΔVWD is still significant in all deciles at the 1 percent level (two-tailed), except for Decile 9, which is significant at the 2 percent level. We thank Raymond Kan for suggesting this improvement.

[11] The evidence presented thus far is inconsistent with the unmeasured capital gains tax liability hypothesis of discounts. This theory predicts that when stocks do well, closed end funds should accrue unrealized capital gains, and discounts should in general widen, holding the turnover rates on fund assets constant. However, Table 3.2 shows that the correlation between returns on the market and changes in discounts is about zero (the statistically insignificant correlation is negative which goes against the tax theory). Table 3.3 also indicates that discounts narrow when small stocks do well which is also inconsistent with the tax explanation.

Table 3.3 The time-series relationship between returns on size-decile portfolios, the market return, and changes in closed end fund discounts

Return on the decile portfolio	Intercept	ΔVWD	VWNY	Adjusted R^2
1 (smallest)	0.0062	−0.0067 (−4.94)	1.238 (18.06)	58.7
2	0.0042	−0.0049 (−4.83)	1.217 (23.66)	70.3
3	0.0036	−0.0039 (−4.20)	1.202 (26.09)	74.0
4	0.0033	−0.0038 (−5.07)	1.163 (30.64)	79.7
5	0.0027	−0.0029 (−4.12)	1.148 (32.90)	81.8
6	0.0024	−0.0028 (−4.65)	1.124 (37.08)	85.1
7	0.0013	−0.0015 (−3.03)	1.134 (45.30)	89.4
8	0.0015	−0.0015 (−3.45)	1.088 (51.32)	91.5
9	0.0003	−0.0010 (−3.14)	1.057 (66.93)	94.8
10 (largest)	−0.0005	0.0010 (3.84)	0.919 (71.34)	95.4
1−10	0.0067	−0.0077 (−4.93)	0.319 (4.05)	13.5

The time series relationship (7/65 to 12/85) between monthly returns on decile portfolios (dependent variables), changes in the monthly discount on a value-weighted portfolio of closed end stock funds (ΔVWD), and the monthly return on a value-weighted portfolio of New York Stock Exchange firms (VWNY). Decile 10 contains the largest firms, Decile 1 the smallest. Membership in each decile is determined at the beginning of year and kept constant for the rest of the year. Returns of each firm are weighted by the beginning-of-month market capitalization. In case of missing returns, a firm is excluded from the portfolio for the current and following month. The dependent variable in the last row is the excess return of small firms over large firms, computed by subtracting Decile 10 returns from Decile 1 returns. The number of observations is 245. t-statistics are shown in parentheses.

per month. Since the median absolute change in the monthly discount index over our study period is 1.40, this means in a typical month the discount factor is associated with a monthly fluctuation of 0.94 percent in the Decile 1 returns. The median monthly absolute return for Decile 1 firms over this period is 3.91 percent. Thus, in a typical month, approximately 24 percent of the monthly small firm returns is accountable by discount changes, even after controlling for general market movements. For Deciles 2 through 9, the effect is in the same direction but weaker. The effect on the returns of Decile 10 firms, while statistically significant, is of a different sign and much smaller: in a typical month, about five percent of the total return is accountable by discount changes.[12]

The coefficients on the change in *VWD* are monotonic in portfolio size. For the smallest stocks, which typically have the highest individual ownership, the comovement with closed end funds is the greatest. For larger capitalization stocks, which have lower individual ownership, this comovement is weaker. Finally, the largest stocks, which by the end of this period had over 50 percent institutional ownership, seem to move in the opposite direction from the discounts.

A final piece of evidence germane to this analysis comes from the seasonal pattern of discounts. Brauer and Chang (1990) present the striking result that prices of closed end funds exhibit a January effect even though prices of the funds' portfolios do not. We confirmed this result in our data: the mean January ΔVWD is significantly negative, meaning discounts shrink in January. Interestingly, Ritter (1988) documents that 40 percent of the year-to-year variation in the turn-of-the-year effect is explained by the buy–sell activities of individual investors. These findings, of course, accord well with the notion that closed end fund prices are affected by individual investor trading, some of which occurs at the end of the year, and not just by fundamentals. To ensure that the Table 3.3 results are not restricted to the turn-of-the-year, we performed the same regressions with January and December observations removed. The coefficients on ΔVWD remained significant for all ten deciles at the 1 percent level and the monotonicity is preserved.

[12] Based on $(1.40 \times 0.10)/2.534$, where 2.534 is the median absolute return on the Decile 10 portfolio.

To summarize, the evidence suggests that discounts on closed end funds narrow when smaller stocks do well. This correlation is the stronger, the smaller are the stocks. These results are consistent with the hypothesis that, in the United States, individual investor sentiment is particularly important for the prices of smaller stocks and of closed end funds.

Before moving on, we need to consider a suggestion that this crucial finding is spurious.

Suppose that closed end funds holdings are concentrated in smaller stocks which are thinly traded. Then prices used in the calculation of net asset value are often stale, whereas closed end fund prices are relatively fresh. This means that when smaller stocks do well, closed end funds that hold these stocks appreciate, but the net asset value does not rise by as much as it should because some of the smaller stock prices used to compute the NAV are stale. Reported NAVs could also be stale if closed end funds report changes in NAV sluggishly. The effect would be the same as if assets were infrequently traded. In their case, the discount narrows (i.e. the stock price of the fund moves up relative to its NAV) precisely when smaller stocks do well. The key finding of Table 3.3 could then result from the mismeasurement of the net asset value.

This objection relies on the critical assumption that closed end funds invest in smaller stocks (so their stock prices move together with the prices of smaller firms). This assumption is suspect in light of Brauer and Chang's (1990) finding that the portfolio holdings of closed end funds do not exhibit a January effect. To evaluate this assumption more directly, we examine the portfolio of TRICON. Table 3.4 describes TRICON's holdings, distributed by decile, every five years starting in 1965. The table shows that TRICON's holdings are concentrated in stocks in the largest two deciles, which, together with short-term holdings and cash equivalents, represent about 80 percent of the fund's holdings. Short-term holdings and stocks in the top five deciles typically represent over 90 percent of the fund's earning assets. In contrast, the fund typically holds less than 4 percent of its assets in stocks from the bottom five deciles. Since the stocks in the top two deciles are virtually never mispriced because of nontrading, and since the stocks in the top five deciles are rarely mispriced, it is hard to believe that TRICON's portfolio is subject to large mistakes in the calculation of net asset value because of nontrading or sluggish reporting.

Table 3.4 Composition of the Tricontinental Corporation investment portfolio

	1985	%	1980	%	1975	%	1970	%	1965	%
Decile 1	0.0	0.0	0.0	0.0	2902.4	0.5	3644.7	0.6	8488.8	1.5
Decile 2	0.0	0.0	3316.5	0.4	548.5	0.1	7514.0	1.2	5856.0	1.0
Decile 3	2793.8	0.2	0.0	0.0	3507.9	0.6	125.8	0.0	0.0	0.0
Decile 4	0.0	0.0	7000.0	0.8	2051.2	0.4	1575.0	0.3	0.0	0.0
Decile 5	2477.9	0.2	19125.0	2.2	9840.5	1.7	9715.5	1.6	8016.2	1.4
Decile 6	4575.0	0.4	38519.2	4.4	5903.5	1.0	14304.3	2.4	0.0	0.0
Decile 7	63575.5	5.3	58238.9	6.6	28283.5	5.0	21934.8	3.7	23832.0	4.3
Decile 8	118981.2	10.0	88204.4	10.1	53320.2	9.4	51241.8	8.5	76452.2	13.7
Decile 9	306874.7	25.7	181298.3	20.7	69407.0	12.2	49787.5	8.3	82263.8	14.7
Decile 10	558993.8	46.8	391753.9	44.7	344500.4	60.7	371398.4	61.7	336612.2	60.2
Short-term holdings and cash equivalents	128745.1	10.8	67978.2	7.8	41905.7	7.4	60690.5	10.1	17940.0	3.2
Other holdings	8143.2	0.7	20890.9	2.3	5474.4	1.0	9702.1	1.6	0.0	0.0
Total value of portfolio	1195160.3	100	876325.3	100	567645.2	100	601633.6	100	559459.2	100

Composition of the investment portfolio of Tricontinental Corporation (TRICON) at the end of the year, distributed by the total market capitalization of the individual investments. To construct this table, each holding in the TRICON portfolio for each of the years listed was identified from the financial statements of the fund. For the majority of holdings, market capitalization was obtained through the CRSP tapes; market capitalization for the remainder were traced to Moody's Security Manuals and manually checked against Decile cutoffs for each year. Values are shown in thousands of dollars. Decile cutoffs for each year are the same as those used on earlier regressions and are obtained from CRSP. Cash and short-term holdings include government T-bills and corporate debt instruments, net of short-term liabilities of the fund. Other holdings represent equity securities for which the market capitalization was not readily obtainable.

Table 3.5 The time series relationship between returns on size-decile portfolios, the market return, and changes in the discount of Tricontinental Corporation

Return on the decile portfolio	Intercept	TRICON	VWNY	Adjusted R^2
1 (smallest)	0.0062	-0.0026 (-2.74)	1.263 (17.52)	56.0
2	0.0044	-0.0021 (-2.98)	1.236 (23.11)	68.9
3	0.0039	-0.0017 (-2.70)	1.214 (25.46)	72.9
4	0.0036	-0.0013 (-2.41)	1.174 (29.39)	78.3
5	0.0030	-0.0011 (-2.40)	1.156 (31.96)	81.0
6	0.0025	-0.0014 (-3.41)	1.135 (36.28)	84.6
7	0.0014	-0.0009 (-2.76)	1.142 (44.99)	89.4
8	0.0016	-0.0010 (-3.54)	1.097 (51.41)	91.7
9	0.0004	-0.0007 (-3.21)	1.062 (66.21)	94.8
10 (largest)	-0.0006	0.0005 (2.94)	0.916 (69.80)	95.4
1-10	0.0069	-0.0031 (-2.85)	0.347 (4.20)	8.9

The time series relationship (7/65 to 12/85) between monthly returns on decile portfolios (dependent variables), changes in the monthly discount on a value-weighted portfolio of Tricontinental (TRICON), and the monthly return on a value-weighted portfolio of New York Stock Exchange firms (VWNY). Decile 10 contains the largest firms, Decile 1 the smallest. Membership in each decile is determined at the beginning of the year and kept constant for the rest of the year. Returns of each firm are weighted by the beginning-of-month market capitalization. In case of missing returns, a firm is excluded from the portfolio for the current and following month. The dependent variable in the last row is the excess return of small firms over large firms, computed by subtracting Decile 10 returns from Decile 1 returns. The number of observations is 241. *t*-statistics are shown in parentheses.

We can now evaluate the validity of the objection by regressing decile returns on VWNY and changes in discounts as in Table 3.3, but this time using changes in TRICON's discount instead of the changes in the value-weighted discount. The results, reported in Table 3.5, are very similar to those in Table 3.3, although parameter estimates are closer to zero, presumably because of a larger idiosyncratic component to TRICON's discounts. Thus smaller stocks do well when TRICON's discount narrows even though TRICON is holding virtually no small stocks. This finding is inconsistent with the hypothesis that our results can be explained by nontrading or delayed reporting.[13] Incidentally, TRICON itself is a Decile 8 stock, and its comovement with small stocks cannot be explained by the size of its own market capitalization.

Discount movements and returns on firms held by individuals

An alternative, and perhaps more direct, way to look at comovement is by focusing on the ownership structure of firms directly and asking whether closed end funds move together with other firms with low institutional (and therefore presumably high individual) ownership. To do this correctly, we have to sort firms by ownership and size separately since, as we have already pointed out, smaller firms also have higher individual ownership. Unfortunately, the ownership data are only available since 1980 and hence we need to change the frequency of observations to weekly rather than monthly data. We have compiled a database using Spectrum data on 13-F SEC filings of institutional holdings in all NYSE firms between 1981 and 1990. At the beginning of each year, we divided all the firms in this sample into size decile

---

[13] We also regressed the difference between the small and large firm returns (Decile 1 returns minus Decile 10 returns) against market movements and the change in discounts for each of ten major funds. For all ten funds, the coefficient on the discount variable was negative, significantly so for eight of the funds. Thus the relationship between small firm excess returns and discount changes is relatively insensitive to the choice of the fund. However, the t-statistics on $\Delta DISC_i$ for individual funds are lower than the t-statistic on ΔVWD in Table 3.3, suggesting that the portfolio approach removes idiosyncratic variations in the individual fund discounts.

portfolios by market capitalization. We then ranked the firms within each decile by institutional ownership, and formed for each decile three equal groups with high, medium, and low institutional holdings. This procedure yielded 30 size-institutional ownership portfolios that are rebalanced annually. With these data, we can directly examine the relationship between returns and changes in discounts by institutional ownership within each size decile.

Table 3.6 reports the results of weekly regressions using these data. Table 3.6 shows very clearly that, within every size decile but the first, low institutional ownership firms comove more strongly with changes in discounts than medium and high institutional ownership firms. The difference in coefficients on change in the value weighted discount between 'high' and 'low' institutional ownership groups is significant in the 6th, 8th, 9th, and 10th size deciles. For all ten size deciles put together, the F-statistic of the hypothesis that the coefficient for low and high institutional ownership firms are the same has the value of 22.70 and a p-value of 0.0001. This result is broadly consistent with the previous finding that what is important about the comovement of small firms and closed end funds is their common structure of predominantly individual ownership. Indeed, the likely reason that we do not see much difference within the first decile in comovement between discounts and the three ownership portfolios is the fact that, during this time period, there was hardly any institutional ownership of first decile stocks (see Chopra *et al.* 1993). Even this evidence, then, is consistent with the view that, in the United States, discounts on closed end funds reflect individual investor sentiment.

Table 3.6 The weekly time series relations between size-institutional ownership portfolio returns, market returns and changes in closed end fund discounts over 1/2/81 to 12/28/90

Size	Inst.	Intercept	VWNY	t-statistic	ΔVWD	t-statistic	Adj.R^2	Mean Institutional Ownership (%)	F-statistic on ΔVWD (H_0:L = H)
1	L	0.00105	0.718	16.57	-0.00206	-2.85	0.3507	0.99	0.018
1	M	0.00031	0.711	17.31	-0.00233	-3.39	0.3712	5.05	(0.892)
1	H	0.00031	0.671	16.79	-0.00216	-3.22	0.3570	16.83	
2	L	-0.00044	0.712	20.98	-0.00249	-4.38	0.4653	2.73	1.550
2	M	0.00021	0.811	25.30	-0.00166	-3.08	0.5586	8.60	(0.214)
2	H	0.00002	0.802	24.79	-0.00192	-3.54	0.5481	23.64	
3	L	-0.00001	0.825	26.42	-0.00228	-4.35	0.5794	3.64	1.340
3	M	-0.00068	0.878	29.28	-0.00186	-3.71	0.6290	12.21	(0.248)
3	H	-0.00024	0.892	30.84	-0.00179	-3.70	0.6531	30.41	
4	L	-0.00082	0.808	29.26	-0.00212	-4.58	0.6285	4.82	1.177
4	M	-0.00070	0.910	34.71	-0.00199	-4.54	0.7045	16.82	(0.279)
4	H	-0.00006	0.966	33.95	-0.00164	-3.44	0.6957	36.06	
5	L	-0.00035	0.814	32.09	-0.00176	-4.15	0.6707	6.64	1.123
5	M	-0.00015	0.899	35.86	-0.00105	-2.50	0.7193	21.73	(0.290)
5	H	-0.00005	0.968	36.05	-0.00132	-2.93	0.7210	42.89	

6	L	0.00004	0.830	36.78	−0.00151	−4.00	0.7284	9.30	3.264
6	M	0.00016	0.932	41.63	−0.00131	−3.49	0.7751	27.76	(0.071)
6	H	−0.00004	0.996	39.97	−0.00080	−1.92	0.7619	50.16	
7	L	−0.00012	0.838	41.21	−0.00137	−4.01	0.7713	10.80	0.866
7	M	0.00030	0.997	48.46	−0.00094	−2.71	0.8245	32.21	(0.352)
7	H	−0.00013	1.095	47.04	−0.00097	−2.48	0.8157	53.25	
8	L	0.00032	0.870	45.21	−0.00123	−3.80	0.8026	15.37	8.706
8	M	0.00010	1.054	66.78	−0.00038	−1.43	0.9000	38.36	(0.003)
8	H	0.00015	1.126	56.89	−0.00002	−0.05	0.8679	58.44	
9	L	0.00005	0.934	51.72	−0.00070	−2.31	0.8429	22.85	6.946
9	M	0.00020	1.048	76.11	−0.00014	−0.61	0.9215	45.16	(0.009)
9	H	−0.00026	1.167	67.28	0.00035	1.20	0.9024	62.21	
10	L	0.00032	0.963	71.10	−0.00008	−0.34	0.9111	28.42	3.490
10	M	0.00019	1.117	95.67	0.00023	1.17	0.9491	49.46	(0.062)
10	H	−0.00026	1.118	78.43	0.00065	2.74	0.9267	66.50	

Source: Chopra *et al.* (1993).

Weekly regression of equally weighted 'size-institutional holding' portfolio returns on the market return (VWNY) and changes in a value-weighted weekly discount index (ΔVWD). All NYSE and AMEX firms with institutional ownership data from the Spectrum database are included. At the beginning of each year, firms are size ranked and divided into Low (L), Medium (M), and High (H) institutional ownership portfolios within each size decile. Portfolios are rebalanced annually. The average number of firms for each portfolio is 64 to 67. Results are based on 10 years (522 weeks) of data: 1/2/81 to 12/28/90. *F*-statistics are for a multivariate test of the null hypothesis that the coefficient on ΔVWD in the Low (L) ownership portfolio is equal to the High (H) ownership portfolio. Two-tailed *p*-values are in parentheses.

3.5 Further evidence

The previous section has found empirical support for all of the
new predictions of the investor sentiment explanation of the
closed end fund puzzles. There is, however, further evidence
bearing on this hypothesis. In this subsection, we briefly review
some of this evidence.

One possible, though not necessarily plausible, argument is
that fluctuations in discounts do reflect an additional risk from
holding a fund rather than its portfolio, but that this risk is not
noise trader risk of Chapter 2, but rather some sort of fundamental risk. For example, if discounts comove with small stocks, as
we have shown they do, perhaps closed end funds are affected by
the same allegedly 'fundamental' risk factor as the small firms.
This explanation is tenuous since, as the analysis of the TRICON
portfolio has shown, this fund holds large stocks, is an 8th decile
stock itself, and yet it comoves with smaller stocks. If 'fundamentals' refer to the actual cash flow characteristics of TRICON, its
fundamentals are those of a large, not a small stock, and hence on
the fundamental risk theory it should trade like a large stock. The
fact that it does not presents a serious challenge to this
explanation.

Lee *et al.* (1991) pursue the fundamental risk story further by
looking at the relationship between the value-weighted discount
and the fundamental 'risk' factors identified by Chen *et al.* (1986).
If the discounts are highly correlated with measures of fundamental risk, then the investor sentiment interpretation may be
suspect. Chen *et al.* (1986) present a number of macroeconomic
variables that affect stock returns in time series regressions. They
interpret the variables to be risk factors. The variables include
'innovations' in: industrial production, risk premia on bonds, the
term structure of interest rates, and expected inflation. Lee *et al.*
(1991) find that changes in discounts are not correlated with
changes in 'fundamental' factors, except for a weak and not obviously interpretable correlation with changes in the expected inflation rate. The 'fundamental risk' theory thus does not appear to
explain the data.

But there is some further evidence consistent with the investor
sentiment interpretation. Malkiel (1977) found that discounts on

closed end funds narrow when purchases of open end funds out-strip redemptions. His interpretation of this finding is that similar shifts in investor demand drive open fund purchases and closed end fund appreciation. Lee *et al.* (1991) confirm Malkiel's findings during their sample period. The evidence suggests that the investors whose sentiment changes are also investors in open end funds. These tend to be individual rather than institutional investors.

As indicated earlier, conceptually the most important evidence in favor of investor sentiment theory is the comovement of fundamentally unrelated securities (or, alternatively, of comovement after the 'fundamentals' are controlled for). Some of the strongest evidence along these lines has come from examining closed end country funds, which are funds traded in the United States that hold securities traded in specific countries' markets outside the United States. For example, there are funds holding German, Mexican, or Korean securities. Bodurtha *et al.* (1993) and Hardouvelis *et al.* (1994) present striking evidence that the prices of closed end funds traded in the United States are 'excessively sensitive' to U.S. stock returns. That is, the fact that the funds trade in the United States imparts a U.S.-component to their returns unrelated to the returns on their portfolios. For example, the price of German fund shares rises when the U.S. market rises, even when the German market does not. This result again suggests that factors unrelated to fundamentals, such as sentiment, influence returns. It cannot be easily explained by a fully rational model, but is broadly consistent with the analysis of this chapter.

3.6 Conclusion

In this chapter, we applied the theory developed in Chapter 2 to the pricing of closed end funds in the United States, and found substantial evidence that investor sentiment, and particularly individual investor sentiment, influences the prices of these securities. The analysis is perhaps a useful illustration of how the theory works, but it also has two broader implications. First, it stresses a crucial—and testable—idea of comovement of fundamentally unrelated securities as a manifestation of investor sentiment influencing prices in the world of limited arbitrage. Evidence of such comovement—in both closed end fund and other markets—turns out to be very difficult to reconcile with market efficiency. Second, and at an even broader level, this analysis illustrates the all-important proposition that the theory of inefficient markets can and does produce new empirical hypotheses that can be brought to the data. The research on which Chapter 2 was based came several years before the tests discussed in this chapter were performed. While this is certainly not the only case of behavioral finance theory generating predictions that are subsequently tested empirically, it should put to rest the contention that behavioral finance theories are untestable.

Appendix I

This appendix comprises a list of the twenty closed end stock funds used in constructing the monthly changes in the value-weighted index of discounts (earlier name in parentheses).

ASA Ltd. (American South African)
Abacus Fund, Inc.
Adams Express Co.
Advance Investors Corp.
American International Corp.
Carriers and General Corp.
Dominick Fund, Inc.
Eurofund International, Inc. (Eurofund, Inc.)
General American Investors, Inc.
MA Hanna Co.
International Holdings Corp.
Japan Fund, Inc.
Lehman Corp.
Madison Resources, Inc. (Madison Fund, Inc.)
Niagara Shares Corp.
Petroleum and Resources Corp. (Petroleum Corp. of America)
Surveyor Fund, Inc. (General Public Service Corp.)
Tricontinental Corp.
United Corp.
United States and Foreign Securities Corp.

4

Professional Arbitrage

In Chapter 2, we considered arbitrageurs who used their own wealth to trade, and were limited only by their own risk aversion. More commonly, arbitrage is conducted by relatively few professional, highly specialized investors who combine their knowledge with resources of outside investors to take large positions. The fundamental feature of such arbitrage is that brains and resources are separated by an agency relationship. For example, mutual and pension funds manage money for millions of individual investors. Hedge funds take money from wealthy individuals, banks, endowments, and other investors with only a limited knowledge of individual markets and invest it using highly specialized knowledge. In this chapter, we examine such arbitrage and its effectiveness in achieving market efficiency.

The implications of the fact that arbitrage requires capital become extremely important in the agency context. In models without agency problems, such as that in Chapter 2, arbitrageurs become more aggressive when prices move further away from fundamental values. When, in contrast, the arbitrageur manages other people's money, and his investors do not know or understand exactly what he is doing, they only observe him losing money when prices move further out of line. They may infer from this loss that the arbitrageur is not as competent as they previously thought, refuse to provide him with more capital, and even withdraw some of the capital although the expected return from the trade has increased.

We refer to the phenomenon of responsiveness of funds under management to past returns as performance based arbitrage. Unlike the arbitrageurs investing their own money, who allocate funds based on expected returns from trades, investors may rationally allocate money based on past returns of arbitrageurs, and withdraw funds after poor past performance. This problem is even more extreme for lenders to an arbitrageur, who typically call their loans when the value of securities used as collateral declines, as it does after poor performance. Poor performance can thus erode both the equity base and the borrowing capacity of an arbitrageur, regardless of the attractiveness of arbitrage opportunities he faces.

As a consequence, when arbitrage requires debt or equity capital, arbitrageurs can become most constrained precisely when they have the best opportunities, i.e., when the mispricing they have bet against widens. The fear of such a scenario would make arbitrageurs more cautious when they put on their initial trades, and hence less aggressive in betting against the mispricing. This chapter argues that this feature of arbitrage can limit its effectiveness in achieving market efficiency well beyond the limitations noted in Chapter 2. We show that performance-based arbitrage is particularly ineffective in extreme circumstances, when prices are significantly out of line and arbitrageurs are fully invested. In such panics, arbitrageurs might bail out of the market—voluntarily or not—when their participation is most needed. Performance based arbitrage brings about the deepening of financial panics rather than an amelioration of price collapses.

We begin with a very simple model that illustrates the mechanics of performance based arbitrage. The model has a much simpler dynamic structure than the one in Chapter 2, but focuses explicitly on the agency relationship between arbitrageurs and their financiers. For simplicity, we examine the case where mispricing may deepen in the short run, even though there is no long run fundamental risk in the trade. We then demonstrate the ineffectiveness of arbitrage when prices move very far from fundamentals. The remainder of the chapter discusses the relevance of the model to financial markets, particularly in times of crisis.

4.1 An agency model of limited arbitrage

We focus on the market for a specific asset with three types of participants: noise traders, arbitrageurs, and investors in arbitrage funds who do not trade on their own. Arbitrageurs specialize in trading only in this market, whereas investors allocate funds between arbitrageurs operating in both this and many other markets. The fundamental value of the asset is V, which arbitrageurs, but not their investors, know. There are three time periods: 1, 2, and 3. At time 3, the value V becomes known to arbitrageurs and noise traders, and hence the price is equal to that value. Since the price is equal to V at $t = 3$ for sure, there is no long run fundamental risk in this trade (this is not risk arbitrage). For $t = 1, 2$, the price of the asset at time t is p_t. For concreteness, we only consider pessimistic noise traders. Unlike in Chapter 2, we do not formally model their beliefs, but rather consider a reduced form demand function. In each of periods 1 and 2, noise traders may experience a pessimism shock S_t, which generates for them, in the aggregate, the demand for the asset given by:

$$QN(t) = [V - S_t] /p_t. \tag{4.1}$$

At time $t = 1$, the first period noise trader shock S_1 is known to arbitrageurs, but the second period noise trader shock is uncertain. In particular, there is some chance that $S_2 > S_1$, i.e. that noise trader misperceptions deepen before they correct at $t = 3$. Chapter 2 stressed the role of such noise trader risk for the analysis of arbitrage.

Both arbitrageurs and their investors are fully rational. Risk-neutral arbitrageurs take positions against the mispricing generated by the noise traders. Each period, arbitrageurs have cumulative resources under management (including their borrowing capacity) given by F_t. These resources are limited, for reasons we describe below. We assume that F_1 is exogenously given, and specify the determination of F_2 below. The assumption of limited arbitrage resources distinguishes this model from that in Chapter 2, where arbitrageurs could invest all they wanted in the risky asset subject only to their own risk tolerance.

At time $t = 2$, the price of the asset either recovers to V, or does not. If it recovers, arbitrageurs invest in cash. If noise traders continue to be confused, then arbitrageurs want to invest all of F_2 in the underpriced asset, since its price rises to V at $t = 3$ for sure. In this case, the arbitrageurs' demand for the asset $QA(2) = F_2/p_2$ and, since the aggregate demand for the asset must equal the unit supply, the price is given by:

$$p_2 = V - S_2 + F_2. \tag{4.2}$$

We assume that $F_2 < S_2$, so the arbitrage resources are not sufficient to bring the period 2 price to fundamental value, unless of course noise trader misperceptions have corrected anyway.

In period 1, arbitrageurs do not necessarily want to invest all of F_1 in the asset. They might want to keep some of the money in cash in case the asset becomes even more underpriced at $t = 2$, so they could invest more in that asset. Accordingly, denote by D_1 the amount that arbitrageurs invest in the asset at $t = 1$. In this case, $QA(1) = D_1/p_1$, and

$$p_1 = V - S_1 + D_1. \tag{4.3}$$

We again assume that, in the range of parameter values we are focusing on, arbitrage resources are not sufficient to bring prices all the way to fundamental values, i.e. $F_1 < S_1$.

To complete the model, we need to specify the organization of the arbitrage industry and the relationship between arbitrageurs and their investors, which determines F_2. Recall that we are focusing on a particular narrow market segment in which a given set of arbitrageurs specialize. A 'segment' here should be interpreted as a particular arbitrage strategy. We assume that there are many such segments and that within each segment there are many arbitrageurs, so that no arbitrageur can affect asset prices in a segment. For simplicity, we can think of T investors each with one dollar available for investment with arbitrageurs. We are concerned with the aggregate amount $F_2 \ll T$ that is invested with the arbitrageurs in a particular segment.

Arbitrageurs compete in the price they charge for their services. For simplicity, we assume constant marginal cost per dollar invested, such that all arbitrageurs in all segments have the same marginal cost. We also assume that each arbitrageur has at least one competitor who is viewed as a perfect substitute, so that Bertrand competition drives price to marginal cost. Each of the T risk-neutral investors allocates his $1 investment to maximize expected consumer surplus, i.e. the difference between the expected return on his dollar and the price charged by the arbitrageur. Investors are Bayesians and have prior beliefs about the expected return of each arbitrageur. Since prices are equal, an investor gives his dollar to the arbitrageur with the highest expected return according to his beliefs. Different investors hold different beliefs about various arbitrageurs' abilities, so one arbitrageur does not end up with all the funds. The market share of each arbitrageur is just the total fraction of investors who believe that he has the highest expected return. The total share of money allocated to a given segment is just the sum of these market shares across all arbitrageurs in the segment. Importantly, we assume that arbitrageurs across many segments have, on average, earned high enough returns to convince investors to invest with them rather than to pursue passive indexing strategies.

The key remaining question is how investors update their beliefs about the future expected returns of an arbitrageur. We assume that investors have no information about the structure of the model determining asset prices in any segment. In particular, they do not know the trading strategy employed by any arbitrageur. This assumption is meant to capture the idea that arbitrage strategies are difficult to understand, and a lot of specialized knowledge is needed for investors to evaluate them. In part, this is because arbitrageurs do not share all their knowledge with investors, and cultivate secrecy to protect their knowledge from imitation. Even if the investors were told more about what arbitrageurs were doing, they would have a difficult time deciding whether what they heard was true. Implicitly, we are assuming that the underlying structural model is sufficiently nonstationary and high dimensional that investors are unable to infer the underlying structure of the model from past returns data. As a result, they only use simple updating rules based on past performance. In particular, investors are assumed to form posterior beliefs about future returns of the arbitrageur based only on their prior and any observations of his arbitrage returns.

Under these informational assumptions, individual arbitrageurs who experience relatively poor returns in a given period lose market share to those with better returns. Moreover, since all arbitrageurs in a given segment are taking the same positions, they all attract or lose investors simultaneously, depending on the performance of their common arbitrage strategy. Specifically, investors' aggregate supply of funds to the arbitrageurs in a particular segment at time 2 is an increasing function of arbitrageurs' gross return between time 1 and time 2 (call this performance-based-arbitrage or PBA). Denoting this function by G, and recognizing that the return on the asset is given by p_2/p_1, the arbitrageurs' supply of funds at $t = 2$ is given by:

$$F_2 = F_1 * G[(D_1/F_1) * (p_2/p_1) + (F_1 - D_1)/F_1], \qquad (4.4)$$

with $G(1) = 1, G' \geq 1, G'' \leq 0$.

If arbitrageurs do as well as some benchmark given by performance of arbitrageurs in other markets, which for simplicity we assume to be zero return, they neither gain nor lose funds under management. They gain (lose) funds if they outperform (underperform) that benchmark. Because of the poor quality of investors' information, past performance of arbitrageurs completely determines the resources they get to manage, regardless of the actual opportunities available in their market.

The responsiveness of funds under management to past performance (as measured by G') is the solution to a signal extraction problem in which investors are trying to ascribe an arbitrageur's poor performance to one of three causes: (1) a random error, (2) a deepening of noise trader sentiment (bad luck), or (3) inferior ability. High cross-sectional variation in ability across arbitrageurs will tend to increase the responsiveness of invested funds to past performance. High variance of the noise trader sentiment relative to the variation in (unobserved) ability will tend to decrease the responsiveness to past performance. In the limit, if ability is known or does not vary across arbitrageurs, poor performance could be ascribed only to a deepening of the noise trader shock (or a pure noise term), which would only increase the investor's estimate of the arbitrageur's future return. The seemingly perverse behavior of taking money away from an arbitrageur after noise trader sentiment deepens, i.e. precisely when his expected return is the highest, is a rational response to the problem of trying to infer the arbitrageur's (unobserved) ability and future opportunities jointly from past returns.

Since our results do not rely on the concavity of the G function, we focus on a linear G, given by

$$G(x) = ax + 1 - a, \text{ with } a \geq 1, \qquad (4.5)$$

where x is the arbitrageur's gross return. In this case, period 2 funds under management become:

$$F_2 = a\{D_1(p_2/p_1) + (F_1 - D_1)\} + (1 - a)F_1 = F_1 - aD_1(1 - p_2/p_1).$$
(4.6)

With this functional form, if $p_2 = p_1$ so the arbitrageur earns a zero net return, he neither gains nor loses funds under management. If $p_2 > p_1$, he gains funds and if $p_2 < p_1$, he loses funds. The higher is a, the more sensitive are the resources under management to past performance. The case of $a = 1$ corresponds to the arbitrageur not getting any more money when he loses some, whereas if $a > 1$, funds are actually withdrawn in response to poor performance.

More complicated incentive contracts would in principle allow arbitrageurs to signal their opportunities or abilities and attract funds based not just on past performance. For example, arbitrageurs who feel that they have superior investment opportunities might try to offer contracts to investors that pay arbitrageurs a fixed price below marginal cost and a share of the upside. That is, if at a particular point of time arbitrageurs believe that they can earn extremely high returns with a high probability (as happens artificially at $t = 2$ in our model), they can try to attract investors by partially insuring them against further losses. We do not consider such 'separating' contracts in our model, since they are unlikely to emerge in equilibrium under plausible circumstances. First, with limited liability, arbitrageurs might be unwilling or unable after mispricing worsens to completely retain (or increase) funds under management by insuring the investor against losses, or pricing below marginal cost. Second, these contracts are less attractive when the risk-averse arbitrageur himself is highly uncertain about his own ability to produce a superior return. We could model this more realistically by adding some noise into the third period return. In sum, under plausible conditions, the use of incentive contracts does not eliminate the influence of past performance on the market shares of arbitrageurs.

Empirically, most money managers in the pension and mutual fund industries work for fees proportional to assets under management and rarely get a percentage of the upside. One exception is hedge fund managers, who typically do get a large incentive component in their compensation. We are not aware of increases in that component and cuts in fees to avert withdrawal of funds from the hedge funds. For mutual funds, Ippolito (1989) and Warther (1995) find that managers lose funds under management when they perform poorly. Warther (1995) also shows that fund flows in and out of mutual funds affect contemporaneous returns of securities these funds hold, consistent with the results established below.

PBA is critical to our model. In conventional arbitrage, capital is allocated to arbitrageurs based on expected returns from their trades. Under PBA, in contrast, capital is allocated based on past returns, which in the model are low precisely when expected returns are high. At that time, arbitrageurs face fund withdrawals, and are not very effective in betting against the mispricing. Breaking the link between greater mispricing and higher expected returns perceived by those allocating capital drives our main results.

To complete the model, we need to set up an arbitrageur's optimization problem. For simplicity, we assume that the arbitrageur maximizes expected time 3 profits. Since arbitrageurs are price-takers in the market for investment services and marginal cost is constant, maximizing expected time 3 profit is equivalent to maximizing expected time 3 funds under management. For concreteness, we examine a specific form of uncertainty about S_2. We assume that, with probability q, $S_2 = S > S_1$—noise trader misperceptions deepen. With a complementary probability $1 - q$, noise traders recognize the true value of the asset at $t = 2$, so $S_2 = 0$ and $p_2 = V$. When $S_2 = 0$, arbitrageurs liquidate their position at a gain at $t = 2$ and hold cash until $t = 3$. In this case, $W = a(D_1 * V/p_1 + F_1 - D_1) + (1 - a)F_1$.

When $S_2 = S$, in contrast, arbitrageurs' third period funds are given by $W = (V/p_2) * [a\{D_1 * p_2/p_1 + F_1 - D_1\} + (1 - a)F_1]$. Arbitrageurs then maximize:

$$EW = (1 - q) \left\{ a\left(\frac{D_1 * V}{p_1} + F_1 - D_1 \right) + (1 - a)F_1 \right\}$$
$$+ q \left(\frac{V}{p_2} \right) * \left\{ a\left(\frac{D_1 * p_2}{p_1} + F_1 - D_1 \right) + (1 - a)F_1 \right\}. \tag{4.7}$$

4.2 Performance-based arbitrage and market efficiency

Before analyzing the pattern of prices in our model, we specify some benchmarks. The first benchmark is efficient markets, in which arbitrageurs have access to all the capital they want. In this case, noise trader shocks are fully counteracted by arbitrageurs and $p_1 = p_2 = V$. An alternative benchmark is one in which arbitrageurs resources are limited, but PBA is inoperative, so arbitrageurs can always raise F_1. Even if they lose money, they can replenish their capital up to F_1. In this case, $p_1 = V - S_1 + F_1$ and $p_2 = V - S + F_1$. Prices fall one for one with noise trader shocks in each period. This case corresponds most closely to that in Chapter 2. One final interesting benchmark is $a = 1$. In this case, arbitrageurs cannot replenish the funds they have lost, but do not suffer withdrawals beyond what they have lost.

The first order condition to the arbitrageur's optimization problem is given by:

$$(1 - q)\left(\frac{V}{p_1} - 1\right) + q\left(\frac{p_2}{p_1} - 1\right)\frac{V}{p_2} \geq 0, \qquad (4.8)$$

with strict inequality holding if and only if $D_1 = F_1$, and equality holding if $D_1 < F_1$. The first term of equation (4.8) is an incremental benefit to arbitrageurs from an extra dollar of investment if the market recovers at $t = 2$. The second term is the incremental loss if the price falls at $t = 2$ before recovering at $t = 3$, and so they have forgone the option of being able to invest more in that case. Condition (4.8) holds with a strict equality if the risk of price deterioration is high enough, and this deterioration is severe enough, that arbitrageurs choose to hold back some funds for the option to invest more at time 2. On the other hand, condition (4.8) holds with a strict inequality if q is low, if p_1 is low relative to V (S_1 is large), if p_2 is not too low relative to p_1 (S not too large relative to S_1). That is to say, the initial displacement must be very large and prices should be expected to recover with a high probability rather than fall further. If they do fall, it cannot be by too much. Under these circumstances, arbitrageurs choose to be fully invested at $t = 1$ rather than hold spare reserves for $t = 2$. We describe the case in which mispricing is so severe at $t = 1$ that arbitrageurs choose to be fully invested as 'extreme circumstances,' and discuss it at some length.

This discussion can be summarized more formally in:

> PROPOSITION 1: For a given V, S_1, S, F_1, and a, there is a q^* such that, for $q > q^*$, $D_1 < F_1$, and for $q < q^*$, $D_1 = F_1$.

If equation (4.8) holds with equality, the equilibrium is given by equations (4.2), (4.3), (4.6), and (4.8). If equation (4.8) holds with inequality, then equilibrium is given by $D_1 = F_1$, $p_1 = V - S_1 + F_1$, as well as equations (4.2) and (4.6). To illustrate the fact that both types of equilibria are quite plausible, consider a numerical example. Let $V = 1$, $F_1 = 0.2$, $a = 1.2$, $S_1 = 0.3$, $S_2 = 0.4$. For this example, $q^* = 0.35$. If $q < 0.35$, then arbitrageurs are fully invested and $D_1 = F_1 = 0.2$, so that the first period price is 0.9. In this case, regardless of the exact value of q, we have $F_2 = 0.1636$ and $p_2 = 0.7636$ if noise trader sentiment deepens, and $F_2 = 0.227$ and $p_2 = V = 1$ if noise trader sentiment recovers. On the other hand, if $q > 0.35$, then arbitrageurs hold back some of the funds at time 1, with the result that p_1 is lower than it would be with full investment. For example, if $q = 0.5$, then $D_1 = 0.1743$ and $p_1 = 0.8743$ (arbitrage is less aggressive at $t = 1$). If noise trader shock deepens, then $F_2 = 0.1766$ and $p_2 = 0.7766$ (arbitrageurs have preserved more funds to invest at $t = 2$), whereas if noise trader sentiment recovers then $F_2 = 0.23$ and price returns to $V = 1$. This example illustrates that both the corner solution and the interior equilibrium are quite plausible. In fact, both occur for most parameters we have tried.

In this simple model, we can show that the larger are the shocks, the further are the prices from fundamental values (the proof of this proposition is tedious and is omitted).

> PROPOSITION 2: At the corner solution ($D_1 = F_1$), $dp_1/dS_1 < 0$, $dp_2/dS < 0$, and $dp_1/dS = 0$. At the interior solution, $dp_1/dS_1 < 0$, $dp_2/dS < 0$, and $dp_1/dS < 0$.

This proposition captures the simple intuition, common to all noise trader models, that arbitrageurs' ability to bear against mispricing is limited, and larger noise trader shocks lead to less efficient pricing. At the interior solution, arbitrageurs spread out the effect of a deeper period 2 shock by holding more cash at $t = 1$ and thus allowing prices to fall more at $t = 1$. As a result, they have more funds at $t = 2$ to counter mispricing at that time. The interior solution bears some resemblance to the model in Chapter 2, in which arbitrageurs limit their betting against the mispricing because they are risk-averse. Here the reason for holding back is not risk aversion but rather the option to invest more in the future if mispricing deepens. The agency problem can thus be an alternative to risk aversion for explaining why arbitrage is limited in normal circumstances. The most interesting results of the model in this Chapter are for the case where arbitrageurs are fully invested at time 1, which we call extreme circumstances.

We can say more about the effectiveness of arbitrage under such circumstances. In particular, we can analyze whether arbitrageurs become more aggressive when mispricing worsens. There are two ways to measure this. One is to ask whether arbitrageurs invest more total dollars in the asset at $t = 2$ than at $t = 1$, i.e., is $D_1 < F_2$? The second is whether arbitrageurs actually hold proportionally more of the asset at $t = 2$, i.e., is $D_1/p_1 < F_2/p_2$? In principle, it is possible that because $p_2 < p_1$ arbitrageurs hold more of the asset at $t = 2$ even though they spend less on it. Perhaps the clearest case of less aggressive arbitrage at $t = 2$ would occur if arbitrageurs actually hold fewer shares at $t = 2$, and are liquidating their holdings, even though prices have fallen from $t = 1$. In the rest of this section, we focus on these liquidation problems.

We focus on a sufficient condition for liquidation at $t = 2$ when the noise trader shock deepens, namely, that arbitrageurs are fully invested at $t = 1$. Specifically, we have:

> PROPOSITION 3: If arbitrageurs are fully invested at $t = 1$, and noise trader misperceptions deepen at $t = 2$, then for $a > 1$ we have $F_2 < D_1$ and $F_2/p_2 < D_1/p_1$.

Proposition 3 describes the extreme circumstances in our model, in which fully invested arbitrageurs experience an adverse price shock, face equity withdrawals, and so liquidate their holdings of the extremely underpriced asset. Arbitrageurs bail out of the market when opportunities are the best.

Before analyzing this case in more detail, we note that full investment at $t = 1$ is a sufficient, but not a necessary condition for liquidation at $t = 2$. In general, for q's in the neighborhood above q^*, where $F_1 - D_1$ is positive but small, investors still liquidate some of their holdings when $a > 1$. The reason is that their cash holdings are not high enough to maintain their holdings of the asset despite equity withdrawals. The cash holdings ameliorate but do not eliminate these withdrawals. For higher q's, however, D_1 is high enough that $F_2/p_2 > D_1/p_1$.

We can illustrate this with our previous numerical example, with $V = 1$, $S_1 = 0.3$, $S_2 = 0.4$, $F_1 = 0.2$, and $a = 1.2$. In this example, we had $q^* = 0.35$. One can show that asset liquidations occur for $q < 0.39$, i.e. when arbitrageurs are fully invested as well as in a small region where they are not. For $q > 0.39$, arbitrageurs increase their holdings of the asset at $t = 2$.

For concreteness, it is easier to focus on the case of Proposition 3, when arbitrageurs are fully invested. In this case, we have that:

$$p_2 = [V - S - aF_1 + F_1]/[1 - aF_1 /p_1], \qquad (4.9)$$

as long as $aF_1 < p_1$. The condition that $aF_1 < p_1$ is a simple stability condition in this model, which basically says that arbitrageurs do not lose so much money that in equilibrium they bail out of the market completely. If $aF_1 > p_1$, then at $t = 2$ the only equilibrium price is $p_2 = V - S$, and arbitrageurs bail out of the market completely. In the stable equilibrium, arbitrageurs lose funds under management as prices fall, and hence liquidate some holdings, but they still stay in the market. For this equilibrium, simple differentiation yields the following result:

> PROPOSITION 4: At the fully invested equilibrium, $dp_2/dS < -1$ and $d^2p_2/(dS)^2 < 0$.

This proposition shows that when arbitrageurs are fully invested at time 1, prices fall more than one for one with the noise trader shock at time 2. Precisely when prices are furthest from fundamental values, arbitrageurs take the smallest positions. Moreover, as PBA intensifies, i.e. as a rises, the price decline per unit increase in S gets greater. If we think of dp_2/dS as a measure of the resiliency of the market (equal to zero for an efficient market and to -1 when $a = 0$ and there is no PBA), then Proposition 4 says that a market driven by PBA loses its resiliency in extreme circumstances. The analysis thus shows that the arbitrage process can be quite ineffective in bringing prices back to fundamental values in extreme circumstances.

This result contrasts with those in Chapter 2, where arbitrageurs are most aggressive when prices are furthest away from fundamentals. This point relates to Friedman's (1953) observation that 'to say that arbitrage is destabilizing is equivalent to saying that arbitrageurs lose money on average,' which is implausible. The model here is consistent with Friedman in that on average arbitrageurs make money and move prices toward fundamentals. The fact that they make money on average does not however mean that they make money always. The model shows that the times when they lose money are precisely the times when prices are far away from fundamentals, and in those times the trading by arbitrageurs has the weakest stabilizing effect.

These results are intimately related to the recent studies of fire sales (Shleifer and Vishny 1992, Stein 1996, Pulvino 1998). As in these studies, an asset here is liquidated involuntarily at a time when the best potential buyers — other arbitrageurs of this asset — have limited funds and external capital is not easily forthcoming. As a result of such fire sales, the price falls even further below fundamental value holding the noise trader shock constant. The implication of limited resiliency is that arbitrage does not bring prices close to fundamental values in panics.

This discussion raises an obvious question: are there markets that arbitrageurs would prefer and markets that they will avoid because of these risks of involuntary liquidation? Casual empiricism suggests that a great deal of professional arbitrage activity, such as that by hedge funds, is concentrated in a few markets, such as the bond market and the foreign exchange market. These also tend to be the markets where extreme leverage, short selling, and performance-based fees are common. In contrast, such activity is less evident in the stock market, either in the United States or abroad. Why is that so? Which markets attract arbitrage?

Part of the answer is the ability of arbitrageurs to ascertain value with confidence and to realize it quickly. In the bond market, calculations of relative values of different fixed income instruments are manageable, since future cash flows of securities are almost certain and can usually be replicated with other securities. As a consequence, there is little fundamental risk in arbitrage. In foreign exchange markets, calculations of relative values are more difficult, and arbitrage becomes riskier. Arbitrageurs put on their largest trades, however, and appear to make the most money, when central banks attempt to maintain nonmarket exchange rates, so it is possible to bet that prices are not equal to fundamental values and to profit quickly. In stock markets, in contrast, both the absolute and the relative values of different securities are harder to calculate, and as we know from Roll (1988) and Wurgler and Zhuravskaya (1999) substitute portfolios are far from perfect. As a consequence, arbitrage opportunities are harder both to identify and to benefit from in stock markets than in bond and foreign exchange markets. One example of this is the value/growth anomaly discussed in Chapter 1. Although value stocks have outperformed growth stocks by a significant amount on average, they have historically shown superior returns only about two thirds of the time, and there is no way to construct a riskless arbitrage portfolio. Such risky arbitrage is not attractive to specialized arbitrageurs. They can find lower-hanging fruit in bond and foreign exchange markets.

In addition, unlike the well-diversified arbitrageurs of Chapter 2, the specialized arbitrageurs here might avoid extremely volatile markets. Although highly volatile markets sometimes offer better arbitrage opportunities, the odds of extreme adverse events in these markets are also higher. If the costs of such events to arbitrageurs are enormous, these markets will be avoided. Although diversification alleviates this problem to some extent, arbitrageurs may not be able to diversify too much if their knowledge is specialized. Moreover, as we discuss below, the correlations in returns between different asset classes that arbitrageurs are interested in might rise sharply during crises, rendering diversification an inadequate protection against liquidation. All this suggests that arbitrageurs will choose to swim in relatively calm markets, and that volatility deters arbitrage even when it comes with significant opportunities.

4.3 Discussion of performance-based arbitrage

In our model performance-based arbitrage (PBA) delinks the arbitrageurs' demand for an asset from its expected return, and is consequently very limited. Even if PBA plays some role in the world, are its consequences as significant as our model suggests? In fact, one can raise a number of objections to the potential empirical importance of PBA. First, even if funds under management decline in response to poor performance, they do so with a lag. For most price moves, arbitrageurs might be able to hold out and not liquidate until the price recovers. Second, if arbitrageurs are at least somewhat diversified, not all of their holdings lose money at the same time, suggesting again that they might be able to avoid forced liquidations. Third, arbitrageurs with relatively long and successful track records might be able to avoid equity withdrawals by investors. Perhaps they can step in and stabilize prices even as other arbitrageurs are liquidating their holdings.

Each of these objections has merit. Yet despite them, the case for the quantitative importance of PBA remains strong. First, the lag on fund withdrawals in reality is often short. In many arbitrage funds, investors have the option to withdraw at least some of their funds at will and are likely to do so quite rapidly if performance is poor. To some extent, this problem is mitigated by contractual restrictions on withdrawals, which are either temporary (as in the case of hedge funds that do not allow investors to take the money out for one to three years) or permanent (as in the case of closed end funds). Because these restrictions expose investors to being stuck with a bad fund manager for a long time, they are relatively uncommon. Most hedge funds, for example, allow investors to withdraw their funds with only a few weeks' notice. Moreover, there may be an agency problem inside an arbitrage organization. If the boss is unsure of the ability of the subordinate taking a position, and the position loses money, the boss may force a liquidation of the position before the uncertainty works itself out.

A further factor that shortens the lags is voluntary liquidations. The model shows how arbitrageurs might be forced to liquidate their positions when prices move against them. One effect that the model does not capture is that risk-averse arbitrageurs might *choose* to liquidate in this situation even when they do not have to, for fear that a possible further adverse price move will cause a really dramatic outflow of funds later on, or a forced liquidation by creditors. Such risk aversion by arbitrageurs, which is not modeled here, would make them likely to liquidate rather than double up when prices move further away from fundamentals, making the problem we are identifying even worse. In this way, the fear of future withdrawals might have a similar effect to withdrawals themselves. Even when arbitrageurs are not fully invested in a particular arbitrage strategy, significant losses in that strategy may induce a voluntary liquidation in extreme circumstances that look very much like the involuntary liquidation in the model.

Perhaps the most important reason why poor performance leads to quick asset sales is liquidation by creditors. Creditors usually demand immediate repayment, or else liquidate the collateral, when the value of this collateral gets near the debt level. Unlike the equity investors in funds, who may either have to or choose to wait to withdraw their capital, creditors have every incentive to rush to get their money back ahead of the equity investors. This phenomenon is a source of considerable instability, for arbitrageurs need to come up with cash to satisfy their creditors and avoid liquidation precisely when they are fully invested and do not have any spare cash. If the arbitrageurs cannot come up with the cash, the securities in the fund are liquidated, often in fire sales that fetch extremely low prices, with the result that the markets become still less efficient, and the position of an arbitrageur still more precarious. Moreover, such liquidations often spill over across markets as funds attempt to liquidate their positions in other markets to meet the lenders' call for funds and avoid liquidations of the most illiquid securities. Creditors are far more important than equity investors in precipitating liquidations.

There are several further problems associated with liquidations by creditors. First, if the creditors have the right to liquidate collateral themselves but the amount owed to them is lower than the value of this collateral, they do not care at what price they liquidate, since the difference belongs to the borrower. Suppose, for example, that a hedge fund borrows $80 from a bank, collateralized by $100 of securities for which the fund must put up 20 percent, or $20, of its own equity capital. Suppose the market value of securities drops to $90, on which the bank is still only willing to lend 80 percent, or $72, and so it demands an immediate repayment of $8. If the fund does not have the necessary cash, the bank, which has control of the securities, has the right to sell them to pay itself back. The key point is that the bank has no incentive to sell for any price above $80, since the difference belongs to the fund. And while the bank does have some obligation to solicit multiple bids, it can often get them from other investors it does business with, and to whom it may well wish to sell the securities at lower—rather than higher—prices. The outcome of such a liquidation might be to push the transaction value of the securities all the way down to $80, causing the fund to lose its full equity investment in these securities. This is another way in which forced liquidation puts downward pressure on prices.

A further potential moral hazard on the part of the creditors is front running. If the bank in question knows what some of the holdings of the fund are, and knows in advance that the fund might be liquidating these holdings involuntarily, it has an incentive to sell short the securities owned by the fund only to buy them back at lower prices when the fund is actually liquidating, possibly from the fund itself. The result of such short-selling is to put downward pressure on prices and to accelerate liquidation. It is not known how important this problem is empirically, but the theoretical potential for significant collapses in prices of less than perfectly liquid securities is clearly present. In this and other ways, creditors might precipitate price collapses in extreme circumstances regardless of the lags on withdrawals by arbitrage fund investors.

Moral hazard problems on the part of the creditors raise some interesting contractual and policy questions, which we can only briefly mention. For example, it is often said that transparency and disclosure on the part of arbitrageurs is a good idea. Who can be against transparency and disclosure? But disclosure by arbitrageurs who have sparse cash and borrowing capacity might only precipitate front running and premature liquidation of these arbitrageurs' positions. Disclosure can make markets less stable, especially near a panic.

What about the role of diversification by arbitrageurs in preventing crises? If a panic is restricted to a market that represents a small share of the total, diversification is a good safeguard against liquidations. Arbitrageurs would just sell their most liquid securities to meet cash demands by their creditors, and equilibrium would be restored. Note, however, that as this happens there is downward pressure on the prices of all the securities that arbitrageurs are liquidating to meet the calls for cash.

Liquidations in one market may then turn into liquidations in other markets. The panic might spill over across markets, particularly if shocks are large enough to stimulate substantial voluntary as well as involuntary liquidations. At the extremes, all securities move down together, and diversification does not solve the problem, especially when arbitrageurs are highly leveraged. This model points to a possibility of financial contagion without any fundamental reason why different markets should move together.

Finally, our model assumes that all arbitrageurs have the same sensitivity of funds under management to performance, and that all invest in the mispriced asset from the beginning. In fact, arbitrageurs differ. Some may have access to resources independent of past performance, and as a result might be able to invest more when prices diverge further from fundamentals. A substantial number of such arbitrageurs can undo the effects of performance based liquidations. If the new arbitrageurs reverse the price decline, the already invested arbitrageurs make money and hence no longer need to liquidate their holdings. After a large noise trader shock that we have in the model, however, most arbitrageurs operating in a market are likely to find themselves fully committed. Even if some of them have held back initially, at some point most of them entered and even accumulated substantial debts to bet against the mispricing. As the mispricing gets deeper withdrawals and feared future withdrawals cause them to liquidate. Admittedly, the total amount of capital available for arbitrage is huge, and perhaps outsiders can come in when insiders liquidate. But in practice, arbitrage markets are specialized and arbitrageurs typically lack the experience and reputations to engage in arbitrage across multiple markets with other people's money. In the extreme circumstances, the few specialist arbitrageurs whose resources are relatively insensitive to past performance are unlikely to stabilize the market.

This discussion has one further implication. The sensitivity to past returns of funds under management must be higher for young, unseasoned arbitrage (hedge) funds than for older, more established funds, with a long reputation for performance. As a result, the established funds will be able to earn higher returns in the long run, since they have more funds available when prices have moved way out of line, which is when the returns to arbitrage are the greatest. In contrast, new arbitrageurs lose their funds precisely when the potential returns are the highest, and hence their average returns would be lower than those of the older funds.

To summarize, this analysis has established that performance based arbitrage leads to potential instability of financial markets, particularly in extreme circumstances. This instability comes from both voluntary and involuntary liquidations of money-losing positions by arbitrageurs and their creditors, even when these positions have positive risk-adjusted expected returns. This instability manifests itself in substantial deviations of security prices from fundamental values in times of crisis, but also in large losses of the arbitrageurs, their counterparties, and other financial market participants. Although lags in liquidations, diversification, and the presence of arbitrageurs whose resources are not responsive to past performance ameliorate this problem, they are unlikely to do so completely, especially in a crisis.

While we have not modeled the economic consequences of such large losses, it is easy to see how they lead to chains of liquidations, and to financial distress of many market participants. When these market participants are financial intermediaries, they may curtail their lending to firms, thereby engendering a recession. When firms hold financial or other assets whose collateral value declines, they might have to cut down their borrowing, investment, and production. Financial panics can thus have severe real consequences. This model, then, provides a potential justification for the Central Bank or another institution becoming the lender of last resort that can step in at the time of crisis and stop the chain of liquidations (Bagehot 1872, Kindleberger 1978). In this model, such intervention would improve the efficiency of financial markets. In a more general model, it can perhaps preserve the integrity of the financial system as well, and even prevent an economic rather than just a financial meltdown.

4.4 A postscript on Long Term Capital Management

On August 16, 1998—a year and a half after the article on which this chapter is based was published—Russia defaulted on most of its ruble-denominated debt and sharply devalued the ruble.

In addition, it imposed a moratorium that froze Western investors' accounts in which these ruble-denominated bonds were held, as well as disabled Russian banks from paying off their private debts to Western creditors. Russia did not, however, default on its foreign debt. The consequences of these actions were manifold. The International Monetary Fund (IMF) suspended its program in Russia. Nearly all the reformers who were a substantial presence in the Russian government since 1992 were fired and replaced by Gorbachev-era 'moderates.' More germane to the subject of this book, world capital markets were severely shaken.

A substantial fraction of Russia's ruble-denominated debt at the time was held by Western hedge funds and other investors involved in emerging markets, and attracted by high yields on that debt. Many of the hedge funds anticipated the likelihood of Russian default on this debt and hedged their risks by selling short Russia's foreign debt (on the theory that Russia is unlikely to default on domestic debt without defaulting on foreign debt), as well as selling the rubles (forward) to Russian banks (on the theory that if Russia devalues, they can at least benefit from their short position in the ruble). The fact that Russia did not default on its foreign debt and imposed a moratorium on payments by its banks meant that neither of these hedges worked. As a consequence, most hedge funds investing in Russia suffered severe losses.

Some of the hedge funds leveraged their Russian positions and many used non-Russian securities as collateral. Following the default, these funds had to come up with cash to pay off their debts and meet their collateral requirements or else face the seizure and liquidation of collateral. Many of them, therefore, started liquidating other emerging markets positions, or even had these positions liquidated for them. In the meantime, the bad news from Russia and the concerns about the capability of the IMF to deal with emerging markets crises reduced the valuation of emerging markets securities, quite aside from the fact that the positions in these securities were being liquidated in fire sales. Moreover, the liquidations, both voluntary and involuntary, spread to other markets where arbitrageurs were active, such as mortgage backed securities. A *bona fide* fire sale liquidation of hedge fund portfolios by creditors had begun.

Perhaps the best known hedge fund caught in this wave of

liquidations was Long Term Capital Management (LTCM), a fund known for its large size, extreme use of leverage, and extraordinary talent it employed. According to reports, the fund lost nearly half of its $3–4 billion in equity in August 1998. The fund was left with virtually no cash, vast losses on its portfolio, and enormous demands by creditors for cash or additional collateral. As a consequence, its many creditors began to seize and liquidate its portfolio. On September 23, 1998, following several failed attempts to raise cash from new or old investors, LTCM was rescued by a group of its creditors, who injected $3.6 billion into the portfolio, took 90 percent of the equity and the control of the fund, and wiped out the existing shareholders other than LTCM's partners. This rescue was conducted under the auspices of the Federal Reserve Bank and has evidently slowed down the liquidation of LTCM's portfolio.

Other hedge funds were not so lucky. Under the pressure on prices resulting both from bad fundamental news and security sales by other funds, many smaller hedge funds suffered enormous losses and were liquidated. The ones that survived were the ones that were more diversified, less leveraged, and better positioned *vis-à-vis* the creditors. The panic appeared to subside only in November, as better fundamental news (including the IMF's rescue of Brazil) and significant interest rate cuts by the Federal Reserve brought new liquidity to the markets.

From the economic perspective, it made a lot of sense for the LTCM to be rescued by a committee of its creditors. After all, by liquidating LTCM's portfolio at fire-sale prices, the creditors were only reducing the value of their collateral and thus suffering huge losses on their loans to LTCM. Indeed, many of the largest commercial and investment banks reported poor profits for the third quarter of 1998 stemming from their losses on loans to the hedge funds. The committee of creditors could thus address the central problem arising in any liquidation: the uncoordinated efforts by separate creditors to grab and liquidate their collateral, which results in large losses to all of them. Whether the oversight by the Federal Reserve was essential for the achievement of this coordinated outcome remains an open question.

In his testimony to the U.S. House of Representatives on the LTCM rescue, the Federal Reserve Chairman Alan Greenspan analyzed the situation as follows:

Had the failure of LTCM triggered the seizing up of markets, substantial damage would have been inflicted on many market participants, including some not directly involved with the firm, and could have potentially impaired the economies of many nations, including our own. With credit spreads already elevated and the market prices of risky assets under considerable downward pressure, Federal Reserve officials moved more quickly to provide their good offices to help resolve the affairs of LTCM than would have been the case in more normal times. In effect, the threshold of action was lowered by the knowledge that markets had recently become fragile. Moreover, our sense was that the consequences of a fire sale triggered by cross-default clauses, should LTCM fail on some of its obligations, risked a severe drying up of market liquidity. The plight of LTCM might scarcely have caused a ripple in financial markets or among Federal regulators 18 months ago—but in current circumstances it was judged to warrant attention...

Quickly unwinding a complicated portfolio that contains exposure to all manner of risks, such as that of LTCM, in such market conditions amounts to conducting a fire sale. The prices received in a time of stress do not reflect longer term potential, adding to the losses incurred. Of course, a fire sale that transfers wealth from one set of sophisticated market players to another, without any impact on the financial system over all, should not be a concern for the central bank. Moreover, creditors should reasonably be expected to put some weight on the possibility of a large market swing when making their risk assessments. Indeed, when we examine banks we expect them to have systems in place that take account of outsized market moves. However, a fire sale may be sufficiently intense and widespread that it seriously distorts markets and elevates uncertainty enough to impair the overall functioning of the economy. Sophisticated economic systems cannot thrive in such an atmosphere.

During the fall of 1998, the LTCM rescue appeared to be a successful investment for the creditors as the fund earned substantial positive returns (consistent with the prediction of the model that, in a crisis, arbitrageurs' positions are liquidated even though they have a positive expected return). It remains uncertain whether the relative calm of emerging markets in late 1998 will be sustained through the possible withdrawal of investments in hedge funds by their shareholders, and whether the system has already experienced all the shocks of this crisis. It is far more certain that arbitrage in these particular circumstances was extremely limited.

5

A Model of Investor Sentiment

PREVIOUS chapters have focused on the limits of arbitrage. They concluded that financial markets should not in general be presumed to be efficient. Moreover, some predictions could be made about the actual behavior of security prices, such as closed end funds, solely from an understanding of the limits of arbitrage. Yet the models in these chapters did not allow strong predictions about stock returns. For that, as we argued in Chapter 1, we need a more elaborate model of investor sentiment—of how investors form beliefs. This chapter presents one such model that is consistent with both the available evidence on stock returns and some of the most robust psychological theories of belief formation.

As a first step in this argument, this chapter briefly reviews some recent empirical research in finance. This research has identified two families of pervasive regularities apparently inconsistent with weak and semi-strong form market efficiency. These regularities, already mentioned in Chapter 1, are conveniently called underreaction and overreaction. The underreaction evidence shows that security prices underreact to news such as earnings announcements. If the news is good, prices keep trending up after the initial positive reaction; if the news is bad, prices keep trending down after the initial negative reaction. Put differently, current news has power in predicting not just the returns on the announcement of these news, but also returns in the future, when the news is already stale. The momentum evidence briefly described in Chapter 1 is closely related to underreaction, since the positive autocorrelations of returns over relatively short horizons may reflect slow incorporation of news into stock prices.

The overreaction evidence shows that over longer horizons of perhaps three to five years, security prices overreact to consistent patterns of news pointing in the same direction. That is, securities that have had a long record of good news tend to become overpriced and have low average returns afterwards. Securities with strings of good performance, however measured, receive extremely high valuations, and these valuations, on average, return to the mean.[1]

In Chapter 1, we have already mentioned some research in this area, such as the reversals in returns of extreme winners and losers documented by De Bondt and Thaler (1985), and the predictability of returns from accounting ratios such as book to market.

In this chapter we propose a model of investor sentiment consistent with this evidence. The model is motivated by experimental psychological evidence on failures of individual judgment under uncertainty. Our specification is motivated by the results of Tversky and Kahneman (1974) on the important behavioral heuristic known as representativeness, or the tendency of experimental subjects to view events as typical or representative of some specific class and to ignore the laws of probability in the process. An important manifestation of the representativeness heuristic is that people think that they see patterns in truly random sequences. Our model also relates to another phenomenon documented in psychology, conservatism, defined as the slow updating of models in the face of new evidence (Edwards 1968). We consider both representativeness and conservatism in the context of investors' interpretation of the news about corporate earnings.

At an intuitive level, our model works as follows. Investors have some prior views about the company in question. When they receive earnings news about this company, they tend not to react to this news in revaluing the company as much as Bayesian statistics warrants, because they exhibit conservatism. This behavior gives rise to underreaction of prices to earnings announcements, and to short horizon trends. At the same time, when investors are hit over the head repeatedly with similar news—such as good earnings surprises—they not only give up their old model but, because of representativeness, attach themselves to a new model, in which earnings trend. In doing so, they

---

[1] There is also evidence of non zero return autocorrelations at very short horizons such as a day (Lehmann 1990). We do not believe that it is essential for a behavioral model to confront this evidence because it can be plausibly explained by market microstructure considerations such as the fluctuation of recorded prices between the bid and the ask.

underestimate the likelihood that the past few positive surprises are the result of chance rather than of a new regime. This gives rise to overreaction. The model presented below incorporates these two elements into a formal story.

The next section summarizes the empirical findings that we try to explain. We then discuss the psychological evidence that motivates the model that follows. The empirical evidence seems to be broadly consistent with the predictions of that model.

5.1 The evidence

The volume of statistical evidence of underreaction and overreaction in security returns is enormous. We devote only minor attention to the behavior of aggregate stock and bond returns because these data often do not provide enough information to reject the hypothesis of efficient markets. Most of the anomalous evidence that our model tries to explain comes from the cross-section of stock returns. Much of this evidence is from the United States, although some recent research has found similar patterns in other countries.

Statistical evidence of underreaction

To begin, we need to define underreaction to news announcements. Suppose that in each time period, the investor hears news about a particular company. We denote the news he hears in period t by z_t. This news can be either good or bad, i.e. $z_t = G$ or $z_t = B$. By underreaction we mean that the average return on the company's stock in the period following an announcement of good news (i.e. after the initial price reaction to the news) is *higher* than the average return in the period following bad news:

$$E(r_{t+1}|z_t = G) > E(r_{t+1}|z_t = B) \tag{5.1}$$

In other words, the stock underreacts to the announcement of news, a mistake which is at least partly corrected in the following period, spreading the impact of the announcement on the price over time. Because the stock underreacts to the actual announcement, profits can potentially be earned by trading in the stock *after* the news is announced, a violation of semi-strong form market efficiency. In this chapter, news consists of earnings announcements, although we also discuss considerable evidence of underreaction to other types of news as well.

Empirical analysis of the aggregate time series of security returns has produced some evidence of underreaction. Cutler *et al.* (1991) examine autocorrelations in excess returns on various indexes over different horizons. They look at returns on stocks, bonds, and foreign exchange in different markets over the period 1960–1988 and generally, though not uniformly, find positive, and often statistically significant, autocorrelations in excess index returns over horizons of between one month and one year. For example, the average one-month autocorrelation in excess stock returns across the world is around 0.1 (and is also around 0.1 in the United States alone), and that in excess bond returns is around 0.2 (and around zero in the United States). This evidence is consistent with the underreaction hypothesis.

More convincing support for the underreaction hypothesis comes from the studies of the cross-section of stock returns in the United States, which look at the actual news events as well as the predictability of returns. Bernard (1992) surveys one class of such studies, those dealing with the underreaction of stock prices to announcements of company earnings. Suppose we sort stocks into groups (say deciles) based on how much of a surprise is contained in their earnings announcement. One naive way to measure an earnings surprise is to look at standardized unexpected earnings (SUE) defined as the difference between a company's earnings in a given quarter and its earnings during the quarter a year before, scaled by the standard deviation of the company's earnings. One can then look at the average net-of-market returns on deciles of stocks grouped by their SUEs over some period following earnings announcements. Figure 5.1 presents the results of such an analysis from Bernard (1992), who examined a sample of 84,792 earnings announcements by U.S. companies between 1974 and 1986.

An unsurprising finding in Figure 5.1 is that stocks with positive earnings surprises also earn relatively high returns in the period *prior to* the earnings announcement, as information about earnings is incorporated into prices. An equally unsurprising finding is that stocks with positive earnings surprises earn positive returns *on* the

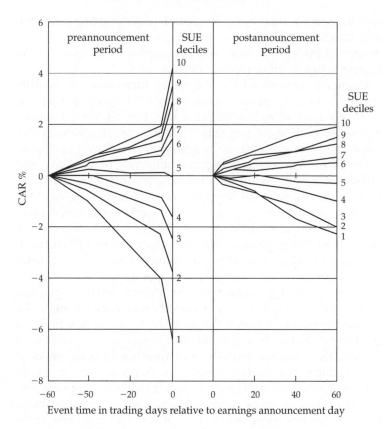

FIG. 5.1 Cumulative abnormal returns (CAR) for SUE portfolios (84,792 earnings announcements, 1974–86).
Source: Bernard (1992).

announcement as some news is incorporated into prices. The surprising finding is that stocks with higher earnings surprises also earn higher returns in the period *after* the announcement and therefore after the portfolios are actually formed: the market underreacts to the earnings announcement in revising a company's stock price. Over the 60 trading days after portfolio formation, stocks with the highest SUE earn a 4.2 percent higher cumulative risk-adjusted return than do stocks with the lowest SUE. Stale information, namely the SUE or the past earnings announcement return, has predictive power for future risk-adjusted returns. Put differently, information about earnings is only slowly incorporated into stock prices.

Bernard also summarizes some evidence on the actual properties of the time series of earnings and provides an interpretation for his findings. The relevant series is changes in a company's earnings in a given quarter relative to the same calendar quarter in the previous year. Over the period 1974–86, using a sample of 2,626 firms, Bernard and Thomas (1990) find that these series exhibit an autocorrelation of about 0.34 at a lag of one quarter, 0.19 at two quarters, 0.06 at three quarters, and −0.24 at four quarters. Earnings changes exhibit a slight trend at one-, two-, and three-quarter horizons and a slight reversal after a year. In interpreting the evidence, Bernard conjectures that market participants do not recognize the positive autocorrelations in earnings changes, and in fact believe that earnings follow a random walk. This belief causes them to underreact to earnings announcements. Our model uses a related idea for generating underreaction: we suppose that earnings follow a random walk but that investors typically assume that earnings are mean-reverting. The key idea that generates underreaction, which Bernard's and our analyses share, is that investors typically (but not always) believe that earnings are more stationary than they really are. As we show below, this idea is consistent with psychological evidence.

Further evidence of underreaction comes from Jegadeesh and Titman (1993), who examine a cross-section of U.S. stock returns and find reliable evidence that over a six-month horizon stock returns are positively autocorrelated. Similar to the earnings drift evidence, they interpret their finding of the 'momentum' in stock returns as pointing to underreaction to information and slow incorporation of information into prices. Chan *et al.* (1996) extend this evidence to a large sample of U.S. stocks between 1977 and 1993. Table 5.1 presents a sampling of their results. Chan *et al.* (1996) find that, during their sample period, the decile portfolio of worst performing stocks over a previous six-month period underperforms on average the decile portfolio of best performing stocks in the future. For example, in the six months after portfolio formation, the past six-month loser portfolio underperforms the past six-month winner portfolio by nearly nine percent. Chan *et al.* (1996) also show that stocks in the loser portfolio on average had negative earnings surprises

Table 5.1 Mean returns and characteristics for portfolios classified by prior six-month return

	1-low	2	3	4	5	6	7	8	9	10-high
Panel A—Returns										
Past 6-month return	−0.308	−0.126	−0.055	0.000	0.050	0.099	0.153	0.219	0.319	0.696
Return 6 months after portfolio information	0.061	0.086	0.093	0.096	0.102	0.104	0.105	0.111	0.120	0.149
Return first year after portfolio formation	0.143	0.185	0.198	0.208	0.214	0.222	0.223	0.235	0.248	0.297
Return second year after portfolio formation	0.205	0.201	0.205	0.206	0.208	0.208	0.204	0.208	0.207	0.199
Return third year after portfolio formation	0.194	0.196	0.197	0.196	0.199	0.202	0.205	0.201	0.208	0.206
Panel B—Standardized Unexpected Earnings										
Most recent quarter	−0.879	−0.336	−0.092	0.046	0.196	0.316	0.433	0.570	0.670	0.824
Next quarter	−1.052	−0.414	−0.147	0.034	0.192	0.350	0.479	0.613	0.744	0.919

Panel C—Abnormal Return around earnings announcements

Most recent announcement	−0.027	−0.013	−0.007	−0.003	0.000	0.004	0.007	0.012	0.018	0.035
First announcement after portfolio formation	−0.011	−0.004	−0.001	0.000	0.002	0.003	0.004	0.006	0.009	0.015
Second announcement after portfolio formation	−0.002	0.000	0.000	0.001	0.001	0.003	0.003	0.003	0.005	0.008
Third announcement after portfolio formation	0.002	0.001	0.002	0.001	0.002	0.001	0.003	0.003	0.003	0.005
Fourth announcement after portfolio formation	0.003	0.001	0.002	0.001	0.001	0.000	0.001	0.002	0.001	0.001

Source: Chan *et al.* (1996).

At the beginning of every month from January 1977 to January 1993, all stocks are ranked by their compound return over the prior six months and assigned to one of ten portfolios. The assignment uses breakpoints based on New York Stock Exchange (NYSE) issues only. All stocks are equally weighted in a portfolio. The sample includes all NYSE, American Stock Exchange (AMEX), and Nasdaq domestic primary issues with coverage on the Center for Research in Security Prices (CRSP) and COMPUSTAT. Panel A reports the average past six-month return for each portfolio, and buy-and-hold returns over periods following portfolio formation (in the following six months and in the first, second, and third subsequent years). Panel B reports each portfolio's most recent past and subsequent values of quarterly standardized unexpected earnings (the change in quarterly earnings per share from its value four quarters ago, divided by the standard deviation of unexpected earnings over the last eight quarters). Panel C reports abnormal returns around earnings announcements dates. Abnormal returns are relative to the equally-weighted market index and are cumulated from two days before to one day after the beginning date of earnings announcement.

prior to portfolio formation and, more impressively, on average have negative earnings surprises *following* portfolio formation. This evidence suggests that the momentum results are closely related to earnings announcements evidence in that both reflect underreaction of stock prices to new information. More recent work by Rouwenhorst (1997) documents the presence of momentum in international equity markets as well.

In addition to the evidence of stock price underreaction to earnings announcements and the related evidence of momentum in stock prices, there is also a body of closely related evidence on stock price drift following other announcements and events. For example, Ikenberry *et al.* (1995) find that stock prices rise on the announcement of share repurchases but then continue to drift in the same direction over the next few years. Michaely *et al.* (1995) find similar evidence of drift following dividend initiations and omissions, while Ikenberry *et al.* (1996) document such a drift following stock splits. Finally, Loughran and Ritter (1995) and Spiess and Affleck-Graves (1995) find evidence of a drift following seasoned equity offerings. A theory of investor sentiment should presumably come to grips with this pervasive evidence of underreaction.

Statistical evidence of overreaction

Analogous to the definition of underreaction at the start of the previous subsection, we define overreaction as occurring when the average return following not one but a series of announcements of good news is *lower* than the average return following a series of bad news announcements. Using the same notation as before,

$$E(r_{t+1} \mid z_t = G, z_{t-1} = G, \ldots, z_{t-j} = G)$$

$$< E(r_{t+1} \mid z_t = B, z_{t-1} = B, \ldots, z_{t-j} = B), \tag{5.2}$$

where j is at least one and probably higher. The idea here is that after a series of announcements of good news, the investor becomes overly optimistic that future news announcements will also be good and hence overreacts, sending the stock price to unduly high levels. Subsequent news is likely to contradict his optimism, leading to lower returns. Again, the idea is that trading on stale information, in this case a series of good or bad news, can earn superior returns.

Empirical studies of predictability of aggregate index returns over long horizons are extremely numerous. Early papers include Fama and French (1988) and Poterba and Summers (1988); Cutler *et al.* (1991) examine some of this evidence for a variety of markets. The thrust of the evidence is that, over horizons of three to five years, there is a relatively slight negative autocorrelation in stock returns in many markets. Moreover, over similar horizons, some measures of stock valuation, such as the aggregate dividend yield or the aggregate book to market ratio, have predictive power for returns in a similar direction: a low dividend yield or book to market ratio tend to predict a low subsequent return (Campbell and Shiller 1988; Pontiff and Schall 1998; Kothari and Shanken 1997).

As before, the more convincing evidence comes from the cross-section of stock returns. In an early paper, mentioned in Chapter 1, De Bondt and Thaler (1985) discover from looking at U.S. data dating back to 1933 that portfolios of stocks with extremely poor returns over the previous three years dramatically outperform portfolios of stocks with extremely high returns, even after making the standard risk adjustments. De Bondt and Thaler's findings are corroborated by later work (e.g. Chopra *et al.* 1992). In the case of earnings, Zarowin (1989) finds that firms that have had a sequence of bad earnings realizations subsequently outperform firms with a sequence of good earnings. This evidence suggests that stocks with a consistent record of good news, and hence extremely high past returns, are overvalued, and that an investor can therefore earn abnormal returns by betting against this overreaction to consistent patterns of news. Similarly, stocks with a consistent record of bad news become undervalued and subsequently earn superior returns.

Subsequent work has changed the focus from past returns to other measures of valuation, such as the ratio of market value to book value of assets (De Bondt and Thaler, 1987; Fama and French, 1992), market value to cash flow (Lakonishok *et al.* 1994), and other accounting measures. All this evidence points in the same direction. Stocks with very high valuations relative to their assets or earnings (growth or glamour stocks), which tend to be stocks of companies with extremely high earnings growth over the previous several years, earn relatively low risk-adjusted returns in the future, whereas stocks with low valuations (value stocks) earn relatively high returns. Table 5.2 presents some evidence from Lakonishok *et al.* who look at the U.S. stocks between 1968 and 1990, and consider a number of risk-adjustments in calculating abnormal returns, as well as control for size. As an example, Lakonishok *et al.* find spreads of 8–10 percent per year between returns of the extreme value and glamour deciles measured by either book to market ratio or cash flow to price ratio. Moreover, their study finds that the glamour portfolios typically have prolonged prior records of high earnings growth, whereas value portfolios have records of consistent poor earnings growth. This evidence points to overreaction by investors to a prolonged record of extreme company performance, whether good or bad: the prices of stocks with such extreme performance tend to be too extreme relative to what these stocks are worth and relative to what the subsequent returns actually deliver. Recent research extends the evidence on value stocks to other countries, including those in Europe, Japan, and emerging economies (Fama and French 1998; Haugen and Baker 1996).

Fama and French (1993, 1996) propose to interpret this evidence as pointing to the higher risk from investing in high book to market and small stocks. In effect, they define the glamour stocks as less risky, and the value stocks as more risky, thereby denying that the superior average returns from investing in value stocks are actually superior on the risk-adjusted basis. Fama and French also take the position that the risk that a high book to market ratio proxies for is 'distress' risk, although direct evidence of this conjecture has not yet been provided. This research represents the Fama (1970) critique of the tests of market efficiency, because it argues that profits from value investing are not superior on the risk-adjusted basis for no other reason than that value investing is riskier by definition.

An important piece of evidence taken by Fama and French (1993) as supporting the risk explanation is the comovement between securities of similar size or book to market ratio. This comovement points to systematic influences on broad groups of securities with similar characteristics, which Fama and French interpret as evidence of common fundamental risk. The results of

Table 5.2 Decile returns based on book to market and cashflow to price

Decile returns based on book to market

BM	Growth 1	2	5	6	9	Value 10
R1	0.110	0.117	0.131	0.154	0.183	0.173
R2	0.079	0.107	0.153	0.156	0.182	0.188
R3	0.107	0.132	0.165	0.172	0.196	0.204
R4	0.081	0.133	0.170	0.169	0.213	0.207
R5	0.088	0.137	0.171	0.176	0.206	0.215
AR	0.093	0.125	0.158	0.166	0.196	0.198
CR5	0.560	0.802	1.082	1.152	1.449	1.462
SAAR	−0.043	−0.020	0.006	0.012	0.033	0.035

Decile returns based on cash flow to price

BM	Growth 1	2	5	6	9	Value 10
R1	0.084	0.124	0.153	0.148	0.183	0.183
R2	0.067	0.108	0.156	0.170	0.183	0.190
R3	0.096	0.133	0.170	0.191	0.193	0.204
R4	0.098	0.111	0.166	0.172	0.223	0.218
R5	0.108	0.134	0.187	0.177	0.212	0.208
AR	0.091	0.122	0.166	0.171	0.199	0.201
CR5	0.543	0.779	1.158	1.206	1.476	1.494
SAAR	−0.049	−0.025	0.013	0.019	0.037	0.039

Using the universe of stocks from the New York Stock Exchange and the American Stock Exchange, at the end of each April between 1968 and 1989, 10 decile portfolios are formed in ascending order based on B/M and C/P. B/M for each stock is the ratio of book value of equity to market value of equity; C/P is the ratio of cash flow to market value of equity. The returns presented in the table are averages over all formation periods. Rt is the average return in year t after formation, $t=1, \ldots, 5$. AR is the average annual return over 5 post-formation years. CR5 is the compounded 5-year return assuming annual rebalancing. SAAR is the average annual size-adjusted return computed over 5 post-formation years. The growth portfolio refers to the decile portfolio containing stocks ranking lowest on B/M and C/P, respectively. The value portfolio refers to the decile portfolio containing stocks ranking highest on B/M and C/P, respectively.
Source: Lakonishok *et al.* (1994).

Chapters 2 and 3 show, however, that noise trader risk that influences security prices is likely to be systematic as well, so that we would expect *from behavioral theory* to see comovement between securities affected by the same investor sentiment. If small stocks, for example, are affected by the same sentiment, the returns on small stocks will be correlated. The evidence of comovement thus does not distinguish the various interpretations of the evidence.

Still, the Fama critique is powerful as usual. Indeed, there have been some recent relatively direct attempts to distinguish risk from overreaction. Perhaps the most direct and obvious implication of the rational explanation of the value/glamour evidence is that investors in glamour stocks who receive low average returns from glamour stocks actually *expect such low returns* because glamour stocks have attractive risk characteristics. A variety of evidence casts doubt on this prediction. If anything, investors are too optimistic about glamour stocks. To begin, Lakonishok *et al.* (1994) present evidence that points to a systematic pattern of expectational errors on the part of investors that is capable of explaining the differential stock returns across glamour and value stocks. Investor expectations of future growth implied by the pricing multiples appear to be excessively tied to past growth despite the fact that future growth rates are more stationary. Investors expect earnings of glamour firms to continue growing much faster than those of value firms in the foreseeable future despite the fact that future growth rates move sharply closer to each other than they have been in the past.

La Porta (1996) focuses on expectations directly. He sorts a large sample of U.S. stocks on the basis of long-term earnings growth rate forecasts made by professional analysts. He finds that analysts are excessively bullish about the stocks they are most optimistic about and excessively bearish about the stocks they are most pessimistic about. As Figure 5.2 shows, stocks with the highest growth forecasts earn much lower future returns than stocks with the lowest growth forecasts. Moreover, on average, stocks with high growth forecasts earn negative returns when they subsequently announce earnings and stocks with low growth forecasts earn high returns. This evidence points to overreaction not just by analysts but in prices as well: in an efficient market, stocks with optimistic growth forecasts should not earn low returns.

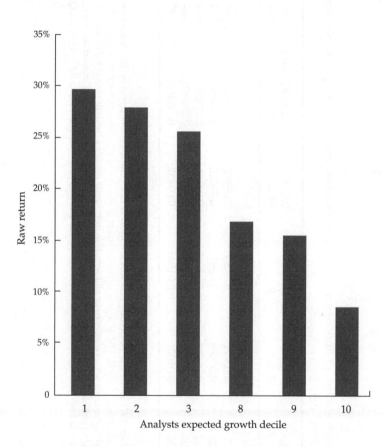

Fig. 5.2 Portfolios formed on analysts' expected earnings growth (1982–91).
Source: La Porta (1996).

Table 5.3 Annual cumulative earnings announcement returns on value and glamour portfolios classified by book-to-market ratios, 1971–1992 (full sample)

BM	Glamour 1	2	9	Value 10	Mean difference 10–1	t-stat for mean difference 10–1
Event Returns						
Q01–Q04	−0.00472	0.00772	0.03200	0.03532	0.04004	5.65
Q04–Q08	−0.00428	0.00688	0.02828	0.03012	0.03440	7.14
Q09–Q12	0.00312	0.00796	0.02492	0.03136	0.02824	5.12
Q13–Q16	0.00804	0.00812	0.02176	0.02644	0.01840	3.67
Q17–Q20	0.00424	0.01024	0.01368	0.02432	0.02008	4.49

Source: La Porta *et al.* (1997).

At the end of each June between 1971 and 1992, 10 decile portfolios are formed in ascending order based on the ratio of the book value of equity to market value of equity (BM). The glamour portfolio refers to the decile portfolio containing stocks ranking lowest on BM. The returns presented in the table are averages over all formation periods. It contains (equally-weighted) earnings announcement returns for each portfolio. These are measured quarterly over a 3-day window ($t-1$, $t+1$) around the *Wall Street Journal* publication date and then summed up over the four quarters in each of the first five post-formation years (Q01–Q04, ..., Q17–Q20).

Finally, La Porta *et al.* (1997) find direct evidence of over-reaction in glamour and value stocks defined using account-ing variables. Specifically, glamour stocks earn negative returns on the days of their future earnings announcements and value stocks earn positive returns (Table 5.3). The market learns when earnings are announced that its valuations have been too extreme. It is very difficult to reconcile this evi-dence with a risk story in which expectations are by definition rational, and hence earnings announcements should be *on average* unsurprising. Moreover, as Fama (1998, p. 283) himself points out, the event study evidence is particularly compelling since the Fama critique has little bite: 'because daily returns are close to zero, the model of expected returns does not have a big effect on inferences about abnormal returns.'

In sum, the cross-sectional overreaction evidence, like the cross-sectional underreaction evidence, presents rather reliable regularities. These regularities taken in their entirety are difficult to reconcile with the efficient markets hypothesis. In the case of overreaction, there is considerable evidence inconsistent with the fundamental risk explanation and no direct evidence to support it. In the case of underreaction, an efficient markets explanation has not even been proposed. The two regularities challenge behavioral finance to provide a model of how investors form beliefs that can account for the empirical evidence.

5.2 Some psychological evidence

Our model is motivated by two important phenomena docu-mented by psychologists: *conservatism* and the *representativeness heuristic*.

Edwards (1968) identifies a phenomenon known as conser-vatism. Conservatism states that individuals are slow to change their beliefs in the face of new evidence. Edwards benchmarks a subject's reaction to new evidence against that of an idealized rational Bayesian in experiments in which the true normative value of a piece of evidence is well defined. In his experiments, individuals update their posteriors in the right direction, but *by too little* in magnitude relative to the rational Bayesian benchmark. This finding of conservatism is actually more pronounced the more objectively useful is the new evidence. In Edwards' own words: 'It turns out that opinion change is very orderly, and usually proportional to numbers calculated from the Bayes Theorem—but it is insufficient in amount. A conventional first approximation to the data would say that it takes anywhere from two to five observations to do one observation's worth of work in inducing a subject to change his opinions (Edwards 1968, p. 359).'

Conservatism is extremely suggestive of the underreaction evidence described above. Individuals subject to conservatism might disregard the full information content of an earnings (or some other public) announcement, perhaps because they believe that this number contains a large temporary component and still cling at least partially to their prior estimates of earnings. As a consequence, they might adjust their valuation of shares only partially in response to the announcement. Edwards would describe such behavior in Bayesian terms as a failure to properly aggregate the information in the new earnings number with investors' own prior information to form a new posterior earnings estimate. In particular, individuals tend to underweight useful statistical evidence relative to the less useful evidence used to form their priors.

A second important phenomenon documented by psychologists is the representativeness heuristic (Tversky and Kahneman 1974): 'A person who follows this heuristic evaluates the probability of an uncertain event, or a sample, by the degree to which it is (i) similar in its essential properties to the parent population, (ii) reflects the salient features of the process by which it is generated' (p. 33). For example, if a detailed description of an individual's personality matches up well with the subject's experiences with people of a particular profession, the subject tends to significantly overestimate the actual probability that the given individual belongs to that profession. In overweighting the representative description, the subject underweights the statistical base rate evidence of the small fraction of the population belonging to that profession.

An important manifestation of the representativeness heuristic, discussed in detail by Tversky and Kahneman, is that people think they see patterns in truly random sequences. This aspect of the representativeness heuristic is suggestive of the overreaction evidence described above. When a company has a consistent history of earnings growth over several years, accompanied as it may be by salient and enthusiastic descriptions of its products and management, investors might conclude that the past history is representative of an underlying earnings growth potential. While a consistent pattern of high growth may be nothing more than a random draw for a few lucky firms, investors see 'order in chaos' and infer from the in-sample growth path that the firm belongs to a small and distinct population of firms whose earnings just keep growing. As a consequence, investors using the representativeness heuristic might disregard the reality that a history of high earnings growth is unlikely to repeat itself, overvalue the company, and become disappointed in the future when the forecasted earnings growth fails to materialize. This, of course, is what overreaction is all about.

To illustrate the general interplay of conservatism and representativeness, consider an individual who observes the outcomes of consecutive tosses of an unfair coin, one toss at a time. Suppose that, in reality, the coin comes out heads 70 percent of the time. The individual knows that the coin is unfair, but he begins with a prior that it is equally likely to be a 70 percent-heads coin or a 70 percent-tails coin. Consider what happens after n trials in which the coin *always comes up heads*. Figure 5.3 shows how a true Bayesian would update his beliefs, as well as how a person whose conduct is consistent with experimental evidence, called a subject, would update. It portrays the probability that each type would attach to the coin being 70 percent-heads as a function of n heads in a row. The solid line shows the Bayesian updating. The dotted line shows that, relative to a Bayesian, a subject first does not update his probability enough (conservatism), but having seen a few heads in a row, jumps to a conclusion that the coin is even more likely to be 70 percent-heads than it really is because the string of heads is 'representative' of what would come from such a coin. This series of trials, consistent with experimental evidence, shows a subject underreacting to individual pieces of information, but overreacting to conspicuous patterns.

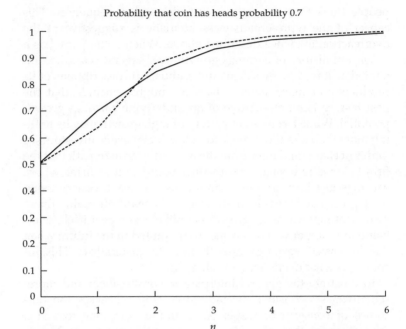

FIG. 5.3 The figure shows the probability that two observers assign to a coin being biased with a 0.7 chance of showing heads, after observing n heads in a row. The subjects are told in advance that the coin is biased and has either a 0.7 chance of showing heads or 0.7 chance of showing tails. They assign 0.5 prior probability to each. The solid line shows the probabilities as computed by a rational Bayesian, while the dashed line comes from someone subject to conservatism and representativeness biases

5.3 Informal description of the model

The model we present in this section attempts to capture the empirical evidence summarized in Section 5.1 using the ideas from psychology discussed in Section 5.2. We consider a model with a representative, risk-neutral investor with discount rate δ. We can think of this investor's beliefs as reflecting the 'consensus,' even if different investors have different beliefs. There is only one security, which pays out 100 percent of its earnings as dividends; in this context, the equilibrium price of the security is equal to the net present value of future earnings, as forecasted by the representative investor. In contrast to models with heterogeneous agents, there is no information in prices over and above the information already contained in earnings.

Given the assumptions of risk-neutrality and a constant discount rate, returns are unpredictable if the investor knows the correct process followed by the earnings stream (Samuelson 1965). If our model is to generate the kind of predictability in returns documented in the empirical studies, the investor must be using the wrong model to form expectations.

We suppose that the earnings stream follows a random walk. This assumption is not entirely accurate, as we discussed above, since earnings growth rates at one- to three-quarter horizons are slightly positively autocorrelated (Bernard and Thomas 1990). We make this assumption only for concreteness: all that is essential for the results is that investors sometimes believe that earnings are more stationary than they really are—the idea stressed by Bernard and captured in the model below. This relative misperception is the key to underreaction.

The investor in our model does not realize that earnings follow a random walk. He thinks that the world moves between two 'states' or 'regimes' and that there is a different model governing earnings in each regime. When the world is in regime 1, Model 1 determines earnings; in regime 2, Model 2 determines them. Neither of the two models is a random walk. Rather, under Model 1, earnings are mean-reverting; in Model 2, they trend. For simplicity, we specify these models as Markov processes: that is, in each model the change in earnings in period t depends only on the change in earnings in period $t - 1$. The only difference between the two models lies in the transition probabilities. Under Model 1, earnings shocks are likely to be reversed in the following period, so that a positive shock to earnings is more likely to be followed in the next period by a negative shock than by another positive shock. Under Model 2, shocks are more likely to be followed by another shock of the same sign.

The idea that the investor believes that the world is governed by one of the two incorrect models is a crude way of capturing the psychological phenomena of the previous section. An investor using Model 1 to forecast earnings reacts too little to an individual earnings announcement, as would an investor exhibiting conservatism. In contrast, the investor who believes in Model 2 behaves as if he is subject to the representativeness heuristic, as he takes past earnings growth to be representative of the future as well. After a string of positive or negative earnings changes, the investor uses Model 2 to forecast future earnings, extrapolating past performance too far into the future.

The investor also believes that there is an underlying regime-switching process that determines which regime the world is in at any time. We specify this underlying process as a Markov process as well, so that whether the current regime is Model 1 or Model 2 depends only on what the regime was last period. We focus attention on cases in which regime switches are relatively rare. That is, if Model 1 determines the change in earnings in period t, it is likely that it determines earnings in period $t + 1$ also. The same applies to Model 2. With some small probability, though, the regime changes, and the other model begins generating earnings. For reasons that will become apparent, we often require the regime-switching probabilities to be such that the investor thinks that the world is in the mean-reverting regime of Model 1 more often than he believes it to be in the trending regime of Model 2.

The transition probabilities associated with Models 1 and 2 and with the underlying regime-switching process are fixed in the investor's mind. In order to value the security, the investor needs to forecast future earnings. To do this, he uses the earnings stream he has observed to update his beliefs about which regime is generating earnings. Once this is done, he uses the regime-switching model to forecast future earnings. The investor updates in a Bayesian fashion even though his model of earnings is incorrect. For instance, if he observes two consecutive earnings shocks of the same sign, he believes more strongly that he is in the trending earnings regime of Model 2. If the earnings shock this period is of the opposite sign to last period's earnings shock, he puts more weight on Model 1, the mean-reverting regime.

Unlike in a typical learning setup, the investor here never changes the model he is using to forecast earnings, but rather uses the same regime-switching model, with the same regimes and transition probabilities throughout. Even after observing a very long stream of earnings data, he does not change his model to something more like a random walk, the true earnings process.

His only task is to figure out which of the two regimes of his model is currently generating earnings. This is the only sense in which he is learning from the data.[2]

A model of such an investor facing a random walk process for earnings can generate the empirical phenomena discussed earlier, including both underreaction to earnings announcements and long-run overreaction. A natural way of capturing overreaction is to say that the average realized return following a string of positive shocks to earnings is lower than the average realized return following a string of negative shocks to earnings. Indeed, after our investor sees a series of positive earnings shocks, he puts a high probability on Model 2 generating current earnings. Since he believes regime switches to be rare, this means that Model 2 is also likely to generate earnings in the next period. The investor then expects the shock to earnings next period to be positive again. Earnings, however, follow a random walk: next period's earnings are equally likely to go up or down. If they go up, the return will not be large, as the investor is expecting exactly such a rise in earnings. If they fall, however, the return is large and negative as the investor is taken by surprise by the negative announcement.[3] The average realized return after a string of positive shocks is therefore negative; symmetrically, the average return after a string of negative earnings shocks is positive. The negative difference between the average returns in the two cases is consistent with the observed overreaction.

Following our earlier discussion, underreaction refers to the fact that the average realized return following a positive shock to earnings is greater than the average realized return following a negative shock to earnings. Underreaction obtains in our model as long as the investor places more weight on Model 1

---

[2] From a mathematical perspective, the investor would eventually learn the true random walk model for earnings if it were included in the support of his prior; from the viewpoint of psychology, though, there is much evidence that people learn *slowly* and find it difficult to shake off pervasive biases such as conservatism and representativeness.

[3] This is exactly the empirical finding of Dreman and Berry (1995). They find that glamour stocks earn small positive event returns on positive earnings surprises and large negative event returns on negative earnings surprises. The converse holds for value stocks.

than on Model 2, on average. Consider the realized return following a positive earnings shock. Since, by assumption, the investor on average believes Model 1, he on average believes that this positive earnings shock will be partly reversed in the next period. In reality, however, a positive shock is as likely to be followed by a positive as by a negative shock. If the shock is negative, the realized return is not large, since this is the earnings realization expected by the investor. If the shock is positive, the realized return is large and positive, since this shock is unexpected. Similarly, the average realized return following a negative earnings shock is negative, and hence the difference in the average realized returns is indeed positive, consistent with the evidence of post-earnings announcement drift and short-term momentum.

The empirical studies indicate that underreaction is a broader phenomenon than simply the delayed reaction to earnings news. Although we formulate the model in terms of earnings news, delayed reaction to announcements of dividends and share repurchases can be understood just as easily in our framework. Just as the investor displays conservatism when adjusting his beliefs in the face of a new earnings announcement, so he may also underweight the information in the announcement of a dividend cut or a share repurchase.

5.4 A model of investor sentiment

A formal model

Suppose that earnings at time t are $N_t = N_{t-1} + y_t$, where y_t is the shock to earnings at time t, which can take one of two values, $+y$ or $-y$. Assume that all earnings are paid out as dividends. The investor believes that the value of y_t is determined by one of two models, Model 1 or Model 2, depending on the 'state' or 'regime' of the economy. Models 1 and 2 have the same structure: they are both Markov processes, in the sense that the value taken by y_t depends only on the value taken by y_{t-1}. The essential difference between the two processes lies in the transition probabilities. To be precise, the transition matrices for the two models are:

Model 1	$y_{t+1} = y$	$y_{t+1} = -y$	Model 2	$y_{t+1} = y$	$y_{t+1} = -y$
$y_t = y$	π_L	$1 - \pi_L$	$y_t = y$	π_H	$1 - \pi_H$
$y_t = -y$	$1 - \pi_L$	π_L	$y_t = -y$	$1 - \pi_H$	π_H

The key is that π_L is small and π_H is large. We think of π_L as falling between zero and 0.5, with π_H falling between 0.5 and one. In other words, under Model 1 a positive shock is likely to be reversed; under Model 2, a positive shock is likely to be followed by another positive shock.

The investor is convinced that he knows the parameters π_L and π_H; he is also sure that he is right about the underlying process controlling the switching from one regime to another, or equivalently from Model 1 to Model 2. It, too, is Markov, so that the state of the world today depends only on the state of the world in the previous period. The transition matrix is:

	$s_{t+1} = 1$	$s_{t+1} = 2$
$s_t = 1$	$1 - \lambda_1$	λ_1
$s_t = 2$	λ_2	$1 - \lambda_2$

The state of the world at time t is written s_t. If $s_t = 1$, we are in the first regime and the earnings shock in period t, y_t, is generated by Model 1; similarly if $s_t = 2$, we are in the second regime and the earnings shock is generated by Model 2. The parameters λ_1 and λ_2 determine the probabilities of transition from one state to another. We focus particularly on small λ_1 and λ_2, which means that transitions from one state to another occur rarely. In particular, we assume that $\lambda_1 + \lambda_2 < 1$. We also think of λ_1 as being smaller than λ_2. Since the unconditional probability of being in state 1 is $\lambda_2 / (\lambda_1 + \lambda_2)$, this implies that the investor thinks of Model 1 as being more likely than Model 2, on average. Our results do not depend, however, on λ_1 being smaller than λ_2. The effects that we document can also obtain if $\lambda_1 > \lambda_2$.

To value the security, the investor needs to forecast earnings into the future. Since the model he is using dictates that earnings at any time are generated by one of two regimes, the investor sees his task as trying to understand which of the two regimes is currently governing earnings. He observes earnings each period and uses that information to make as good a guess as possible about which regime he is in. In particular, at time t, having observed the earnings shock y_t, he calculates q_t, the probability that y_t was generated by Model 1, using the new data to update his estimate from the previous period, q_{t-1}. Formally, $q_t = \Pr(s_t = 1 | y_t, y_{t-1}, q_{t-1})$. We suppose that the updating follows Bayes Rule, so that

$$q_{t+1} = \frac{((1-\lambda_1)q_t + \lambda_2(1-q_t))\Pr(y_{t+1} | s_{t+1} = 1, y_t)}{((1-\lambda_1)q_t + \lambda_2(1-q_t))\Pr(y_{t+1} | s_{t+1} = 1, y_t) + (\lambda_1 q_t + (1-\lambda_2)(1-q_t))\Pr(y_{t+1} | s_{t+1} = 2, y_t)}. \quad (5.3)$$

In particular, if the shock to earnings in period $t+1$, y_{t+1}, is the same as the shock in period t, y_t, the investor updates q_{t+1} from q_t using

$$q_{t+1} = \frac{((1-\lambda_1)q_t + \lambda_2(1-q_t))\pi_L}{((1-\lambda_1)q_t + \lambda_2(1-q_t))\pi_L + (\lambda_1 q_t + (1-\lambda_2)(1-q_t))\pi_H}, \quad (5.4)$$

and we show in the Appendix that in this case, $q_{t+1} < q_t$. In other words, the investor puts more weight on Model 2 if he sees two consecutive shocks of the same sign. Similarly, if the shock in period $t+1$ has the opposite sign to that in period t,

$$q_{t+1} = \frac{((1-\lambda_1)q_t + \lambda_2(1-q_t))(1-\pi_L)}{((1-\lambda_1)q_t + \lambda_2(1-q_t))(1-\pi_L) + (\lambda_1 q_t + (1-\lambda_2)(1-q_t))(1-\pi_H)}, \quad (5.5)$$

and, in this case, $q_{t+1} > q_t$ and the weight on Model 1 increases.

To aid intuition about how the model works, we present a simple illustrative example. Suppose that in period 0, the shock to earnings y_0 is positive and the probability assigned to Model 1 by the investor, i.e. q_0, is 0.5. For a randomly generated earnings stream over the next 20 periods, Table 5.4 presents the investor's belief q_t that the time t shock to earnings is generated by Model 1. The particular parameter values chosen here are $\pi_L = 1/3 < 3/4 = \pi_H$, and $\lambda_1 = 0.1 < 0.3 = \lambda_2$. Note again that the earnings stream is generated using the true process for earnings, a random walk.

In periods 0 through 4, positive shocks to earnings alternate with negative shocks. Since Model 1 stipulates that earnings shocks are likely to be reversed in the following period, we observe an increase in q_t, the probability that Model 1 is generating the earnings shock at time t, rising to a high of 0.94 in period 4. From periods 10 to 14, we observe five successive positive

Table 5.4 Investor beliefs as a function of observed earnings

t	y_t	q_t	t	y_t	q_t
0	y	0.50			
1	$-y$	0.80	11	y	0.74
2	y	0.90	12	y	0.56
3	$-y$	0.93	13	y	0.44
4	y	0.94	14	y	0.36
5	y	0.74	15	$-y$	0.74
6	$-y$	0.89	16	y	0.89
7	$-y$	0.69	17	y	0.69
8	y	0.87	18	$-y$	0.87
9	$-y$	0.92	19	y	0.92
10	y	0.94	20	y	0.72

Source: Barberis *et al.* (1998).

This table shows the probability q_t the investor assigns to current earnings being generated by a mean-reverting model after observing the change in earnings y_t at time t.

shocks; since this is behavior typical of that specified by Model 2, q_t falls through period 14 to a low of 0.36. One feature that is evident in the above example is that q_t rises if the earnings shock in period t has the opposite sign from that in period $t-1$ and falls if the shock in period t has the same sign as that in period $t-1$.

Basic results

To analyze the implications of the model for prices, note that, with a representative agent, the price of the security is simply this agent's valuation of the security. In other words

$$P_t = E_t \left\{ \frac{N_{t+1}}{1+\delta} + \frac{N_{t+2}}{(1+\delta)^2} + \ldots \right\}. \tag{5.6}$$

The expectations in this expression are the expectations of the investor who does not realize that the true process for earnings is a random walk. Indeed, if the investor did realize this, the series above would be simple enough to evaluate since, under a random walk, $E_t(N_{t+j}) = N_t$, and price equals N_t/δ. In our model, the price deviates from this correct value because the investor does not use the random walk model to forecast earnings, but rather some combination of Models 1 and 2, neither of which is a random walk. The following proposition, proved in the Appendix, summarizes the behavior of prices in this context, and shows that they depend on the state variables in a particularly simple way.

PROPOSITION 1: If the investor believes that earnings are generated by the regime-switching model described above, then prices satisfy

$$P_t = \frac{N_t}{\delta} + y_t(p_1 - p_2 q_t),$$

where p_1 and p_2 are constants that depend on π_L, π_H, λ_1, and λ_2. The full expressions for p_1 and p_2 are given in the Appendix.[4]

The formula for P_t has a very simple interpretation. The first term, N_t/δ, is the price that would obtain if the investor used the true random walk process to forecast earnings. The second term, $y_t(p_1 - p_2 q_t)$, gives the deviation of price from this fundamental value.

Proposition 2 below gives sufficient conditions on p_1 and p_2 to ensure that this price function exhibits the empirical phenomena we are after. As a first step, we try to build intuition for those conditions. First, note that if the price function P_t is to exhibit underreaction to earnings news, on average, then p_1 cannot be too large in relation to p_2. Suppose the latest earnings shock y_t is positive. Underreaction means that, on average, the stock price does not react sufficiently to this shock, leaving the price below fundamental value. This means that, on average, $y_t(p_1 - p_2 q_t)$, the deviation from fundamental value, must be negative. If q_{avg} denotes an average value of q_t, this implies that we must have $p_1 < p_2 q_{avg}$. This is the sense in which p_1 cannot be too large in relation to p_2.

On the other hand, if P_t is also to display overreaction to sequences of similar earnings news, then p_1 cannot be too small in relation to p_2. Suppose that the investor has just observed a series of good earnings shocks. Overreaction would require that price now to be above fundamental value. Moreover, we know that

---

[4] It is difficult to prove general results about p_1 and p_2, although numerical computations show that p_1 and p_2 are both positive over most of the range of values of π_L, π_H, λ_1, and λ_2 we are interested in.

after a series of shocks of the same sign, q_t is normally low, indicating a low weight on Model 1 and a high weight on Model 2. If we write q_{low} to represent a typical low value of q_t, overreaction then requires that $y(p_1 - p_2 q_{low})$ to be positive, or that $p_1 > p_2 q_{low}$. This is the sense in which p_1 cannot be too small in relation to p_2. Putting the two conditions together, we obtain $p_2 q_{low} < p_1 < p_2 q_{avg}$.

In Proposition 2, we provide sufficient conditions on p_1 and p_2 for prices to exhibit both underreaction and overreaction, and their form is very similar to what we have just obtained. In fact, the argument in Proposition 2 is essentially the one we have just made, although some effort is required to make the reasoning rigorous.

Recall that overreaction means that the expected return following a sufficiently large number of positive shocks should be lower than the expected return following the same number of successive negative shocks. In other words, there exists some number $J \geq 1$, such that for all $j \geq J$,

$$E_t(P_{t+1} - P_t | y_t = y_{t-1} = \cdots = y_{t-j} = y)$$
$$-E_t(P_{t+1} - P_t | y_t = y_{t-1} = \cdots = y_{t-j} = -y) < 0. \tag{5.7}$$

Underreaction means that the expected return following a positive shock should exceed the expected return following a negative shock. In other words,

$$E_t(P_{t+1} - P_t | y_t = +y) - E_t(P_{t+1} - P_t | y_t = -y) > 0. \tag{5.8}$$

Proposition 2 provides sufficient conditions on π_L, π_H, λ_1, and λ_2 for these two inequalities to hold.[5]

PROPOSITION 2: If the underlying parameters π_L, π_H, λ_1, and λ_2 satisfy

---

[5] For the purposes of Proposition 2, we have made two simplifications in our mathematical formulation of under- and overreaction. First, we examine the absolute price change $P_{t+1} - P_t$ rather than the return. Second, the good news is presumed here to be the event $y_t = +y$, i.e. a positive change in earnings, rather than better-than-expected earnings. Since the expected change in earnings $E_t(y_{t+1})$ always lies between $-y$ and $+y$, a positive earnings change is in fact a positive surprise. Therefore, the results are qualitatively the same in the two cases. In the simulations below, we calculate returns in the usual way, and condition on earnings surprises as well as raw earnings changes.

$$\underline{k}p_2 < p_1 < \bar{k}p_2,$$

$$p_2 \geq 0,$$

then the price function in Proposition 1 exhibits both under-reaction and overreaction to earnings; $\underline{k}$ and $\bar{k}$ are positive constants that depend on π_L, π_H, λ_1, and λ_2 (the full expressions are given in the Appendix).

Barberis _et al._ (1998) evaluate the conditions in Proposition 2 numerically for a large range of parameter values. They find that, for most reasonable parameter values, both conditions of Proposition 2 are satisfied, implying that the model can easily generate both underreaction and overreaction.

Some simulation experiments

One way of evaluating our model is to try to replicate the empirical evidence using artificial data sets of earnings and prices simulated from our model. First, we fix parameter values, setting the regime-switching parameters to $\lambda_1 = 0.1$ and $\lambda_2 = 0.3$. We set $\pi_L = 1/3$ and $\pi_H = 3/4$: these parameters comfortably satisfy the conditions of Proposition 2.

To simulate earnings, prices, and returns for a large number of firms over time, we choose an initial level of earnings N_1 and use the true random walk model to simulate 2,000 independent earnings sequences, each one starting at N_1. Each sequence represents a different firm and contains six earnings realizations. We think of a period in our model as corresponding roughly to a year, so that our simulated data set covers six years. For the parameter values chosen, we then apply the formula derived above to compute prices and returns.

The random walk model we use for earnings imposes a constant volatility for the earnings shock y_t, rather than making this volatility proportional to the level of earnings N_t. While this makes our model tractable enough to calculate the price function in closed form, it also allows earnings, and hence prices, to turn negative. In the simulations, we choose the absolute value of the earnings change y to be small relative to the initial earnings level N_1 so as to avoid generating negative earnings. Since this choice has the effect of reducing the volatility of returns in our simulated samples, we pay more attention to the *sign* of the numbers we present than to their absolute magnitudes.

This aspect of our model also motivates us to set the sample length at a relatively short six years. For any given initial level of earnings, the longer the sample length, the greater is the chance of earnings turning negative in the sample. We choose the shortest sample that still allows us to condition on earnings and price histories of the length typical in empirical analyses.

A natural starting point is to use the simulated data to calculate returns following particular realizations of earnings. For each n-year period in the sample, where n can range from one to four, we form two portfolios. One portfolio consists of all the firms with positive earnings changes in each of the n years, and the other of all the firms with negative earnings changes in each of the n years. We calculate the difference between the returns on these two portfolios in the year after formation. We repeat this procedure for all the n-year periods in the sample and calculate the time series mean of the difference in the two portfolio returns, which we call $r_+^n - r_-^n$.

The calculation of $r_+^n - r_-^n$ for the case of $n = 1$ essentially replicates the empirical analysis in studies such as that of Bernard and Thomas (1989). This quantity should therefore be positive, matching our definition of underreaction to news. Furthermore, to match our definition of overreaction, we need the average return in periods following a long series of consecutive positive earnings shocks to be *lower* than the average return following a similarly long series of negative shocks. Therefore, we hope to see $r_+^n - r_-^n$ *decline* as n grows, or as we condition on a progressively longer string of earnings shocks of the same sign, indicating a transition from underreaction to overreaction. Table 5.5 reports the results.

Table 5.5 Earnings sort

$r_+^1 - r_-^1$	0.0391
$r_+^2 - r_-^2$	0.0131
$r_+^3 - r_-^3$	−0.0072
$r_+^4 - r_-^4$	−0.0309

Source: Barberis *et al.* (1998).

The results display the pattern we expect. The average return following a positive earnings shock is greater than the average return following a negative shock, consistent with underreaction. As the number of shocks of the same sign increases, the difference in average returns turns negative, consistent with overreaction.

While the magnitudes of the numbers in the table are quite reasonable, their absolute values are smaller than those found in the empirical literature. This is a direct consequence of the low volatility of earnings changes imposed to prevent earnings from turning negative in our simulations. Moreover, we report only point estimates and do not try to address the issue of statistical significance. Doing so would require more structure than we have imposed so far, such as assumptions about the cross-sectional covariance properties of earnings changes.

An alternative computation to the one reported in Table 5.5 is to condition not on raw earnings but on the size of the surprise in the earnings announcement, measured relative to the investor's forecast. This calculation yields very similar results.

Jegadeesh and Titman (1993) and De Bondt and Thaler (1985) calculate returns conditional not on previous earnings realizations but on previous realizations of returns. To replicate these studies, for each n-year period in our simulated sample, where n again ranges from one to four, we group the 2,000 firms into deciles based on their cumulative return over the n years and compute the difference between the return of the best- and the worst-performing deciles for the year after portfolio formation. We repeat this for all the n-year periods in our sample, and compute the time series mean of the difference in the two portfolio returns, $r_W^n - r_L^n$. We hope to find that $r_W^n - r_L^n$ decreases with n, with $r_W^1 - r_L^1$ positive just as in Jegadeesh and Titman and $r_W^4 - r_L^4$ negative as in De Bondt and Thaler. The results, shown in Table 5.6, are precisely these.

Finally, we can also use our simulated data to try to replicate one more widely reported empirical finding, namely the predictive power of earnings–price (E/P) ratios for the cross-section of returns. Each year, we group the 2,000 stocks into deciles based on their E/P ratio and compute the difference between the return on the highest E/P decile and the return on the lowest E/P decile in the year after formation. We repeat this for each of the years in our sample and compute the time series mean of the difference in

Table 5.6 Returns sort

$r_W^1 - r_L^1$	0.0280
$r_W^2 - r_L^2$	0.0102
$r_W^3 - r_L^3$	−0.0094
$r_W^4 - r_L^4$	−0.0181

Source: Barberis *et al.* (1998).

the two portfolio returns, which we call $r_{E/P}^{hi} - r_{E/P}^{low}$. This mean, equal to 0.0435, is large and positive matching the empirical fact. Note that this difference in average returns cannot be the result of a risk premium since in our model the representative investor is assumed to be risk neutral.

5.5 Concluding comments

We have presented a parsimonious model of investor sentiment, or of how investors form expectations of future earnings. This model is consistent with a variety of empirical findings in finance on underreaction and overreaction of prices to information. In this concluding section, we briefly discuss both some possible extensions of the model, and some alternative ways to generate the same predictions.

Regime 1 in our model is consistent with the almost universal finding across different information events that stock prices drift in the same direction as the event announcement return for a period of six months to five years, with the length of the time period dependent on the type of event. An important question is whether our full model, and not just regime 1, is consistent with all of the event study evidence. Michaely *et al.* (1995) find that stock prices of dividend-cutting firms decline on the announcement of the cut but then continue falling for some time afterwards. This finding is consistent with our regime 1 in that it involves underreaction to the new and useful information contained in the cut. But we also know that dividend cuts generally occur after a string of bad earnings news. If a long string of bad earnings news pushes investors towards believing in regime 2, another piece of bad news such as a dividend cut would perhaps cause an overreaction rather than an underreaction in our model.[6]

To explain such findings, it would be useful to extend the model to consider different kinds of news. Our model predicts an overreaction when the new information is part of a long string of similar numbers, such as earnings or sales figures. An isolated information event such as a dividend cut, an insider sale of stock, or a primary stock issue by the firm may not constitute part of the string, even though it could superficially be classified as good news or bad news like the earnings numbers that preceded it. Investors need not simply classify all information events, whatever their nature, as either good or bad news and then claim to see a trend on this basis. Instead, they may form forecasts of earnings or sales using the time series for those variables and extrapolate past trends too far into the future. A model with different types of news may well be consistent with an overreaction to a long string of bad earnings news and the underweighting of informative bad news of a different type which arrives shortly afterwards.

Another important extension is to add risk-averse arbitrageurs to this model. It is quite obvious that such arbitrageurs would not eliminate market inefficiency because arbitrage here is risky. It is risky both because the fundamental value is unpredictable and because investor sentiment can get further out of line, as it does when an investor overpricing the asset gets another positive surprise. Arbitrage in this model raises interesting questions. For example, suppose that arbitrageurs know 'the model,' i.e. exactly the form of behavior that the noise traders follow, and trade with the noise traders to take advantage of their misperceptions. Would such arbitrageurs bring the price of an asset closer to its fundamental value? At least in principle, it is possible that in some situations it pays arbitrageurs to anticipate future noise trader demand, and to 'jump on the bandwagon' when prices are high rather than sell the asset. In Chapter 6, we illustrate this idea in a much simpler

---

[6] A similar puzzle is presented by Ikenberry *et al.* (1996), who find that the positive price reaction to the announcement of a stock split is followed by a substantial drift in the same direction over the next few years. The split is also often preceded by a persistent run-up in the stock price, suggesting an overreaction that should ultimately be reversed.

model, but here only note that the effects of arbitrage in this chapter's model are not entirely straightforward.

Although we take our approach to modeling beliefs to be extremely plausible, ours is not the only way to model investor behavior that generates both underreaction and overreaction. Daniel *et al.* (1998) present a model in which noise traders are overconfident and also suffer from biased self-attribution in their evaluation of their own performance. Hong and Stein (1999) consider a market in which different classes of investors pay attention to different information: some only look at fundamental news while others only look at past price trends. Earlier models by Frankel and Froot (1988), Cutler, Poterba, and Summers (1991), and De Long *et al.* (1990a) focus on the interaction between trend-chasing noise traders and arbitrageurs, and derive predictions similar to those examined here. The next chapter in fact focuses on a model taken from the last of these papers, which offers another perspective on the evidence.

Appendix 5.1

PROPOSITION 1: If the investor believes that earnings are generated by the regime-switching model described in Section 4, then prices satisfy

$$P_t = \frac{N_t}{\delta} + y_t(p_1 - p_2 q_t),$$

where p_1 and p_2 are given by the following expressions:

$$p_1 = \frac{1}{\delta}(\gamma_0'(1 + \delta)[I(1 + \delta) - Q]^{-1}Q\gamma_1),$$

$$p_2 = -\frac{1}{\delta}(\gamma_0'(1 + \delta)[I(1 + \delta) - Q]^{-1}Q\gamma_2),$$

where

$$\gamma_0' = (1, -1, 1, -1),$$
$$\gamma_1' = (0, 0, 1, 0),$$
$$\gamma_2' = (1, 0, -1, 0),$$

$$Q =$$

$$\begin{pmatrix} (1-\lambda_1)\pi_L & (1-\lambda_1)(1-\pi_L) & \lambda_2\pi_L & \lambda_2(1-\pi_L) \\ (1-\lambda_1)(1-\pi_L) & (1-\lambda_1)\pi_L & \lambda_2(1-\pi_L) & \lambda_2\pi_L \\ \lambda_1\pi_H & \lambda_1(1-\pi_H) & (1-\lambda_2)\pi_H & (1-\lambda_2)(1-\pi_H) \\ \lambda_1(1-\pi_H) & \lambda_1\pi_H & (1-\lambda_2)(1-\pi_H) & (1-\lambda_2)\pi_H \end{pmatrix}$$

PROOF OF PROPOSITION 1: The price will simply equal the value as gauged by the uniformed investors which we can calculate from the present value formula:

$$P_t = \mathrm{E}_t\left\{\frac{N_{t+1}}{1+\delta} + \frac{N_{t+2}}{(1+\delta)^2} + \ldots\right\}.$$

Since

$$\mathrm{E}_t(N_{t+1}) = N_t + \mathrm{E}_t(y_{t+1}),$$
$$\mathrm{E}_t(N_{t+2}) = N_t + \mathrm{E}_t(y_{t+1}) + \mathrm{E}_t(y_{t+2}), \text{ and so on,}$$

we have

$$P_t = \frac{1}{\delta}\left\{N_t + \mathrm{E}_t(y_{t+1}) + \frac{\mathrm{E}_t(y_{t+2})}{1+\delta} + \frac{\mathrm{E}_t(y_{t+3})}{(1+\delta)^2} + \ldots\right\}.$$

So the key is to calculate $\mathrm{E}_t(y_{t+j})$. Define

$$q^{t+j} = (q_1^{t+j}, q_2^{t+j}, q_3^{t+j}, q_4^{t+j})',$$

where

$$q_1^{t+j} = \Pr(s_{t+j} = 1, y_{t+j} = y_t | \Phi_t),$$
$$q_2^{t+j} = \Pr(s_{t+j} = 1, y_{t+j} = -y_t | \Phi_t),$$
$$q_3^{t+j} = \Pr(s_{t+j} = 2, y_{t+j} = y_t | \Phi_t),$$
$$q_4^{t+j} = \Pr(s_{t+j} = 2, y_{t+j} = -y_t | \Phi_t),$$

where Φ_t is the investor's information set at time t consisting of the observed earnings series $(y_0, y_1, \ldots, y_t)$, which can be summarized as (y_t, q_t).
Note that

$$\Pr(y_{t+j} = y_t | \Phi_t) = q_1^{t+j} + q_3^{t+j} = \bar{\gamma}' q^{t+j}$$
$$\bar{\gamma}' = (1, 0, 1, 0).$$

The key insight is that

$$q^{t+j} = Qq^{t+j-1},$$

where Q is the transpose of the transition matrix for the states (s_{t+j}, y_{t+j}), i.e.

$Q' =$

	(1)	(2)	(3)	(4)
(1)	$(1-\lambda_1)\pi_L$	$(1-\lambda_1)(1-\pi_L)$	$\lambda_1\pi_H$	$\lambda_1(1-\pi_H)$
(2)	$(1-\lambda_1)(1-\pi_L)$	$(1-\lambda_1)\pi_L$	$\lambda_1(1-\pi_H)$	$\lambda_1\pi_H$
(3)	$\lambda_2\pi_L$	$\lambda_2(1-\pi_L)$	$(1-\lambda_2)\pi_H$	$(1-\lambda_2)(1-\pi_H)$
(4)	$\lambda_2(1-\pi_L)$	$\lambda_2\pi_L$	$(1-\lambda_2)(1-\pi_H)$	$(1-\lambda_2)\pi_H$

where, for example,

$$\Pr(s_{t+j} = 2, y_{t+j} = y_t | s_{t+j-1} = 1, y_{t+j-1} = y_t) = \lambda_1\pi_H.$$

Therefore,

$$q^{t+j} = Q^j q^t = Q^j \begin{pmatrix} q_t \\ 0 \\ 1-q_t \\ 0 \end{pmatrix}.$$

(Note the distinction between q_t and q^t). Hence,

$$\Pr(y_{t+j} = y_t | \Phi_t) = \bar{\gamma}' Q^j q^t,$$

and

$$E_t(y_{t+j} | \Phi_t) = y_t (\bar{\gamma}' Q^j q^t) + (-y_t)(\underline{\gamma}' Q^j q^t),$$

$$\underline{\gamma}' = (0, 1, 0, 1).$$

Substituting this into the original formula for price gives:

$$p_1 = \frac{1}{\delta} (\gamma_0'(1+\delta)[I(1+\delta)-Q]^{-1}Q\gamma_1),$$

$$p_2 = -\frac{1}{\delta} (\gamma_0'(1+\delta)[I(1+\delta)-Q]^{-1}Q\gamma_2),$$

$$\gamma_0' = (1, -1, 1, -1),$$

$$\gamma_1' = (0, 0, 1, 0),$$

$$\gamma_2' = (1, 0, -1, 0),$$

PROPOSITION 2: Suppose the underlying parameters π_L, π_H, λ_1, and λ_2 satisfy

$$\underline{k}p_2 < p_1 < \bar{k}p_2,$$

$$p_2 \geq 0,$$

where

$$\underline{k} = \underline{q} + \tfrac{1}{2}\bar{\Delta}(\underline{q}),$$

$$\bar{k} = \underline{q}^e + \tfrac{1}{2}(c_1 + c_2 q_*),$$

$$c_1 = \frac{\bar{\Delta}(\underline{q})\bar{q} - \underline{\Delta}(\bar{q})\underline{q}}{\bar{q} - \underline{q}},$$

$$c_2 = \frac{\underline{\Delta}(\bar{q}) - \bar{\Delta}(\underline{q})}{\bar{q} - \underline{q}},$$

$$q_* = \begin{cases} \bar{q}^e & \text{if } c_2 < 0, \\ \underline{q}^e & \text{if } c_2 \geq 0, \end{cases}$$

where $\underline{q}^e$ and $\bar{q}^e$ are bounds on the unconditional mean of the random variable q_t. Then the conditions for both underreaction and overreaction given in Section 5.1 are satisfied. (Functions and variables not yet introduced will be defined in the proof.)

PROOF OF PROPOSITION 2: Before we enter the main argument of the proof, we present a short discussion of the behavior of q_t, the probability assigned by the investor at time t to being in regime 1. Suppose that the earnings shock at time $t + 1$ is of the opposite sign to the shock in period t. Let the function $\bar{\Delta}(q_t)$ denote the increase in the probability assigned to being in regime 1, i.e.

$$\bar{\Delta}(q) = q_{t+1} - q_t \big|_{y_{t+1} = -y_t,\ q_t = q}$$

$$= \frac{((1 - \lambda_1)q + \lambda_2(1 - q))(1 - \pi_L)}{\begin{array}{l}((1 - \lambda_1)q + \lambda_2(1 - q))(1 - \pi_L) \\ + (\lambda_1 q + (1 - \lambda_2)(1 - q))(1 - \pi_H)\end{array}} - q.$$

Similarly, the function $\underline{\Delta}(q)$ measures the size of the fall in q_t if the period $t + 1$ earnings shock should be the same sign as that in period t, as follows:

$$\underline{\Delta}(q) = q_t - q_{t+1}\big|_{y_{t+1}=y_t,\, q_t=q}$$

$$= q - \frac{((1-\lambda_1)q + \lambda_2(1-q))\,\pi_L}{((1-\lambda_1)q + \lambda_2(1-q))\,\pi_L + (\lambda_1 q + (1-\lambda_2)(1-q))\,\pi_H}.$$

By checking the sign of the second derivative, it is easy to see that both $\overline{\Delta}(q)$ and $\underline{\Delta}(q)$ are concave. More important, though, is the sign of these functions over the interval $[0,1]$. Under the conditions $\pi_L < \pi_H$ and $\lambda_1 + \lambda_2 < 1$, it is not hard to show that $\overline{\Delta}(q) \geq 0$ over an interval $[0, \bar{q}]$, and that $\underline{\Delta}(q) \geq 0$ over $[\underline{q}, 1]$, where $\underline{q}$ and $\bar{q}$ satisfy $0 < \underline{q} < \bar{q} < 1$.

The implication of this is that over the range $[\underline{q}, \bar{q}]$, the following is true: if the time t earnings shock has the same sign as the time $t + 1$ earnings shock, then $q_{t+1} < q_t$, or the probability assigned to regime 2 rises. If the shocks are of different signs, however, then $q_{t+1} > q_t$, and regime 1 will be seen as more likely.

Note that if $q_t \in [\underline{q}, \bar{q}]$, then $q_\tau \in [\underline{q}, \bar{q}]$, for $\forall \tau > t$. In other words, the investor's belief will always remain within this interval. If the investor sees a very long series of earnings shocks, all of which have the same sign, q_t will fall every period, tending towards a limit of $\underline{q}$. From the updating formulas, this means that $\underline{q}$ satisfies

$$\underline{q} = \frac{((1-\lambda_1)\underline{q} + \lambda_2(1-\underline{q}))\,\pi_L}{((1-\lambda_1)\underline{q} + \lambda_2(1-\underline{q}))\,\pi_L + (\lambda_1\underline{q} + (1-\lambda_2)(1-\underline{q}))\,\pi_H}.$$

Similarly, suppose that positive shocks alternate with negative ones for a long period of time. In this situation, q_t will rise every period, tending to the upper limit $\bar{q}$, which satisfies

$$\bar{q} = \frac{((1-\lambda_1)\bar{q} + \lambda_2(1-\bar{q}))(1-\pi_L)}{((1-\lambda_1)\bar{q} + \lambda_2(1-\bar{q}))(1-\pi_L)}$$
$$\xi + \pm \div + (\lambda_1\bar{q} + (1-\lambda_2)(1-\bar{q}))(1-\pi_H)$$

In the case of the parameters used for Table 5.2, $\underline{q} = 0.28$ and $\bar{q} = 0.95$.

There is no loss of generality in restricting the support of q_t to the interval $[\underline{q}, \bar{q}]$. Certainly, an investor can have prior beliefs that lie outside this interval, but with probability one, q_t will eventually belong to this interval, and will then stay within the interval forever.

We are now ready to begin the main argument of the proof. Underreaction means that the expected return following a positive shock should exceed the expected return following a negative shock. In other words,

$$E_t(P_{t+1} - P_t | y_t = +y) - E_t(P_{t+1} - P_t | y_t = -y) > 0.$$

Overreaction means that the expected return following a series of positive shocks is smaller than the expected return following a series of negative shocks. In other words, there exists some number $J \geq 1$, such that for all $j \geq J$,

$$E_t(P_{t+1} - P_t | y_t = y_{t-1} = \cdots = y_{t-j} = y)$$
$$- E_t(P_{t+1} - P_t | y_t = y_{t-1} = \cdots = y_{t-j} = -y) < 0.$$

Proposition 2 provides sufficient conditions on p_1 and p_2 so that these two inequalities hold. A useful function for the purposes of our analyis is:

$$f(q) = E_t(P_{t+1} - P_t | y_t = +y, q_t = q)$$
$$- E_t(P_{t+1} - P_t | y_t = -y, q_t = q).$$

The function $f(q)$ is the difference between the expected return following a positive shock and that following a negative shock, where we also condition on q_t equaling a specific value q. It is simple enough to write down an explicit expression for this function. Since

$$P_{t+1} - P_t = \frac{y_{t+1}}{\delta} + (y_{t+1} - y_t)(p_1 - p_2 q_t) - y_t p_2(q_{t+1} - q_t)$$
$$- (y_{t+1} - y_t) p_2(q_{t+1} - q_t),$$

we find

$$E_t(P_{t+1} - P_t | y_t = +y, q_t = q) = \tfrac{1}{2}\left(\frac{y}{\delta} + yp_2 \, \underline{\Delta}(q)\right)$$
$$+ \tfrac{1}{2}\left(-\frac{y}{\delta} - 2y(p_1 - p_2 q) - yp_2 \bar{\Delta}(q) + 2yp_2 \bar{\Delta}(q)\right)$$
$$= y(p_2 q - p_1) + \tfrac{1}{2} yp_2(\bar{\Delta}(q) + \underline{\Delta}(q))$$

Further, it is easily checked that

$$E_t(P_{t+1} - P_t | y_t = +y, q_t = q) = -E_t(P_{t+1} - P_t | y_t = -y, q_t = q)$$

and hence that

$$f(q) = 2y(p_2 q - p_1) + yp_2(\bar{\Delta}(q) + \underline{\Delta}(q)).$$

First, we show that a sufficient condition for overreaction is $f(q) < 0$.

If this condition holds, it implies

$$E_t(P_{t+1} - P_t | y_t = +y, q_t = \underline{q}) < E_t(P_{t+1} - P_t | y_t = -y, q_t = \underline{q}).$$

Now as $j \to \infty$,

$$E_t(P_{t+1} - P_t | y_t = y_{t-1} = \cdots$$
$$= y_{t-j} = y) \to E_t(P_{t+1} - P_t | y_t = +y, q_t = \underline{q})$$

and

$$E_t(P_{t+1} - P_t | y_t = y_{t-1} = \cdots = y_{t-j} = -y)$$
$$\to E_t(P_{t+1} - P_t | y_{t-1} = -y, q_t = \underline{q}).$$

Therefore, for $\forall j \geq J$ sufficiently large, it must be true that

$$E_t(P_{t+1} - P_t | y_t = y_{t-1} = \cdots = y_{t-j} = y)$$
$$< E_t(P_{t+1} - P_t | y_t = y_{t-1} = \cdots = y_{t-j} = -y),$$

which is nothing other than our original definition of overreaction.

Rewriting the condition $f(\underline{q}) < 0$ as:

$$2y(p_2 \underline{q} - p_1) + yp_2(\bar{\Delta}(\underline{q}) + \underline{\Delta}(\underline{q})) < 0,$$

we obtain

$$p_1 > p_2 \left(\underline{q} + \frac{\bar{\Delta}(\underline{q})}{2} \right),$$

which is one of the sufficient conditions given in the Proposition.

We now turn to a sufficient condition for underreaction. The definition of underreaction can also be succinctly stated in terms of $f(q)$ as:

$$E_q(f(q)) > 0,$$

where E_q denotes an expectation taken over the unconditional distribution of q.

Rewriting this, we obtain:

$$2yp_2 E(q) - 2yp_1 + yp_2 E_q(\overline{\Delta}(q) + \underline{\Delta}(q)) > 0,$$

and hence,

$$p_1 < p_2 \left(E(q) + \frac{E_q(\overline{\Delta}(q) + \underline{\Delta}(q))}{2} \right).$$

Unfortunately, we are not yet finished because we do not have closed form formulas for the expectations in this expression. To provide sufficient conditions, we need to bound these quantities. In the remainder of the proof, we construct a number $\bar{k}$ where

$$\bar{k} < E(q) + \frac{E_q(\overline{\Delta}(q) + \underline{\Delta}(q))}{2}.$$

This makes $p_1 < p_2 \bar{k}$ a sufficient condition for A.2. Of course, this assumes that $p_2 \geq 0$, and so we impose this as an additional constraint to be satisfied. In practice, we find that for the ranges of π_L, π_H, λ_1, and λ_2 allowed by the model, p_2 is always positive. However, we do not attempt a proof of this.

The first step in bounding the expression $E(q) + \frac{1}{2} E_q (\overline{\Delta}(q) + \underline{\Delta}(q))$ is to bound $E(q)$. To do this, note that:

$$\begin{aligned}
E(q_t) = E(q_{t+1}) &= E_{q_t}(E(q_{t+1} \mid q_t)) \\
&= E_{q_t}(\tfrac{1}{2}(q_t + \overline{\Delta}(q_t)) + \tfrac{1}{2}(q_t - \underline{\Delta}(q_t))) \\
&= E_q(g(q)).
\end{aligned}$$

Consider the function $g(q)$ defined on $[\underline{q}, \bar{q}]$. The idea is to bound this function above and below over this interval by straight lines, parallel to the line passing through the endpoints of $g(q)$, namely $(\underline{q}, g(\underline{q}))$ and $(\bar{q}, g(\bar{q}))$. In other words, suppose that we bound $g(q)$ above by $\bar{g}(q) = a + bq$. The slope of this line is:

$$b = \frac{g(\bar{q}) - g(\underline{q})}{\bar{q} - \underline{q}} = \frac{(\bar{q} - \underline{q}) - \frac{1}{2}(\underline{\Delta}(\bar{q}) + \overline{\Delta}(\underline{q}))}{\bar{q} - \underline{q}} < 1,$$

and a will be such that

$$\inf_{q \in [\underline{q}, \bar{q}]} (a + bq - g(q)) = 0.$$

Given that

$$E_q(g(q) - q) = 0,$$

we must have

$$E_q(\bar{g}(q) - q) \ge 0,$$

or

$$E(a + bq - q) \ge 0$$

$$E(q) \le \frac{a}{1 - b},$$

since $b < 1$. This gives us an upper bound on $E(q)$, which we will call $\bar{q}^e$. A similar argument produces a lower bound $\underline{q}^e$.

The final step before completing the argument is to note that since $\bar{\Delta}(q)$ and $\underline{\Delta}(q)$ are both concave, $\bar{\Delta}(q) + \underline{\Delta}(q)$ is also concave, so that

$$(\bar{\Delta} + \underline{\Delta})(q) > \left(\frac{q - \underline{q}}{\bar{q} - \underline{q}}\right)\underline{\Delta}(\bar{q}) + \left(\frac{\bar{q} - q}{\bar{q} - \underline{q}}\right)\bar{\Delta}(\underline{q}),$$

$$= c_1 + c_2 q$$

where

$$c_1 = \frac{\bar{\Delta}(\underline{q})\bar{q} - \underline{\Delta}(\bar{q})\underline{q}}{\bar{q} - \underline{q}},$$

$$c_2 = \frac{\underline{\Delta}(\bar{q}) - \bar{\Delta}(\underline{q})}{\bar{q} - \underline{q}}.$$

Therefore,

$$E(q) + \tfrac{1}{2}E(\bar{\Delta}(q) + \underline{\Delta}(q)) \ge \underline{q}^e + \tfrac{1}{2}E(c_1 + c_2 q) \ge \underline{q}^e + \tfrac{1}{2}(c_1 + c_2 q_*),$$

where

$$q_* = \begin{cases} \bar{q}^e & \text{if } c_2 < 0, \\ \underline{q}^e & \text{if } c_2 \ge 0, \end{cases}$$

This completes the proof of the Proposition.

6

Positive Feedback Investment Strategies

THE previous chapter has focused on underreaction to news as a source of momentum in stock returns. While underreaction to news is well documented empirically, it may not describe some important instances of momentum. These are the so-called price bubbles, in which prices go up and up without much news just because noise traders are chasing the trend. Noise traders in price bubbles react to past price changes, as opposed to particular news.

A most immediate example of such an apparent bubble is Internet stocks in 1998. Companies providing services related to the Internet, such as Yahoo!, Ebay, and Amazon.com, often have few assets, little market power, and negative earnings, yet during 1998 they kept rising in price and acquired market capitalizations in the tens of billions of dollars. In early 1999 market capitalization of Amazon.com reached $30 billion, increasing 20-fold since the beginning of 1998. To put this in perspective, this capitalization was seven times the combined market values of the two largest book-sellers in the United States, Barnes and Noble and Borders, and 200 times their combined earnings. Amazon.com, which *sold* about $250 million worth of books per quarter over the Internet and lost about $90 million in 1998 had become an object of intense discussions in Internet chatrooms, where anxious investors advanced arguments as to why the price should just keep rising. Ebay, whose market capitalization reached $12 billion, runs online auctions of such objects as Beanie-babies, for which it collects small fees. It too had not yet made money. It is conceivable that, over the next decade, Internet commerce will grow so fast and so profitably as to justify the enormous current valuations of the industry as a whole. Even so, it is virtually inconceivable that the Internet companies traded today, as opposed to the new entrants, will represent most of the value of that industry. Such price bubbles, which exhibit positive return autocorrelations until the crash, are not well described by underreaction to news about fundamentals.

A better description of noise trader behavior in such bubbles is positive feedback trading. Positive feedback investors buy securities after prices rise and sell after prices fall. Many forms of behavior common in financial markets can be described as positive feedback trading. It can result from extrapolative expectations about prices, or trend chasing. It can also result from stop-loss orders, which prompt selling in response to price declines. Another form of positive feedback trading is the liquidation of the positions of investors unable to meet margin calls, described in Chapter 4. Positive feedback trading is also exhibited by buyers of portfolio insurance, a popular investment strategy until the market crash of 1987 whereby institutional investors attempted to increase their exposure to stocks slowly as prices rose, and to diminish it as prices fell. Investors might engage in this practice because their willingness to bear risk rises sharply with wealth (Black 1988), which effectively amounts to positive feedback trading.

Many surveys point to the prevalence of extrapolative expectations that could underlie positive feedback trading. Case and Shiller (1988) find that home buyers in cities where house prices have risen rapidly in the past anticipate much greater future price appreciation than home buyers in cities where prices have been stagnant or have fallen. Shiller (1988) surveys investors in the wake of the 1987 market crash and finds that most sellers of shares cite price declines as the reason that they have sold—presumably because they anticipate further price declines.

Perhaps the most interesting survey evidence on extrapolative expectations of prices is presented in Frankel and Froot's (1988) work on the dollar exchange rate in the 1980s. Frankel and Froot evaluate the forecasts and recommendations of a number of exchange rate forecasting services during the period in the mid-1980s when the dollar had been rising for some time without a widening in the U.S.-rest of world interest rate differentials and with a rising U.S. trade deficit. Frankel and Froot find that during this period the typical forecaster expected the dollar to continue to appreciate over the next month but also to depreciate within a year in accordance with underlying fundamentals. Consistent with these expectations, forecasting services were issuing *buy* recommendations while maintaining that the dollar was overpriced relative to its fundamental value. Such trend-chasing short run expectations, combined with a belief in a long run return to fundamentals, are hard to reconcile with a fully rational model.

In addition to possibly shedding light on price bubbles, positive feedback trading raises another issue crucial to the analysis in this book, namely that of the stabilizing powers of arbitrage. Generally in this book, we have taken the position that arbitrageurs lean against noise trader demands and therefore stabilize prices, though sometimes imperfectly. The one exception, analyzed in Chapter 4, is the case of price collapses where arbitrageurs effectively lose control over their positions and have to liquidate their holdings. A key reason for this generally benign view of arbitrage is that arbitrageurs do not have any superior information about future noise trader demand. If arbitrageurs can anticipate noise trader demand, the analysis changes drastically. Specifically, in the presence of positive feedback traders, arbitrage can be destabilizing. When arbitrageurs receive good news, they recognize that the initial price increase will stimulate buying by positive feedback traders tomorrow. In anticipation of these purchases, informed arbitrageurs buy more today, and so drive prices up today higher than fundamental news warrants. Tomorrow, positive feedback traders buy in response to today's price increase and so keep prices above fundamentals even as arbitrageurs are selling out and stabilizing prices. Although part of the price rise is rational, part of it results from arbitrageurs' anticipatory trades and from positive feedback traders' reaction to such trades. Trading by arbitrageurs destabilizes prices because it triggers positive feedback trading.

An extensive literary tradition describes positive feedback trading and destabilizing arbitrage along these lines. George Soros (1987, 1998) describes his own trading in similar terms. Soros has apparently been successful over the past three decades by betting not on fundamentals but, he claims, on future crowd behavior. Soros finds clear examples of the trading opportunities he seeks in the 1960's conglomerate and the 1970's Real Estate Investment Trust (REIT) booms.[1] In his view, the 1960s saw a number of poorly informed investors become excited about rises in the reported annual earnings of conglomerates. The truly informed investment strategy in this case, says Soros, was not to sell short in anticipation of the eventual collapse of conglomerate shares (which did not happen until 1970) but instead to buy in anticipation of further

---

[1] For similar accounts, see Tobias (1971) and Goodman (1968).

buying by uninformed investors. The initial price rise in conglomerate stocks, caused in part by purchases by speculators like Soros, stimulated the appetites of uninformed investors since it created a trend of increasing prices and allowed conglomerates to report earnings increases through acquisitions. As uninformed investors bought more, prices rose further. Eventually price increases stopped, conglomerates failed to perform up to uninformed investors' expectations, and stock prices collapsed. Although in the end disinvestment and perhaps short sales by arbitrageurs brought the prices of conglomerate stocks down to fundamentals (or even below), the initial buying by smart money, by raising the expectations of noise traders about future returns, may have amplified the total move of prices away from fundamentals. Soros's analysis of REITs tells the same story.

Soros's view of self-feeding bubbles has a distinguished history, dating back at least to Bagehot (1872). According to Bagehot, 'owners of savings ... rush into anything that promises speciously, and when they find that these specious investments can be disposed of at a high profit, they rush into them more and more. The first taste is for high interest [i.e. large fundamental returns], but that taste soon becomes secondary. There is a second appetite for large gains to be made by selling the principal which is to yield the interest. So long as such sales can be effected the mania continues.' Kindleberger (1978) also sees speculative price movements as involving 'insiders [who] destabilize by driving the price up and up, selling out at the top to the outsiders who buy at the top and sell out at the bottom. ... The professional insiders initially destabilize by exaggerating the upswings and the falls, while the outsider amateurs who buy high and sell low are ... the victims of euphoria, which infects them late in the day.' More recently, John Train (1987) in his profiles of successful U.S. investors refers to the activity of one of his protagonists as 'pumping up the tulips.' Investment pools (common earlier in this century) that were explicitly designed to excite positive feedback traders are yet another example.

The next section of this chapter presents a model that combines arbitrageurs' trading in anticipation of noise demand with positive feedback strategies to show that the addition of rational speculators can destabilize prices. We then briefly present a history of some of the famous price bubbles and argue that our model describes all the events occurring during such bubbles more accurately than do the models of rational price bubbles, which focus exclusively on price increases and crashes (Blanchard and Watson 1982, Tirole 1982).

6.1 A model

Assumptions

We consider a model with four periods—0, 1, 2, and 3—and two assets, cash and stock. Cash is in perfectly elastic supply and pays no net return. Stock is in zero net supply: it should be thought of as side bets that investors make against one another. Stock is liquidated and pays a risky dividend equal to $\Phi + \theta$ in period 3, which is when investors consume all their wealth. θ is distributed normally with mean zero and variance σ_θ^2. No information about θ is released at any time before period 3. Φ has mean zero and can take on three possible values: ϕ, 0, and $-\phi$. The value of Φ becomes public in period 2, and a signal about Φ is released in period 1.

The model includes three types of investors: positive feedback traders, present in a measure of one, denoted 'f'; arbitrageurs who maximize utility as a function of period 3 consumption, present in a measure of μ, denoted 'a'; and passive investors whose demand in all periods depends only on the price relative to its fundamental value, who are present in a measure of $1 - \mu$ and who are denoted 'i.' We keep the total of the last two types of investors constant to derive comparative statics results on the effect of changes in the number of arbitrageurs holding constant the risk-bearing capacity of the market.

It is easiest to describe the structure of the model and the behavior of investors from period 3 backwards. Table 6.1 summarizes the assumptions.

Table 6.1 Structure of the Model

Period	Event	Total Demands of:		
		Positive Feedback Traders	Passive Investors	Arbitrageurs
0	None, benchmark period	0	0	optimally chosen ($=0$)
1	Arbitrageurs receive a signal ε of the period 2 fundamental shock Φ	0	$-\alpha p_1$	optimally chosen ($=D_1^a$)
2	Passive investors learn Φ	$\beta(p_1 - p_0)$	$-\alpha(p_2 - \Phi)$	optimally chosen ($=D_2^a$)
3	Liquidation: dividend $\Phi + \theta$ declared, where θ is an unpredictable period 3 fundamental shock	$\beta(p_2 - p_1)$	$-\alpha(p_3 - (\Phi + \theta))$	optimally chosen sets $p_3 = \Phi + \theta$

Quantities demanded by different classes of investors by period and events that reveal information to different classes of investors. β and α are parameters that determine the slopes of positive feedback traders' and passive investors' demand curves. p_0, p_1, p_2 and p_3 are asset prices in periods 0, 1, 2, and 3, respectively. D_1^a and D_2^a are arbitrageurs' period 1 and 2 demands, respectively.

Period 3

In period 3, there is no trading. Investors pay each other according to the positions they hold in the stock and the publicly known dividend $\Phi + \theta$. Since the dividend is known for certain in period 3, arbitrageurs pin the stock price down to its fundamental value of $\Phi + \theta$.

Period 2

In period 2, the value of Φ is revealed to both arbitrageurs and passive investors. We require that the realized value of Φ be sufficiently small so as not to upset the mean–variance approximation used in deriving arbitrageurs' demands.[2]

Positive feedback traders' demand for stock in period 2 is given by

$$D_2^f = \beta(p_1 - p_0) = \beta(p_1), \tag{6.1}$$

where p_1 is the price in period 1, p_0 is the price in period 0 (which is set equal to 0), and β is the positive feedback coefficient. Positive feedback traders' period 2 demands respond to the price change between periods 0 and 1: if the price had risen they buy; if the price had fallen they sell. Importantly, positive feedback traders place a market order today in response to a *past* price change. This formulation does not allow investors to respond instantaneously to price movements; they do not place market orders based on price changes between periods 1 and 2. One way to describe this assumption is that investors react to a past history of capital gains by raising their estimate of the mean rate of return and thus increasing their demand.

In this model, no arbitrageur would follow a positive-feedback trading strategy. Since rational investors know the expected period 3 value of the stock, no rational investor would hold a positive quantity of stocks in period 2 if $p_2 > \Phi$ because such a portfolio is exposed to risk and has a negative expected return. In contrast, positive feedback traders' purchases are invariant to the period 2 price.

---

[2] In our setup, period 2 news is about the fundamental value of stocks. Our conclusions also hold if Φ represents a 'noise' shock—a temporary shock to noise traders' demand but not to the fundamental value of stocks.

Arbitrageurs choose their period 2 demand D_2^a to maximize a mean–variance utility function with risk aversion coefficient γ. In period 2, the aggressiveness of arbitrageurs in betting on reversion to fundamentals is limited only by period 3 dividend risk. The demand of an arbitrageur is given by

$$D_2^a = \frac{\Phi - p_2}{2\,\gamma\,\sigma_\theta^2} = \alpha(\Phi - p_2), \tag{6.2}$$

where we set $\alpha = \dfrac{1}{2\,\gamma\,\sigma_\theta^2}$ for notational convenience.

A passive investor's period 2 demand is also negatively related to price:

$$D_2^i = \alpha(\Phi - p_2), \tag{6.3}$$

where we assume that α is the same as in equation (6.2). We make the slope of passive investors' demands and arbitrageurs' period 2 demands equal and set the numbers of arbitrageurs and passive investors equal to μ and $1 - \mu$, respectively. This allows us to examine the consequences of introducing arbitrageurs without changing the risk-bearing capacity of the market, since changes in μ keep the risk-bearing capacity of the economy constant. In the absence of passive investors, an increase in the number of arbitrageurs has two opposite effects: it destabilizes prices because it enhances the stimulus of arbitrageurs' purchases to positive-feedback trading, and it stabilizes prices because it increases the risk-bearing capacity of the market (as in Chapter 2). In this chapter, however, we abstract from this effect and to this end include passive investors in the model.[3] If we perform the experiment of simply adding arbitrageurs, there are still cases in which the risk-sharing stabilizing effect is less important than the destabilizing effect of anticipatory purchases.

For the model to have stable solutions, we require that $\alpha > \beta$.

---

[3] Passive investors are not simply uninformed arbitrageurs. Since the price in period 1 reveals what arbitrageurs have learned, any rational investor can infer the period 1 signal from prices. Such a rational investor would then want to get into the speculative game as well. Passive investors, by contrast, neither receive the period 1 signal nor infer this signal from prices.

Because arbitrage makes period 1 prices rise one-for-one with expected period 2 prices, unless $\alpha > \beta$ the model has no stable equilibrium: for high correctly anticipated values of p_2, demand exceeds supply.

Period 1

In period 1, arbitrageurs receive a signal $\varepsilon \in \{-\phi, 0, \phi\}$ about period 2 fundamental news Φ. We consider two different assumptions about the signal ε. First, the signal could be noiseless: $\varepsilon = \Phi$. Second, the signal could be noisy and satisfy:

$$\text{Prob } (\varepsilon = \phi, \Phi = \phi) = .25, \qquad \text{Prob } (\varepsilon = \phi, \Phi = 0) = .25,$$
$$\text{Prob } (\varepsilon = -\phi, \Phi = -\phi) = .25, \quad \text{Prob } (\varepsilon = -\phi, \Phi = 0) = .25. \tag{6.4}$$

In the case of a noisy signal, when the arbitrageurs' signal ε is ϕ, the expectation of the subsequent value of Φ is $\phi/2$; when the arbitrageurs' signal ε is $-\phi$, the expectation of the subsequent value of Φ is $-\phi/2$. In period 1, arbitrageurs choose their demand D_1^a to maximize the same mean–variance utility function as in period 2 over the distribution they face as of period 1 of their certain-equivalent wealth in period 2.[4]

Passive investors' demand in period 1 takes the same form as in period 2. They buy low and sell high, and their demand is given by:

$$D_1^i = -\alpha p_1. \tag{6.5}$$

Positive feedback traders' demand in period 1 is equal to zero:

$$D_1^f = 0. \tag{6.6}$$

Since the form of positive feedback behavior we study reacts to past price movements but not to current price changes, positive feedback traders do not trade in period 1.

Period 0

Period 0 is a reference period. No signals are received. As a result, the price is set at its initial fundamental value of zero, and there is no trading. Period 0 provides a benchmark against which the pos-

---

[4] These preferences are time consistent up to the approximation error from using the mean variance formulation.

itive feedback traders can measure the appreciation or deprecia-
tion of stock from period 0 to periods 1 and 2 and so form their positive feedback demands in periods 1 and 2.

Since there is no trading in periods 0 or 3, the market clearing
conditions are automatically satisfied in those periods. For periods
1 and 2, since there are μ arbitrageurs and $1 - \mu$ passive investors,
the market clearing conditions are, respectively,

$$0 = D_1^f + \mu D_1^a + (1 - \mu)D_1^i \tag{6.7}$$

$$0 = D_2^f + \mu D_2^a + (1 - \mu)D_2^i \tag{6.8}$$

Solution with a noiseless signal

We consider the case of a positive demand shock, $\Phi = + \phi$. The
argument is symmetric in the case of a negative demand shock. If
the arbitrageurs' signal ε is perfectly correlated with the period 2
demand shock Φ, then from their point of view there is no uncertainty in period 1 about the period 2 stock price. As long as arbitrageurs are present in positive measure ($\mu > 0$), their trades
guarantee the equality of prices in periods 1 and 2. If no arbitrageurs are present ($\mu = 0$), then the period 1 price equals zero, for
no one has information about the period 3 value of $\Phi + \theta$.

$$p_1 = p_2 \text{ if } \mu > 0$$
$$p_1 = 0 \text{ if } \mu = 0. \tag{6.9}$$

Imposing market clearing in period 2, and substituting in the
period 2 demands (6.1), (6.2), and (6.3) into (6.8), yields the period
2 equilibrium condition:

$$0 = \beta p_1 + \alpha(\phi - p_2) \tag{6.10}$$

Combining (6.9) and (6.10), we obtain

$$p_1 = p_2 = \frac{\alpha\phi}{\alpha - \beta} \text{ if } \mu > 0, \tag{6.11}$$

$$p_1 = 0, p_2 = \phi \text{ if } \mu = 0. \tag{6.12}$$

If $\beta > \alpha/2$, then the price is strictly further away from fundamentals in all periods when arbitrageurs are present than when they are
absent. In the case of a noiseless signal, therefore, the addition of
arbitrageurs can push prices away from fundamentals.

The path of prices in the case of a noiseless signal is discontinuous: $\mu = 0$ and $0 < \mu << 1$ are not nearly equivalent. Moreover, once $\mu \neq 0$, the path of prices is invariant to changes in μ (Figure 6.1). These peculiarities arise from the fact that the period 1 signal of Φ is noiseless. For an arbitrageur, the round-trip trade involving a purchase in period 1 and a sale in period 2 carries no risk since no uncertainty is resolved in period 2. Even a small measure μ of arbitrageurs is consequently willing to put on an arbitrarily large position. To make holding stocks between periods 1 and 2 risky, we next consider the case in which arbitrageurs' signal ε of Φ is imperfect.

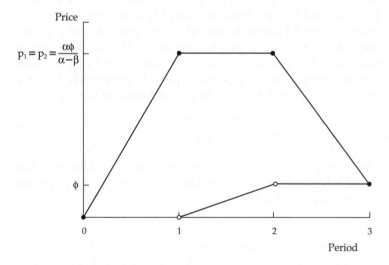

FIG. 6.1 Prices with a noiseless signal.
$\circ$ = Price without arbitrageurs. $\bullet$ = Price with arbitrageurs. Pattern of prices with and without arbitrageurs in the noiseless signal model with a shock Φ to fundamentals. Arbitrageurs perceive the shock in period 1; passive investors perceive the shock in period 2 and fail to learn from period 1 prices. α is the slope of the demand curve of all non-positive feedback investors. β is the responsiveness of positive feedback investors' demand to past price changes.

Solution with an imperfectly informative signal

Suppose that arbitrageurs receive a noisy signal. Once again we consider the case of a (possible) positive shock to fundamentals: $\varepsilon = \phi$, which implies that $\Phi = +\phi$ with probability $1/2$ and that $\Phi = 0$ with probability $1/2$. The symmetric case obtains when $\varepsilon = -\phi$. We call the first resolution of uncertainty state $2a$ and the second resolution state $2b$.

There are now two market clearing conditions for period 2, which together replace equation (6.10) for states $2a$ and $2b$, respectively:

$$0 = \beta p_1 + \alpha(\phi - p_{2a}), \tag{6.13}$$

$$0 = \beta p_1 - \alpha p_{2b}. \tag{6.14}$$

The market clearing condition for period 1 is simply

$$0 = \mu D_1^a - \alpha(1 - \mu)p_1, \tag{6.15}$$

with arbitrageurs' period 1 demand D_1^a still to be determined.

The expected value of the investment opportunities open to arbitrageurs in period 2 is such as to provide them, for given purchases D_1^a in period 1, with certain-equivalent wealth as of period 2 in the two states a and b equal to:

$$W_{2a} = D_1^a(p_{2a} - p_1) + \frac{\alpha(p_{2a} - \phi)^2}{2} = D_1^a\left(\phi + \frac{\beta - \alpha}{\alpha}p_1\right) + \frac{\beta^2 p_1^2}{2\alpha}, \tag{6.16}$$

$$W_{2b} = D_1^a(p_{2b} - p_1) + \frac{\alpha p_{2b}^2}{2} = D_1^a\left(\frac{\beta - \alpha}{\alpha}p_1\right) + \frac{\beta^2 p_1^2}{2\alpha}. \tag{6.17}$$

Maximization of mean–variance utility over the distribution of period 2 certain equivalent wealth yields arbitrageurs' period 1 demand:

$$D_1^a = \frac{(p_{2a} + p_{2b}) - 2p_1}{\gamma(p_{2a} - p_{2b})^2}. \tag{6.18}$$

Arbitrageurs' period 2 demands are simply expected returns divided by the next period's risk; they are proportional to the expected return $\Phi - p_2$ and inversely proportional to the fundamental risk σ_θ^2 borne by holding stocks from period 2 to period 3. Period 1 demands also have a simple return/risk interpretation. Since p_{2a} is equal to $p_{2b} + \phi$, and since the expected fundamental value of stocks in period 2 is higher by ϕ in state 2a than in state 2b, the profit opportunities open in period 2 to arbitrageurs are invariant to realized returns from period 1 to period 2. The arbitrageur's two-period decision problem can accordingly be treated as a sequence of one-period decision problems. Period 1 demand is just the expected one-period return divided by 2γ times the risk.

Equations (6.13), (6.14), (6.15), and (6.18) form a system in four unknowns, the three prices p_1, p_2, and p_{2b}, and arbitrageurs' period 1 demand D_1^a. The solution for the period 1 price is:

$$p_1 = \frac{\phi}{2} \frac{\alpha}{\alpha - \beta} \frac{1}{1 + \dfrac{\phi^2}{4\sigma_\theta^2} \cdot \dfrac{\alpha}{\alpha - \beta} \cdot \dfrac{1 - \mu}{\mu}}. \qquad (6.19)$$

In the special cases where μ is equal to 1 or to 0, this expression reduces to

$$p_1 = \frac{\phi}{2}\left(\frac{\alpha}{\alpha - \beta}\right) \text{ if } \mu = 1, \qquad (6.20)$$

$$p_1 = 0 \text{ if } \mu = 0. \qquad (6.21)$$

When no passive investors are present ($\mu = 1$) in period 1, arbitrageurs' period 1 holdings are zero—there is no one from whom they can buy. For arbitrageurs' period 1 holdings to be zero, there must be no expected profit opportunity from buying in period 1 and selling in period 2. Hence, in (6.20) the period 1 price is simply equal to the expected period 2 price. When no arbitrageurs are present ($\mu = 0$), no one in period 1 foresees the period 2 shock to fundamentals. Hence, in (6.21) the period 1 price is zero.

Rewriting (6.13) and (6.14) makes it obvious that the period 2 deviation of prices from their fundamental value of Φ is monotonically increasing in the period 1 price as long as $\beta > 0$:

$$p_{2a} = \frac{\beta}{\alpha} p_1 + \phi, \qquad (6.22)$$

$$p_{2b} = \frac{\beta}{\alpha} p_1. \qquad (6.23)$$

The effect of arbitrage on the pattern of prices for one set of parameter values is shown in Figure 6.2. Arbitrageurs bet on Φ being high in period 2 and drive the period 1 price up above zero; this in turn raises positive feedback trader demand in period 2 in both states of the world. This betting on future positive feedback trader demand drives the price in period 1 above its fundamental value of $\phi/2$. In period 2, arbitrageurs unload their positions and sell the asset short as positive feedback demand keeps its price above the fundamental value. Interestingly, the way arbitrageurs make money in this model is through short-term trading: they buy in period 1, sell and go short in period 2, and cover in period 3. There is a sense in this model in which short-term trading destabilizes prices.

When $\mu > 0$, the price is always further away from fundamentals in period 2 than when $\mu = 0$, for in the latter case period 2 prices equal fundamentals. The introduction of arbitrageurs always destabilizes period 2 prices.

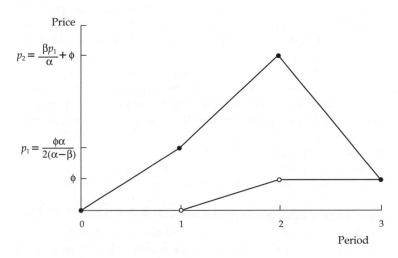

FIG. 6.2. Prices with a noisy signal.
○ = Price without arbitrageurs. ● = Price with arbitrageurs. Pattern of prices with and without arbitrageurs in the noisy signal model with a shock Φ to fundamentals. Arbitrageurs receive a noisy signal of the shock to fundamentals in period 1; passive investors perceive the shock in period 2 and fail to learn from period 1 prices. α is the slope of the demand curve of all non-positive feedback investors. β is the responsiveness of positive-feedback investors' demand to past price changes.

The period 1 price is further away from fundamentals when μ > 0 than when $\mu = 0$ if

$$\frac{1 - \mu}{\mu} < \frac{2\sigma_\theta^2}{\phi^2}\left\{1 - 2\left(\frac{\alpha - \beta}{\alpha}\right)\right\}. \tag{6.24}$$

When a small number of arbitrageurs is introduced into this economy, they always bring the period 1 price closer to its fundamental value. However, as long as $\beta > \alpha/2$, there will always be a μ^* < 1 such that the introduction of more than μ^* arbitrageurs moves the period 1 price further from fundamentals than it would be with $\mu = 0$. The value μ^* is lower when the positive feedback coefficient β is higher and when uncertainty about θ is high relative to uncertainty about Φ. When enough arbitrageurs are trading, both period 1 and period 2 prices are destabilized.

With a noisy period 1 signal, the period 1 price reflects uncertainty about period 2 demand. When arbitrageurs are risk-averse, the period 1 price is lower than the average period 2 price. Short-run price movements from period 0 to period 1 on average continue from period 1 to period 2. Returns are therefore positively correlated at short horizons, even though at long horizons—in period 3 in this model—prices come back to fundamental values and two-period returns are negatively correlated. This pattern is consistent with the evidence of a positive serial correlation of returns over the horizon of several months and mean reversion over several years described in Chapter 5, but of course there is no sense in which prices underreact to news in this model. As importantly, the negative correlation of returns over longer horizons here comes simply from the fact that time ends and prices have to return to fundamentals, rather than from a more basic model of how reality sets in.[5] Despite these reservations, the model does produce a pattern of returns and expectations that appears to be highly relevant in at least some situations.

---

[5] Positive feedback trading would lead to the observed pattern of returns even without the working of the arbitrageurs. The point here is that the arbitrageurs accentuate these price movements away from fundamental values, rather than counter them through their trades.

6.2 Anatomy of a price bubble[6]

The combination of positive return correlation at short horizons and eventual reversion to the mean corresponds to a conventional view of a price bubble, as Figure 6.2 illustrates. Our version of such a bubble relies on the positive feedback investment strategies of a significant number of investors, aggravated by arbitrageurs' anticipatory pumping up of the bubble. This description of price bubbles is not new. For example, Goodman (1968) refers to an 'informal theorem of chartism' that classifies phases of price movements in terms of categories—accumulation, distribution, and liquidation—that correspond one-to-one to the periods in our model. Accumulation involves purchases by informed investors in anticipation of a future price rise and reveals itself through increased volume and upward price pressure; distribution involves 'the smart people who bought it early selling to the dumb people who bought it late'; and liquidation involves the return of prices to fundamental values.

Although the basic structure of a price bubble is similar to the structure of our model, narrative histories of famous price bubbles—presented brilliantly by Kindleberger (1978)—suggest a more elaborate, and interesting, story. In Table 6.2, we summarize the stories of ten world-famous price bubbles and organize them along a number of elements that elaborate Kindleberger's description. The evidence points to important new elements of both noise trading and smart money response in the course of most bubbles.

To begin, just as in the model, most price bubbles start with initial good news, called 'displacement' by Kindleberger, which generate substantial profits for some investors in an asset. In the case of the Dutch Tulipmania, mosaic viruses produced interesting looking tulips which connoisseurs paid high prices for. The Mississippi Bubble was stimulated by expanding trade with the New World. The first British Railway boom arose out of excitement about the new means of transportation. The U.S. stock market boomed in the 1920s as the economy and even more so the industry grew for several years at a remarkable pace. The examples can be continued (see Table 6.2) but the role of the initial major good news is indisputable.

---

[6] This section is based on some old unpublished research with Brad De Long.

Table 6.2 Famous bubbles

Bubble	Initial displacement	Smart-money response	Sustaining the bubble	Authoritative blessing	Crash	Political reaction
Dutch Tulipmania (1630s)	Mosaic viruses produce interesting looking tulips; prosperity of Holland	Selective breeding of tulips; purchase by 'insiders' of broken tulips that can only reproduce slowly and asexually	Development of tulip speculation contracts, which can be signed before notaries; appearance of trading	??	1637	??
South Sea Bubble (1710–20)	Profits from conversion of government debt; supposed monopoly on trade with Spanish ruled parts of America	Insiders buy up debt in advance of the conversion scheme, then profit by presenting debt for full conversion	Development of coffee house network for speculation; new subscriptions	Government approval; royal involvement	1720	ex post facto punishing directors; restrictions on use of the corporate form
Mississippi Bubble (1717–20)	Rapidly growing trade with the New World; Law's success as a financial organizer	Law's plan to make money and acquire power by securitizing the French debt	Government support; large expansion of credit by Law's bank to support further purchases	Official government support. Duke of Orleans imprisons critics of Law — the president of the Parlement de Paris and others	1720	Fall of Law; end of efforts to reform French finances until 1787
British first railway boom (1845–6)	End of depression; excitement over the new means of transportation	Many new railroad projects	Ponzi schemes by George Hudson (i.e. use this railroad's capital to pay the last railroads dividends)	Parliamentary bills passed for every railroad suggesting government approval; close links between George Hudson and London Society	No crash, gradual decline	Reform of accounting standards; requirement that dividends be paid only out of earnings, not out of capital
U.S. 1873 railway boom and crash	End of the Civil War; settlement of the American west	Construction of government subsidized railroads	Additional railroad charters; expectation that subsidies would continue	Henry Varnum Poor and Charles Frances Adams	1873 — Bankruptcy of Jay Cooke & Co., beginning of mid 1870s depression	??

Argentine loans (1880s)	Strong demand on world markets for the staple products of Argentinian agriculture; large profits made by early investors	Investment flows from Britain to Argentina; expansion of railway network; construction of social overhead capital	New issues on the London exchange; creation of joint-stock companies to speculate in Argentinian land	Foreign investors 'grossly misled … by Argentinian president' Barings' express optimism that the situation might improve (hoping to avoid bankruptcy)	Baring Bros. bankruptcy November 1890	Coup d'etat in Argentina; laws discriminating against foreign investment
1920s Florida land boom	Great winter climate; closeness to centers of American population; prosperity of the 1920s	Building of railroads; development of Miami; land development projects	Subdivisions; creation of a network of real estate offices selling Florida land	William Jennings Bryan boosts Florida land; close connections between mayors and developers	1926	Fraud prosecutions
1920s U.S. Stock Market boom	Decade of fast growth in the 1920s; end of fears of post WWI deflation; rapid expansion of mass production	Expansion of supply of shares; growth of margin accounts and brokers' loans	Regional exchanges; creation of new closed end funds	Blessings from Coolidge, Hoover, Mellon and Irving Fisher	October 1929 and following	Glass–Steagall Act; creation of SEC; public utility holding company act; election of FDR
1920s U.S. utility stocks boom	Expansion of demand for power; economies of scale	High leverage; expansion of scale to capture economies	Creation of public utility holding companies with cascades of control	??	October 1929 and following	Breakup of large utilities, TVA a byproduct; substantial government regulation of utility industries
1960s conglomerate mergers in the US	Two decades of a rising stock market during which investing in growth stocks had been profitable	Emergence of professional conglomerates; Harold Geneen's ITT, Textron, Teledyne, etc.	Stock swaps to create apparent earnings growth	Harvard endowment takes large positions in National Student Marketing; McGeorge Bundy urges institutions to invest aggressively	1970–1971	Reform of accounting practices; Williams Act

In response to the initial increases in asset prices, smart money (arbitrageurs) begins by increasing the supply of both the desirable physical assets and the claims to them. To increase the supply of actual assets that are the subjects of excitement, smart money reproduce tulips, build railroads, develop land, organize holding companies and conglomerates, and so on. But smart money also create financial assets to take advantage of noise traders, particularly in the later stages of the bubble as they try to sustain noise trader enthusiasm. In the case of Tulipmania, they developed new speculative contracts; in the case of the Mississippi Bubble, issuance of new securities to replace national debt was accelerated; in the case of the Argentine Loans, Barings floated new issues on the London exchange; in the case of the U.S. stock market boom of the 1920s, new stock issues, including closed end funds and utilities holding companies, were floated to meet the public demand (De Long and Shleifer 1991). In the 1960s, of course, new conglomerates rapidly increased their supply of shares through acquisitions for stock. This form of arbitrage—through meeting noise trader demand by increasing supply—appears to be the critical element of just about every bubble.

Of course, smart investors also take positions in the desirable securities early on, and even make an effort for organized front-running in bubbly markets, just as our model predicts. This happened with John Law and friends in both the South Sea and the Mississippi Bubble, with various political friends of developers in the Florida Land boom, and with railroad speculators in the United States. Perhaps as interestingly, smart investors stimulate positive feedback trading not just by buying the securities themselves, but also by facilitating noise trader speculation. In Tulipmania, futures contracts on tulips were developed. In the South Sea Bubble, a coffee house network of speculation was created. In the Mississippi Bubble, John Law's bank greatly expanded credit to finance purchases of French debt. In the U.S. stock price bubble of the 1920s, closed-end funds were created to provide investors with access to baskets of hot stocks. The opportunities for 'pumping up the tulips' in reality are far more extensive than arbitrageurs just 'jumping on the bandwagon' as they do in the model.

At the very top, something more is perhaps needed to sustain the bubble, and this something in many cases is an authoritative blessing. The Mississippi Bubble received official government support, and in fact some of Law's critics were imprisoned. The U.S. railway boom of 1873 was endorsed and justified by Henry Varnum Poor (of the later Standard and Poor's fame). Florida Land in the 1920s was pumped up by William Jennings Bryan (of the earlier cross of gold fame). The boom in U.S. equities in the 1920s was justified by many people, including at least two U.S. Presidents. Irving Fisher famously declared in the summer of 1929 that 'the stock prices have reached a new and higher plateau.' In the 1960s, McGeorge Bundy encouraged U.S. institutional investors to take positions in growth stocks, and Harvard University took a large position in National Student Marketing. Who could argue against that?

Inevitably, these bubbles have been followed by crashes, with vast losses for the noise traders who have held on to their securities, again pretty much as our model suggests. The crash of a bubble has often been accompanied by a severe financial crisis and a depression, more along the lines of the discussion in Chapter 4. For example, the crash of the U.S. railway boom of 1873 and the Great Crash of 1929 were both followed by severe depressions, which might have been caused by the severe disruption of the financial system. These elements are not captured by the model presented here.

One final twist here is that many of the bubbles were followed by an extremely adverse political response aimed at both the speculators and the organizers of the scheme. The South Sea Bubble in England was followed by an over-century-long prohibition on the formation of joint stock companies without an explicit permission by Parliament, the collapse of the Argentine Loans bubble brought about a coup d'etat, not to mention severe restrictions on foreign investment, and the Crash of 1929 resulted in the Glass–Steagall Act, the Public Utility Holding Company Act, the formation of the SEC and many other new regulations of the financial markets. The bubbles clearly have economic repercussions considerably more extensive than allowed for in the model.

These histories suggest that our model is incomplete, but that it gets at some of the crucial aspects of real-world bubbles. It captures some elements of reality for which the alternative of rational price bubbles, where nothing but the growth of prices takes place, leaves no room. This is not a place to argue with these models, but rather to suggest quite the opposite, namely that a full model of economics and politics of bubbles remains to be built.

6.3 Conclusion

This short chapter has attempted to do three things. First, it presented an alternative view of price patterns observed in the data on security returns, one based on positive feedback trading. Rather than take the view that one theory is right and the other is wrong, it is probably more accurate to say that each applies in somewhat different circumstances. Second, the chapter has argued that, in the presence of positive feedback trading, rational arbitrage can destabilize security prices. Rather than bucking the trends, smart investors might rationally choose to jump on the bandwagon. This aspect of arbitrage, like many others we presented in earlier chapters, is inconsistent with a strong faith in its effectiveness in bringing prices to fundamental values. Finally, the chapter has argued that the particular interaction between positive feedback traders and arbitrageurs modeled here is germane to the study of price bubbles. In this area in particular, much can be learned about what arbitrageurs really do when there is a lot of money to be taken from the noise traders.

7

Open Problems

THE last 20 years have been very exciting for academic finance—perhaps almost as exciting as they were for financial markets. We have learned a lot, and what we think we know now is quite a bit different from what we thought we knew in 1978. Among the many changes of views, the increased skepticism about market efficiency stands out. This skepticism derives from many sources, including the recognition of the limitations of arbitrage, the accumulation of evidence on predictability of security returns, the observation of identical securities trading at different prices in different markets, and the salient but unexplained movements in stock market prices, such as the crash of 1987. Of course, the theories, the evidence, and even the unexplained movements have all been subject to much debate. But the cumulative effect has been to put the new discipline—behavioral finance—on the map.

Behavioral finance has provided both theory and evidence which suggest what the deviations of security prices from fundamental values are likely to be, and why they persist over time without being eliminated by arbitrage. In many cases, behavioral theories have also met the 'scientific' standard of issuing new testable predictions that are subsequently confirmed. Two examples discussed in this book illustrate this crucial point. First, the analysis of limited arbitrage predicted that discounts on different closed end funds should reflect systematic investor sentiment and therefore should move together. Subsequent research, discussed in Chapter 3, confirmed this finding. Second, behavioral theories arguing that high valuation companies are inefficiently overvalued predicted that their subsequent earnings announcements should, on average, disappoint investors. A number of studies discussed in Chapter 5 confirmed this prediction as well. Through this interplay of new theory and evidence, finance has moved from so-called 'anomalies,' a favorite term of efficient market theorists for empirical regularities they have trouble explaining, to 'behavioral explanations' of these, as well as many new, regularities.

Despite these successes, debates over market efficiency continue, and usually take a highly predictable form. First, price predictability is hard to establish with statistical confidence (Summers 1986). By its nature it is imperfect—remember that residual risk must remain for price predictability not to be eliminated by arbitrage. For instance, while value stocks have outperformed growth stocks by a substantial margin on average, there are many individual years and even longer periods in which growth has outperformed value. Second, once predictability is established, the data-snooping discussion inevitably ensues: does this predictability reflect a real economic phenomenon or a chance occurrence (Merton 1987b, Black 1993, Fama 1998)? Although many of the findings discussed in Chapter 5 have been replicated out of sample, using both historical and international data, such replication never entirely eliminates the concerns about data-snooping. Third, even the regularities established with statistical confidence both in and out of sample are subject to the Fama critique and the ex post rationalizations of the new evidence as reflecting fundamental risk. This critique can be addressed in part by looking at the event studies, as we did in Chapter 5, but it never dies. Even the Fama critique, however, does not explain why identical securities sell at different prices in different markets (Chapter 2).

Finally, in a number of instances price predictability eventually disappears, either permanently or for a while, as more arbitrageurs learn about it and more resources are brought to bear against it. In the last 15 years, this happened to the superior returns on small firms in January, which have previously persisted in the United States for seven decades. Such disappearance is very informative. If permanent, it is a huge embarrassment to the view that size is a permanent proxy for fundamental risk, since the higher risk demands the no-longer-available higher average returns. The disappearance surely undermines the view that size is somehow a 'risk factor.' Still, the efficient markets theorists often greet the disappearance of small firm and similar effects as proof that markets are ultimately efficient. If *ultimately* means that totally obvious regularities, such as a portfolio of small firms earning an extra 5 percent during each January, can persist *for seven decades*, then markets might be 'ultimately efficient.' 'Ultimately efficient,' however, does not mean efficient.

A more plausible interpretation of the evidence is that arbitrage eventually catches up with at least some of the most obvious regularities, but it takes arbitrageurs a long time to catch on and to accept the risk that such arbitrage entails. Some 'anomalies' eventually disappear, but it may take a long time for this to happen, especially if the countervailing sentiment that disturbs security prices in the first place is sufficiently strong and pervasive. The *ultimate* effectiveness of arbitrage is not a problem for behavioral finance—in fact this result is strongly supportive of the view that arbitrage is limited by the aggregate risk bearing capacity of arbitrageurs, which for a particular mispricing may increase over time. From the point of view of empirical work, however, the eventual arrival of arbitrageurs—slow as it might be—means that persistent mispricing can only be inferred from a limited time span of data. Statistically, this makes it all the more difficult to establish that mispricing was there in the first place.

Despite considerable progress, our knowledge of determination of security prices remains limited. Although we may reject the null hypothesis of market efficiency with more confidence than before, we still know relatively little about such key determinants of prices as expectations about fundamentals, discount rates, and simple movements of demand. Behavioral finance, and the finance of the determination of valuations more generally, has many years to grow.

In this chapter, we attempt to describe some of the growth opportunities. We begin with a discussion of some of the open issues in security valuation, where the available psychological knowledge is only beginning to be exploited, and many open problems remain. It is interesting to ask why our knowledge in this area is so lacking. Summers (1985) argues that traditional finance is simply uninterested in the determination of security values. He colorfully proposes that traditional finance is more interested in checking that the price of two 8 oz bottles of ketchup is close to the price of one 16 oz bottle of ketchup, than in understanding what determines the actual price of a 16 oz bottle. While there may have been some truth in this assessment 15 years ago, the future looks brighter today. Some of the available knowledge about such matters as attitudes toward risk, forecasting, and movements of uninformed demand is beginning to be used to explain valuation. This area is surely the greatest challenge of behavioral finance.

Understanding security valuation is an important, as well as a lucrative, end it itself. But research into valuation has many additional benefits. Among them, perhaps the crucial, and relatively neglected, issues have to do with real consequences of financial markets. How do firms issue securities, which ones do they issue, and when? How aggressively do they take advantage of favorable sentiment? How do firms use the funds they raise? Do they actually change their investment policies to stimulate favorable sentiment and sell securities? Does market inefficiency have real consequences, or does it just lead to a redistribution of wealth from noise traders to arbitrageurs and firms?

Once it is recognized that market inefficiencies may have real consequences, important policy issues arise. Should anything be done by the government to make financial markets better? Or does the government do more harm than good in intervening in financial markets, even the inefficient ones? These issues have been ignored in the book, largely because relatively little is known about them. This chapter briefly addresses them as well.

7.1 *What determines security prices?*

To fix ideas, consider again the valuation of the S&P 500 at the end of 1998. The price to earnings ratio of the Index at year end was around 32, compared to the post-war average of about 15 (Siegel 1998), making large U.S. stocks at that time roughly twice as expensive as they have been historically. How do financial economists explain such high valuations? Are we in a bubble and, if so, why? The explanations of this phenomenon of both efficient market and behavioral finance variety generally come in two forms. In 1998, either investors—rationally or not—expected future earnings to grow much faster than they have historically, or investors—rationally or not—considered the future to be a lot less risky, or were more tolerant toward that risk, than historically, leading them to accept lower expected returns.

Begin with the rational explanations. It is possible that the earnings of American corporations will grow in the next decade much faster than they have historically, perhaps as a result of improvements in information technology. But such rapid earnings growth, especially on the tails of already huge increases in earnings in the last 15 years, appears unlikely. Campbell and Shiller (1998) report that earnings growth rates implied by extreme market valuations have never materialized in U.S. history, and it is the stock prices that adjust down rather than earnings that adjust up. It is also possible that the U.S. economy is now less volatile than it has been during most of the post-war period, although the recent volatility of the economies outside the United States does not raise confidence in this hypothesis. Instead, recent research has focused on a different idea, namely that after a period of very good times such as the 1980s and the 1990s investors have an extraordinarily high tolerance for risk, and so accept a relatively low expected return to hold stocks (Campbell and Cochrane 1999). This hypothesis is intuitively appealing, and in fact has an even more appealing behavioral counterpart discussed below.

Unfortunately, this hypothesis also has a less plausible empirical prediction that investors *expect* low stock returns in bull markets such as 1998. In contrast to this prediction, survey evidence on investor expectations shows that in good times, when stock prices are high, investors actually expect high returns on stocks, and not low returns that they supposedly accept because they are especially risk-tolerant (Durell 1999). Similar evidence has also been obtained for the 'hot' housing markets, in which investors expect further rapid appreciation rather than low returns (Case and Shiller 1988). Prices are high because investors expect them to go even higher, not because they are ready for prices to go down.

Behavioral finance also offers explanations of the pricing of stocks at the end of 1998 dealing with expected growth of earnings and the discount rates. Barsky and De Long (1993) and Chapter 5 suggest that, when earnings grow rapidly, investors extrapolate past growth rates of earnings into the long run future. The earnings of U.S. corporations have indeed grown much faster than the long run trend over the past 15 years, and hence the conversion to such beliefs by many investors is plausible. Although such an expectation is unlikely to be rational since earnings do not usually grow at a permanently much faster rate (Campbell and Shiller 1998), it is consistent with investor surveys (Durell 1999, Case and Shiller 1988).

Another idea focuses on the way in which investors assess risk. This explanation, due to Barberis *et al.* (1999), combines the Prospect Theory of Kahneman and Tversky (1979) with the idea that investors' willingness to gamble rises with their stock market winnings (Thaler and Johnson 1990). The theory holds that many investors in the United States are now sitting on considerable capital gains in their stock portfolios. Because they are so much ahead of what they paid for their investments, their willingness to bear risk is extremely high. As a consequence, they drive stock prices further up. Like Campbell and Cochrane (1999), this explanation focuses on the movements in tolerance toward risk, but derives them from psychology rather than from the variations in the marginal utility of consumption. The theory can also explain the equity premium puzzle, the historical 7 percent per year difference in returns on stocks and bonds in the U.S. and other markets (Mehra and Prescott 1985). Although investors can become tolerant of stock market risk in very good times, they are on average loss-averse and hence avoid equities (see also Benartzi and Thaler 1995). On the other hand, like Campbell and Cochrane (1999), this theory has trouble explaining high returns on stocks actually expected by investors in boom times.

Another possible view of low discount rates is worth mentioning even though it does not have as distinguished a psychological pedigree, namely that investors *perceive* the world to have become less risky, and hence require a lower rate of return on their stocks. Unlike Prospect Theory, which has to do with the tolerance of a given level of risk, this explanation focuses on the possibly inaccurate evaluation of how risky holding stocks actually is. The false sense of security about the stock market in 1998 may have come from the investors' good fortune with stocks in the last two decades, or from some theory of how the world of global capitalism is safe for corporations. This perception would justify a low required return and hence a high valuation.

Risk perception comes up in other instances in security valuation, such as the value/growth puzzle already discussed in Chapter 5. The underpricing of value stocks may come from the fact that investors perceive individual value stocks—whose past performance after all has been terrible—as likely to go bankrupt, scary, and therefore risky, even though a *portfolio* of value stocks earns a higher average return. In contrast, investors may perceive growth stocks, such as Microsoft and Coca-Cola, to be great, prosperous, and *safe*, even though a portfolio of such stocks performs poorly. Unlike the traditional definition of fundamental risk, perceived risk does not come from poor portfolio performance in bad times, and therefore should not be rewarded with superior returns. But if risk perception affects the demand for securities, it would generate exactly the returns we observe in the data even if the perception has nothing to do with the reality of fundamental risk of a portfolio. The perception of risk is one of the most intriguing open areas in behavioral finance.

The final potentially relevant behavioral idea deals with the demand for stocks by different investors, and thus focuses on the valuation of securities by the marginal rather than the average investor. It begins with an observation that the share of U.S. equities held by institutional investors has grown tremendously in recent years from 26 percent in 1980 to 53 percent in 1996, with the increase being even greater for the largest stocks (Gompers and Metrick 1999). Many of these institutional investors are themselves index funds, which hold stocks in the S&P 500 Index. Many more are pension and mutual funds whose managers are evaluated on their performance relative to the S&P Index, and therefore focus on holding S&P stocks to 'control' the so-called tracking error, the deviation of their performance from that of the Index. Still other institutional investors prefer S&P stocks because they have high liquidity and hence are cheap to trade. The superior performance of U.S. stocks, and in particular of the largest stocks in the S&P 500 Index, may perhaps be attributed to the growing demand for these stocks by institutional investors, who buy them up from individuals with effectively lower valuations. Indeed, many institutional investors simply do not care about the absolute valuations of the stocks they hold, since they are evaluated and compensated not on their absolute performance, but on the performance relative to the very Index they are close to holding.

The idea that the valuation of the S&P 500 Index is driven by institutional demand fits nicely with several of the ideas discussed in this book. It is consistent with the significant jumps in share prices of stocks when they are included into the S&P 500 and with the increases in the magnitude of these jumps over time. Gompers and Metrick (1999) actually find that stocks with higher increases in institutional ownership have earned higher returns over the period they study. This idea is also consistent with the disappearance of the small firm effect in the last 15 years, since, as Gompers and Metrick (1999) demonstrate, institutional investors hold predominantly the larger stocks, and hence the demand shift has been larger for those stocks.

This approach also illustrates how difficult arbitrage in these circumstances might be: if an arbitrageur tried to sell, or sell short, S&P during the last few years—whether he hedged the risk or not—he would have surely been out of business by now (see Chapter 1). In fact, the growth of institutional investing in the Index suggests that investing in stocks out of the Index has become increasingly costly in terms of relative performance. The optimal strategy for a smart investor might be very far from betting against the Index. Instead, the best approach may well be to stick to selecting stocks in the Index to avoid poor relative performance if the Index continues to perform better than other stocks, or even to deliberately shift to investing in the Index to benefit from its rise. In addition, some pension plans, disenchanted with the poor relative performance of their money managers, might switch to passive investing in the S&P 500 themselves. All this would generate arbitrageur behavior in the spirit of Chapter 6—if you can't beat them, join them—and give rise to destabilizing rather than stabilizing speculation.

Of course, there are some stabilizing influences as well. The professional money management industry is becoming segmented, with various active managers choosing to be evaluated relative to more specialized benchmarks, such as value stocks or growth stocks. One reason for this is to be able to measure 'skill' better for a given specialized style; another reason is to avoid having to mimic the S&P 500 Index. As the industry becomes more segmented, institutional investors may move away from the Index, thus slowing down its relative overvaluation. In the longer run, earnings news is likely to take a toll on the valuations of the S&P 500 stocks. When investors realize that earnings are falling, or not rising as rapidly as they have for nearly two decades, they may reconsider valuing stocks at 30 or 40 times earnings. But this may take a very long time.

This explanation of the pricing of U.S. equities at the end of 1998 suggests that the price can be just about anything. As long as institutions keep growing, and as long as sophisticated investors jump on the bandwagon, prices may just keep rising. Arbitrageurs do not help to bring prices to reality, especially since they have no idea when a correction might set in, if at all. Historical valuations provide little guide to what is going to happen in the future. Even the negative earnings surprises in 1998 did not seem to shake the market. Fischer Black (1986) humorously defined a market as efficient if the price falls within a factor of two of fundamental value. When broad enough groups of securities are in demand, the price might move even further away without corrective pressures.

The behavioral explanations presented here have one element in common: they require a model of what investors actually think and do. How do they assess risk? How do they forecast growth? When they invest other people's money, what rules and guidelines do they follow? The emphasis on *investors* is entirely foreign to traditional finance, which has achieved its success by assuming precisely that investors do not matter except for the determination of the equilibrium discount rate, and that security prices can be understood only in terms of their cash flows and the news about these cash flows. Such an approach is internally consistent as long as financial markets are efficient, and as long as one focuses on relative prices of securities (recall Summers on ketchup). But as soon as arbitrage is limited, investor sentiment and conduct begin to matter and it no longer suffices to focus only on cash flows and news. The world of finance becomes much more difficult and less elegant, but perhaps more accurate as well. In this world, different investors form different models of the future and trade with each other. Trading volume is substantial, especially when different models generate different demands. But when models lead to similar predictions, investors try to buy the same securities at the same time, thereby driving up prices without any fundamental news. A complicated world, but also the one that we live in.

It is also an unexplored world, as the multiplicity of explanations of the most striking fact about financial markets today demonstrates. Each explanation has some intuitive appeal, and each may account for some piece of the puzzle. Each, moreover, has some support from the lab or from other market data. Yet we still do not know which one of them is driving U.S. stock prices today, or which will drive them in the future. In fact, we do not even know that we have the right theory on the list.

7.2 Does it matter?

Does inefficiency of financial markets have real consequences? Note first that, even if it does not, and the trading between noise traders and arbitrageurs results merely in a redistribution of wealth from the former to the latter, many thorny issues come up. For example, if individuals are on average poor investors and significantly underperform the market, as they appear to do, then allowing individuals to manage their Social Security savings might be a bad idea. Individual retirement accounts contemplated in some discussions of Social Security reform in the United States may lead to publicly unacceptable wealth losses by poor investors. Here we largely ignore these issues—important as they are—and focus on 'real' consequences.

The channels of influence of financial markets—efficient or otherwise—on 'real life' are extremely numerous: stock values enter aggregate wealth, they help firms and other economic agents forecast the future, they influence financing and investment, and so on. For concreteness, this section takes a more narrow 'corporate finance' view, and asks whether market inefficiency has implications for corporate financing and investment decisions. An analysis of financial markets is incomplete without at least some attention being paid to this issue.

If the world of efficient markets, the central proposition of corporate finance is the Modigliani–Miller (M&M) Theorem (Williams 1938, Modigliani and Miller 1958). It states that the market value of the firm, holding its investment policy constant, is independent of the firm's capital structure. The proof of this proposition is straightforward: if securities are *correctly* valued for their cash flows, then the combined market value of all the securities that the firm issues is equal to the present value of this firm's profits regardless of which securities are issued. Riskless arbitrage also works to render capital structure irrelevant: if two identical firms with different capital structures sell at different aggregate market values, an arbitrageur buys all the securities of the cheap one, and sells short all the securities of the expensive one, thereby locking in a sure profit up front with zero net cash flows in future periods. In this world of M&M, it does not pay firms to tinker with their financial policies by actively choosing whether to issue bonds or stocks, or by marketing the securities they issue. Such activities are largely a waste of time and resources as long as investment is held constant.

When markets are inefficient, the financial structure of the firm is no longer irrelevant, since carving up the cash flows in different ways may attract different clienteles of investors who are willing to pay high prices for the patterns of cash flows they want. For example, if a small group of speculators are wild about a firm's prospects while most market participants expect its future to be relatively stable, the firm might be able to raise the most money by selling very risky equity to the first group and debt to the second. Moreover, the M&M argument that arbitrage ensures the irrelevance of financial structure runs into the very problems discussed in Chapters 2 and 4: such arbitrage is risky even when perfect substitutes for securities or groups of securities are available, and substitutes are typically far from perfect for securities of individual firms (Roll 1988, Wurgler and Zhuravskaya 1999). In this world, it pays firms to alter their financial structure to take advantage of investor sentiment, and to create and market securities that investors want. Selling stocks and bonds becomes very similar to selling encyclopedias and cars.

Dividend policy begins to matter also, unlike in the Miller and Modigliani (1961) world in which it does not matter when and how firms pay out their profits. When markets are not efficient, firms can use their dividend policies to raise demand for their securities. Dividends, like the capital structure, become part of the marketing program of the firm's securities. Lintner (1956) calls attention to the extremely deliberate policies that mature firms use to set dividends, including a slow adjustment of dividends to earnings and an aversion to rapid changes, especially cuts. Lintner's essentially behavioral analysis of dividend policies has not received enough attention, but may come back once behavioral corporate finance is developed.

The evidence on corporate financing policies demonstrates not

186 Open Problems

only that market inefficiency matters, but that it matters in a way suggested by the model in Chapter 2: firms take part in arbitrage by issuing securities in high valuation markets. Such activities as initial and secondary equity offerings, mergers (particularly with stock as a means of payment), and the formation of closed end funds (see Chapter 3) are all heavily concentrated in 'hot' markets about to go down (Baker and Wurgler 2000). *Overvaluation* of new security issues is made more convincing by the fact that such securities themselves—whether of new firms, seasoned firms, or new closed end funds—earn low returns *after* issuance (Stigler 1964, Ritter 1991, Loughran and Ritter 1995, Brav and Gompers 1997, Brav *et al.* 1999).

Figure 7.1 presents the data on the performance of an average IPO issued between 1975 and 1992 and compares it to the S&P 500 Index benchmark as well as a benchmark of firms of comparable

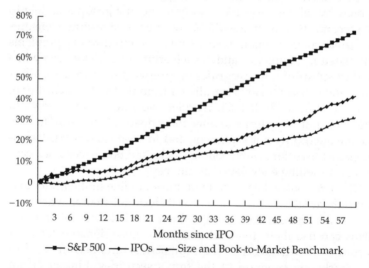

FIG. 7.1 The long run performance after initial public offerings relative to size and book-to-market matched benchmarks and the S&P 500. The sample is all IPOs from 1975 through 1992. Buy and hold returns are calculated from the offering date through five years after the offering. The buy and hold return on benchmarks matched on the basis of size and book-to-market as well as the S&P 500 are also plotted over the same period.

Source: Brav and Gompers (1997).

size and market to book ratio. The figure shows how far the IPOs have fallen behind the S&P 500 index during this period, but also that they are not bad investments relative to matched small growth firms (Brav and Gompers 1997). Similar findings obtain for seasoned equity offerings (Brav *et al.* 1999).

What can we make of these findings? The authors of these studies note that since both the equity offerings and small growth firms are bad investments during this period relative to the S&P 500, the returns on both types of investments may be appropriate once fundamental risk is properly measured. The view that small growth firms and IPOs are expected by the investors who buy them to earn low returns because they are especially good hedges against risk strains credulity, and runs into the many problems of treating size and market to book ratio as proxies for fundamental risk. It is more likely that small growth firms and new issues are both on average overpriced.

Much supplementary evidence points to such overpricing. Not only do firms issue securities when the valuations are unusually high, and not only do these securities earn low returns after the issuance, but firms actively manipulate their accounts to raise valuations prior to selling stock by creating trends of growing earnings (Teoh *et al.* 1998*a*, 1998*b*). Such manipulation appears to work: analysts are excessively optimistic about the earnings potential of recent IPOs and their growth prospects (Rajan and Servaes 1996). And the poor stock performance following both initial and secondary equity offerings is accompanied by announcements of disappointing earnings (Loughran and Ritter 1997). The earnings evidence matches the timing, the expectations, and the returns evidence to suggest that companies both promote and take advantage of overvaluation of their stock to raise capital.

Comparable evidence suggests that firms buy back shares when they feel that these shares are underpriced in the market. Ikenberry *et al.* (1995) find that firms buy back shares when valuations are low, and that firms earn superior returns on both the announcement of a share buyback, and during the period when shares are actually repurchased. Moreover, low valuation firms earn higher returns as a result of the repurchases than high valuation firms. Again, the evidence points to firms engaging in arbitrage in their own shares.

Although the results just described represent some of the most persuasive evidence that corporate financial policies are responsive to market inefficiencies, they have not become a central part of corporate finance thinking. We still, as a consequence, do not know whether taking advantage of market inefficiencies is a small part of how firms raise external funds, or whether it is a central, or even the dominant, aspect of their financing policies. Would many firms choose to raise external equity, or merge for stock, were it not for temporary overpricing of their equity? An interesting question, but one for which the answer is unavailable.

The fact that firms time the market in security issues does not by itself imply that such timing influences their investment. After all, firms may simply issue overpriced securities and invest the proceeds in cash or fairly priced securities, and benefit their existing shareholders and managers without committing more funds to real investment. Conversely, firms may buy back underpriced shares and reduce dividends, thereby benefitting their shareholders without cutting investment. Morck, Shleifer and Vishny (1990) and Stein (1996) suggest that firms should engage in such financial arbitrage while setting real investment without regard for market valuations. On the other hand, De Long *et al.* (1989) present a model in which firms must commit to their investment plans in advance and it is rational for firms to let stock market inefficiencies influence their investment. Which of these theoretical possibilities better describes reality is rather poorly understood at the moment.

Even if market inefficiencies influence investment, as they are likely to in some circumstances, there is an important question of whether this is good or bad for efficiency. In some cases, firms wishing to continue issuing overpriced securities must invest some of the proceeds to convince future buyers that they actually do have good opportunities. To do so, they may have to invest in bad projects. Take the case of price bubbles discussed in Chapter 6, such as the Florida Land Bubble. The evidence shows that this was not a purely financial set of transactions: entrepreneurs invested substantial funds into developing and selling Florida land as part of attracting outside funds. Likewise, railroad builders actually had to build railroads, often too many of them, to raise external finance. In these and other cases, 'pumping up the tulips' requires a distortion in real investment and not just financial arbitrage by firms.

Alternatively, overvaluation may enable firms to finance profitable projects that they could not finance otherwise because of imperfections in the capital markets. When capital markets are not sufficiently developed to enable the financing of all privately profitable projects, bubbles play an extremely positive social role. This benefit only becomes greater when the social return on investment exceeds the private return. Keynes (1931) has pointed this out in his defense of the stock market boom of the 1920s when he wrote: 'While some part of the investment which was going on ... was doubtless ill judged and unfruitful, there can, I think, be no doubt that the world was enormously enriched by the constructions of the quinquennium from 1925 to 1929; its wealth expanded in those five years by as much as in any other ten or twenty years in its history. ... A few more quinquennia of equal activity might, indeed, have brought us near to the economic Eldorado where all our reasonable economic needs would be satisfied.' Comparable arguments can perhaps be made about Latin American and Asian economies in the 1980s and the 1990s. And even a believer that the pricing of Internet stocks in recent years is a bubble would recognize that a large number of creative entrepreneurs have moved into this line of activity as a result, which may well be efficient in light of the possibly significant external benefits from innovation in this area.

The other side of stock market booms is stock market panics (see Chapters 4 and 6). Historically, many of these have been followed by prolonged depressions and severe cuts in real investment. In the United States, the Great Depression following the Crash of 1929, which itself followed the decade of growth of both security prices and economic activity, is the most disturbing example of this problem, but Kindleberger (1978) presents many other equally compelling examples from around the world. Although the stock market crash of 1929 did not overreact to what was to come, and stock prices continued falling for several years, it may have exacerbated the collapse of investment and real activity, and therefore worsened the Depression. More generally, collapses of security prices lead to collapses of collateral values of assets and entail possibly hugely inefficient liquidations and investment collapses. The recent Asian crisis illustrates this problem all too vividly. This too is a largely unexplored subject, but the evidence does point to a potentially large cost of market inefficiency.

The overall state of understanding at this writing seems to be that market inefficiency almost surely matters for corporate finance and is likely to matter for real investment, especially in extreme situations. Finding out how it matters, and how much, is an exciting area of inquiry.

7.3 Is there a role for authorities?

When the inefficiency of any market, including the stock market, is mentioned, economists often have one of the two opposite reactions. Some of them, particularly those who spend time in Washington, get the itch to intervene to correct 'market failures.' In their view, government intervention is nearly always benign and typically effective. Other economists, particularly those who spend time in Chicago, respond to the possibility of government intervention by denying the existence of a market inefficiency in the first place. To them, government intervention is almost never benign and even less often effective. It should be resisted at all costs, perhaps even the cost of denying the reality of market inefficiency in the first place.

It may be better to adopt a more judicious perspective than the two extremes: markets are sometimes inefficient, and some policies may help improve efficiency, but government intervention often makes matters worse and therefore should be viewed with considerable skepticism (Stigler 1964, Shleifer and Vishny 1998). From this perspective, it is possible to say a few things about at least some government interventions in financial markets. Here we briefly consider just three policies where market efficiency considerations enter the discussions: investor protection, lender of last resort, and curbs on trading. In all these debates, market efficiency is only one of several relevant matters, and hence the discussion here is extremely tentative.

One area where the authorities play a crucial role in financial markets is the protection of investors from theft and expropriation by corporate insiders. When insiders are not prevented from stealing from the firm (i.e. from the outside investors) by law or regulation, they often do so in a variety of ways, including excessive compensation, transfer pricing, and asset diversion to related companies controlled by insiders, and simple theft. These problems take a relatively mild form in the U.K. and the United States, a more extreme form in Continental Europe, and become the central reality of financial markets in some Asian countries and Russia. The protection of investors from expropriation requires government intervention in the form of legal rules, such as disclosure requirements, legal recourse against abuse and expropriation by directors, and bankruptcy procedures advantageous to creditors. Effective protection also requires good enforcement of these rules, such as functioning and relatively uncorrupt courts and regulatory agencies. Without investor protection, financial markets simply disintegrate.

In fact, recent research documents significant adverse consequences of the failure of a legal regime to protect investors. Countries with strong legal protections of minority shareholders and creditors have bigger and broader capital markets, larger firms, more initial public offerings, and more dispersed corporate ownership even controlling for firm size (ECGN 1997, La Porta *et al.* 1997, 1998; La Porta *et al.* 1999). They also have more efficient markets, in which prices more accurately reflect the fundamentals of individual companies (Morck *et al.* 2000). The evidence also shows that, when investor protection is poor, investment funds are not allocated efficiently across activities (Wurgler 2000), since entrepreneurs with profitable projects need not be the ones with access to funds and investors do not entrust their funds to entrepreneurs. These failures of markets to work well have significant real consequences. Levine and Zervos (2000) and Rajan and Zingales (1998) show that poor investor protection policies, through their adverse effects on capital market development, retard economic growth. And Johnson *et al.* (1999) find that, during the financial crisis of 1997–98, countries with bad investor protection have experienced greater declines in their financial markets than did the countries with good protection.

In the area of investor protection, more activist governments—such as those in the United States and the U.K.—have done a lot more for the development of financial markets than the less activist governments in Continental Europe, Latin America, and East Asia. This, perhaps, has been the clearest case of advantageous government regulation of financial markets. This is not to say that financial regulations and regulators have been perfect in the United States: Stigler (1964) and Miller (1997) offer stinging criticisms of the Securities and Exchange Commission's interventionism. While the U.S. regulators may be overly zealous, the fact remains that the U.S. (and British) capital markets are tremendously broad and liquid, attract tens of millions of investors, and remain the ultimate place where companies seeking equity funds seek to be listed. The heavy disclosure requirements, and the broad shareholder powers including the right to sue directors, do not deter these firms. It remains an open question whether financial markets in other countries will converge to this model, or whether political and historical obstacles will prevent convergence (Coffee 1999).

Another area where the case for government intervention is fairly strong, though more controversial, is the lender of last resort. This case makes little sense when financial markets are efficient, since in such markets security prices are always at efficient levels and are unaffected by liquidations. In contrast, the model in Chapter 4 shows that financial panics can lead to failures of arbitrage and market inefficiencies. Such inefficiencies may well undermine the financial system as well as the real economy: as collateral values of firms' assets decline, so does their ability to borrow, invest, and produce. The lender of last resort—such as the Bank of England or the Federal Reserve—can inject liquidity into financial institutions that are subject to bank runs or other forms of liquidation, thereby preventing the inefficient collapse of security prices, further liquidations, and a real recession (see Bagehot 1872 and Kindleberger 1978). Here, as well, there is a positive role for government intervention in securities markets, although the risks of governments becoming too soft in their rescue policies are definitely present.

There is an intimate and largely ignored relationship between the quality of investor protection, the susceptibility of financial markets to a crisis, and the need for the lender of last resort. When investor protection works well, creditors can repossess and sell collateral or reschedule their loans to the borrowers, and shareholders can attempt to restructure the company or its management without the fear that the insiders will steal whatever assets remain before the creditors show up. When financial shocks can be worked out privately, or with minimum government intervention, the likelihood of systemic collapses and the need for major bailouts is lower. The Long Term Capital Management (LTCM) example in Chapter 4 illustrates this point extremely well: the creditors were able to take control of an extremely complex company with only a minor intervention from the Federal Reserve and with no public money. When corporate governance mechanisms work effectively, the demands on the lender of last resort are that much smaller. In contrast, when corporate governance mechanisms do not function well, as was the case in Asia in 1998, the financial system itself cannot work out the shocks, and is therefore much more susceptible to a collapse. This, of course, is exactly what Johnson *et al.* (1999) find in their study of the Asian crisis: countries with the best corporate governance experienced the mildest crises.

Perhaps the most controversial area of government intervention in securities markets is policies aimed to stabilize, or even fix, securities prices. The best known example of such policies is fixing the exchange rates, but there are many others. These include government purchases of equities to prevent price collapses, as was done by the Ministry of Finance in Japan in the 1990s and by the Hong Kong Monetary Authority in 1998; trading halts and circuit breakers to prevent panics (Greenwald and Stein 1988); transaction taxes to prevent excess volatility, as practiced in some European countries and advocated by Summers and Summers (1988); and perhaps other measures as well. Relatedly, one can wonder whether opening up new markets improves risk sharing opportunities and arbitrage, or only facilitates speculation.

Generally speaking, advocates of restrictions on trading make two types of argument. The first is alleviation of a panic and financial distress. The second is discouragement of speculation. It is difficult to believe that fixing prices, whether of currencies or equities, or preventing them from falling, is a good way to prevent a panic. Government price stabilization only invites speculation against the government, which often leads to eventual price collapses after the expenditure of enormous funds on price stabilization, as the many currency crises in the 1990s have shown. More direct lender of last resort policies may achieve the same goal without subsidizing the arbitrageurs. Consistent with this skepticism, Roll (1989) examines the magnitude of the 1987 stock market crash in a number of countries, and finds no evidence that countries that had stock market rules limiting price movements experienced smaller crashes.

Policies restricting market trading are extremely controversial. Whether they are desirable depends to some extent on whether they primarily discourage noise traders or arbitrageurs. Even if they primarily discourage the noise traders, such policies may not be desirable. For example, by limiting participation in financial markets, such policies keep stock prices down even when high stock prices encourage both privately and socially desirable investment. The Internet bubble of the late 1990s might be welfare-enhancing. Even aside from the effect of noise traders on prices, discouraging people from investing when they enjoy doing it and there are no clear *negative* externalities is not an obviously good thing for the state to do.

If restrictions on trading primarily discourage arbitrageurs, they may make markets more volatile, and make inefficiencies associated with panics more extreme. If anything, the theoretical presumption is that restrictions on trading do discourage arbitrageurs. As we have shown in Chapters 2 and 4, the aggressiveness of arbitrageurs in countering mispricing depends on how well they can hedge their risks. Continuous trading, low cost trading, and the availability of derivative instruments such as futures and options all facilitate hedging by arbitrageurs and therefore make them more aggressive in betting against the noise traders. Opening up markets makes arbitrage cheaper and more effective, shutting them down keeps arbitrageurs out or even sends them away to other markets, reducing market efficiency. Indeed, the rapid development of financial markets around the world, including the creation of new derivatives and other markets, has been accompanied by significant capital flows to poorer countries, in part because investors could better hedge their risks. Finally, as Keynes (1936) was early to recognize, policies that make trading more expensive reduce market liquidity, and therefore are likely to discourage all investors from participation in markets, raising the cost of capital and discouraging real investment in the first place. In general, security price stabilization by the government appears to be a highly dubious proposition.

7.4 Open problems

Much of this chapter has presented opinions about issues in financial economics that are only beginning to be understood. In conclusion, it seems useful to briefly summarize some of the open problems. The list presented below is highly subjective, and includes without discussion many problems that have been mentioned elsewhere in the book. The goal is to highlight some of the areas of intellectual excitement rather than to point to any solutions.

Twenty broad problems in behavioral finance

Investors

1 How do investors perceive risk? How are perceptions related to the actual fundamental risk, and how are they shaped by investors' own successes and failures and the framing of the investment problem?

2 How do investors evaluate risk? Why do they sometimes gamble, e.g. by investing in Internet stocks, and sometimes reveal extreme caution, e.g. by avoiding equities? Do they have different mental accounts for different investments (Poker Chips and Nest Eggs)?

3 What are the catalysts that prompt people to form an extrapolative (trend-chasing) model of returns on some security, or a group of securities? How do bubbles get started?

4 What are the important psychological phenomena shaping investor demand for stocks, and what, in contrast, are the 'just-so' stories?

5 Why do different investors have such different models of what are good investments? Why do they trade so much with each other?

Markets

1 Why do the mechanisms of borrowing securities and selling them short appear so underdeveloped? Why are some crucial securities that arbitrageurs need missing altogether?

2 How long does it take arbitrage to eliminate a money-making regularity, and what does this depend on? Why do some 'anomalies' persist so much longer than others?

3 What is the life cycle of an investment style? How does it originate, become more popular, and disappear? Is it better to be a lone arbitrageur in a market because the opportunities are the best, or is there strength in numbers because prices converge faster to fundamental values?

4 Where do indexing and quasi-indexing lead us? How big can the index premium get? What, if anything, will eliminate it?

5 How do 'corrections' set in? Do earnings or other news act as a catalyst? Or is there a big self-fulfilling element, whereby small news reveal large amounts of information?

Real consequences

1 How central is investor sentiment for security issuance? What do firms do to market their securities? How are dividends and earnings 'managed' to improve sentiment?

2 What, if any, are the investment distortions arising from market inefficiencies? Do bubbles help finance good investment projects that would not be financed otherwise, or encourage the undertaking of wasteful projects?

3 Does opening markets, or facilitating trading more generally, only increase speculation or does it primarily improve arbitrage? When does it do more harm, more good?

4 What are the benefits of portfolio investment in a country, and what are the costs?

5 What are the consequences of investors doing badly in financial markets—because of unwise investment choices or even ripoffs—for their willingness to participate in the future?

Policy

1 When should the government intervene to 'stabilize' security prices (e.g. fix exchange rates, buy securities, stop trading, etc.)? How can governments be encouraged to intervene when they should and not when they should not?

2 How can noise trading be discouraged (assuming that it should be) without discouraging arbitrage? Who should regulate securities markets and how?

3 Should disclosure by money managers be improved? Is continuous marking portfolios to market desirable, or does it cause trigger-happy front-running and liquidations by creditors, and consequent crashes? Is transparency of intermediaries always good, or does it encourage panics?

4 Who, if anyone, should be rescued in distress, and by whom?

5 Can investor education overcome psychological biases, and if so, how? Why aren't there private 'de-biasing' services?

Many of these problems remain poorly understood. In fact, most of them have trivial answers if financial markets are efficient, and extremely complex answers if they are not. But progress is in sight. We now understand that arbitrage is a costly activity limited by risk aversion and severe agency problems. Viewed as an economic activity itself, arbitrage does not automatically, or even readily, lead to market efficiency even when arbitrageurs fiercely compete with each other for profits. We also understand that investor sentiment influences security prices, and recognize some of the ways in which this sentiment is formed. In particular, when sentiment is correlated across investors and is therefore systematic, its effect on security prices is likely to be large. The evidence and the theory in behavioral finance tell the same story: financial markets are inefficient, *just as an economist would expect*. Moreover, once we begin to see financial markets as places where these different types of investors—some rational, some not—trade, and understand the forces that shape their demands for securities, we can begin to think about many new problems. Tremendous opportunities for both research and intelligent discussions of how to make markets more efficient open up.

Bibliography

Alpert, M. and Raiffa, H. (1982). 'A progress report on the training of probability assessors'. *Judgment under Uncertainty: Heuristics and Biases*. In Daniel Kahneman, Paul Slovic, and Amos Tversky (eds.) Cambridge: Cambridge University Press.

Anderson, S. (1986). 'Closed-end funds versus market efficiency'. *Journal of Portfolio Management*, 13:63–7.

Bagehot, W. (1872). *Lombard Street*. London: Smith, Elder.

Baker, M. and Wurgler, J. (2000). 'The equity share in new issues and aggregate stock returns'. *Journal of Finance*, forthcoming.

Barberis, N., Huang, M., and Santos, T. (1999) 'Prospect theory and asset prices'. Mimeo, University of Chicago.

Barberis, N., Shleifer, A., and Vishny, R. (1998). 'A model of investor sentiment'. *Journal of Financial Economics*, 49:307–43.

Barsky, R., and De Long, J. B. (1993). 'Why does the stock market fluctuate?' *Quarterly Journal of Economics*, 108:291–311.

Benartzi, S. and Thaler, R. (1995). 'Myopic loss aversion and the equity premium puzzle'. *Quarterly Journal of Economics*, 110:73–92.

Bernard, V. (1992). 'Stock price reactions to earnings announcements'. In R. Thaler, (ed.), *Advances in Behavioral Finance*. New York: Russell Sage Foundation.

Bernard, V., and Thomas, J. K. (1989). 'Post-earnings announcement drift: delayed price response or risk premium?' *Journal of Accounting Research*, Supplement 27:1–36.

Bernard, V. and Thomas, J. K. (1990). 'Evidence that stock prices do not fully reflect the implications of current earnings for future earnings'. *Journal of Accounting and Economics*, 13:305–41.

Black, F. (1986). 'Noise'. *Journal of Finance*, 41:529–43.

Black, F. (1988). 'An equilibrium model of the crash'. *NBER Macroeconomics Annual*, 269–76.

Black, F. (1993). 'Beta and return'. *Journal of Portfolio Management*, 20:8–18.

Blanchard, O. and Watson, M. (1982). 'Bubbles, rational expectations, and financial markets'. In P. Wachtel (ed.) *Crises in the Economic and Financial Structure*. Lexington, MA: Lexington Books.

Bodurtha, J., Kim, D., and Lee, C. M. (1993). 'Closed-end country funds and U.S. market sentiment'. *Review of Financial Studies*, 8:879–918.

Boudreaux, K. J. (1973). 'Discounts and premium on closed-end mutual funds: A study in valuation'. *Journal of Finance*, 28:515–22.

Brauer, G. A. (1984). 'Open-ending closed-end funds'. *Journal of Financial Economics*, 13:491–507.

Brauer, G. A. (1988). 'Closed-end fund shares' abnormal returns and the information content of discounts and premiums'. *Journal of Finance*, 43:113–28.

Brauer, G. A. and Chang, E. (1990). 'Return seasonality in stocks and their underlying assets: Tax loss selling versus information explanations'. *Review of Financial Studies*, 3:257–80.

Brav, A. and Gompers, P. (1997). 'Myth or Reality? The long-run underperformance of initial public offerings: Evidence from venture and nonventure capital-backed companies'. *Journal of Finance*, 52:1791–1821.

Brav, A., Geczy, C., and Gompers, P. (1999). 'Is the abnormal return following equity issuances anomalous?' Mimeo, Duke University.

Brickley, J. A. and Schallheim, J. S. (1985). 'Lifting the lid on closed-end investment companies: A case of abnormal returns'. *Journal of Financial and Quantitative Analysis*, 20:107–17.

Campbell, J. Y. and Cochrane, J. (1999). 'By force of habit: A consumption-based explanation of aggregate stock market behavior'. *Journal of Political Economy*, 107:205–51 .

Campbell, J. Y. and Kyle, A. (1993). 'Smart money, noise trading, and stock price behavior'. *Review of Economic Studies*, 60:1–34.

Campbell, J. Y. and Shiller, R. (1988). 'Stock prices, earnings, and expected dividends'. *Journal of Finance*, 43:661–76.

Campbell, J. Y., and Shiller, R. (1998). 'Valuation ratios and the long-run stock market outlook'. *Journal of Portfolio Management*, 24:11–26.

Campbell, J. Y., Grossman, S., and Wang, J. (1993). 'Trading volume and serial correlation in stock returns'. *Quarterly Journal of Economics*, 108:905–39.

Case, K., and Shiller, R. (1988). 'The behavior of home buyers in boom and post boom markets'. In R. Shiller (1989), *Market Volatility*. Cambridge, MA:MIT Press.

Chan, L., Jegadeesh, N., and Lakonishok, J. (1996). 'Momentum strategies'. *Journal of Finance*, 51:1681–713.

Chen, N., Roll, R., and Ross, S. (1986). 'Economic forces and the stock market'. *Journal of Business*, 59:383–403.

Chevalier, J. and Ellison, G. (1997). 'Risk taking by mutual funds as a response to incentives'. *Journal of Political Economy*, 105:1167–200.

Chopra, N., Lakonishok, J., and Ritter, J. (1992). 'Measuring abnormal performance: Do stocks overreact?' *Journal of Financial Economics*, 31:235–68.

Chopra, N., Lee, C. M., Shleifer, A., and Thaler, R. (1993). 'Yes, discounts on closed-end funds are a sentiment index'. *Journal of Finance*, 48:801–08.

Coffee, J. (1999). 'The future as history: The prospects for global convergence in corporate governance and its implications', *Northwestern Law Review*, 93:631–707.

Cutler, D., Poterba, J., and Summers, L. (1991). 'Speculative dynamics'. *Review of Economic Studies*, 58:529–46.

Daniel, K., Hirshleifer, D., and Subrahmanyam, A. (1998). 'Investor psychology and security market under- and overreactions'. *Journal of Finance*, 53:1839–85.

De Bondt, W. F. M. (1993). 'Betting on trends: Intuitive forecasts of financial risk and return'. *International Journal of Forecasting*, 9:355–71.

De Bondt, W. F. M. and Thaler, R. (1985). 'Does the stock market overreact?' *Journal of Finance*, 40:793–805.

De Bondt, W. F. M., and Thaler, R. (1987). 'Further evidence on investor overreaction and stock market seasonality'. *Journal of Finance*, 42:557–81.

De Long, J. B. and Shleifer, A. (1991). 'The stock market bubble of 1929: Evidence from closed-end mutual funds'. *Journal of Economic History*, 51:675–700.

De Long, J. B., and Shleifer, A. (1993). 'Anatomy of a price bubble'. Mimeo, Harvard University.

De Long, J. B., Shleifer, A., Summers, L., and Waldmann, R. (1987). 'Noise trader risk in financial markets'. NBER Working Paper no. 2395. Cambridge, MA:NBER.

De Long, J. B., Shleifer, A., Summers, L., and Waldmann, R. (1989). 'The size and incidence of the losses from noise trading'. *Journal of Finance*, 44:681–96.

De Long, J. B., Shleifer, A., Summers, L., and Waldmann, R. (1990a). 'Noise trader risk in financial markets'. *Journal of Political Economy*, 98:703–38.

De Long, J. B., Shleifer, A., Summers, L., and Waldmann, R. (1990b). 'Positive feedback investment strategies and destabilizing rational speculation'. *Journal of Finance*, 45:375–95.

De Long, J. B., Shleifer, A., Summers, L., and Waldmann, R. (1991). 'The survival of noise traders in financial markets'. *Journal of Business*, 64:1–19.

Dimson, E. and Minio-Kozerski, C. (1998). 'Closed-end funds: A survey'. Manuscript, London Business School.

Dreman, D. and Berry, M. (1995). 'Overreaction, underreaction, and the low-p/e effect'. *Financial Analysts Journal*, 51:21–30.

Durell, A. (1999). 'Consumer confidence and stock market returns'. Manuscript, Harvard University.

Edwards, W. (1968), 'Conservatism in human information processing'. In B. Kleinmutz (ed.), *Formal Representation of Human Judgment*. New York: John Wiley and Sons.

European Corporate Governance Network (1997). 'The separation of ownership and control: A survey of 7 European Countries'. http://www.ecgn.ulb.ac.be/ecgn.

Fama, E. (1965). 'The behavior of stock market prices'. *Journal of Business*, 38:34–106.

Fama, E. (1970). 'Efficient capital markets: A review of theory and empirical work'. *Journal of Finance*, 25:383–417.

Fama, E. (1991). 'Efficient capital markets: II'. *Journal of Finance*, 46:1575–617.

Fama, E. (1998). 'Market efficiency, long-term returns, and behavioral finance'. *Journal of Financial Economics*, 49:283–306.

Fama, E. and French, K. (1988a). 'Dividend yields and expected stock returns'. *Journal of Financial Economics*, 22:3–25.

Fama, E. and French, K. (1988b). 'Permanent and temporary components of stock prices'. *Journal of Political Economy*, 96:246–73.

Fama, E. and French, K. (1992). 'The cross-section of expected stock returns'. *Journal of Finance*, 47:427–65.

Fama, E. and French, K. (1993). 'Common risk factors in the returns on bonds and stocks'. *Journal of Financial Economics*, 33:3–56.

Fama, E. and French, K. (1996). 'Multifactor explanations of asset pricing anomalies'. *Journal of Finance*, 51:55–84.

Fama, E. and French, K. (1998). 'Value versus growth: the international evidence'. *Journal of Finance*, 53:1975–99.

Fama, E., Fisher, L., Jensen, M., and Roll, R. (1969). 'The adjustment of stock prices to new information'. *International Economic Review*,10:1–21.

Figlewski, S. (1979). 'Subjective information and market efficiency in a betting market'. *Journal of Political Economy*, 87:75–88.

Frankel, J. and Froot, K. (1988). 'Explaining the demand for dollars: International rates of return and the expectations of chartists and fundamentalists'. In R. Chambers and P. Paarlberg, (eds.), *Agriculture, Macroeconomics, and the Exchange Rate.* Boulder, CO:Westfield Press.

Friedman, M. (1953). 'The case for flexible exchange rates'. In *Essays in Positive Economics.* Chicago: University of Chicago Press.

Froot, K. A. and Dabora, E. (1999). 'How are stock prices affected by the location of trade'. *Journal of Financial Economics*, 53:189–216.

Gompers, P. and Metrick, A. (1999). 'Institutional investors and equity prices'. Mimeo, Harvard University.

Goodman, G. [Adam Smith] (1968). *The Money Game.* New York: McGraw-Hill.

Graham, B. (1974). *The Intelligent Investor.* New York: Harper and Row.

Graham, B. and Dodd, D. (1934). *Security Analysis.* New York: McGraw-Hill.

Greenwald, B. and Stein J. (1988). 'The task force report: The reasoning behind the recommendations'. *Journal of Economic Perspectives*, 2:3–24.

Griffin, D. and Tversky, A. (1992). 'The weighing of evidence and the determinants of confidence'. *Cognitive Psychology*, 24:411–35.

Grossman, S. and Hart, O. (1980). 'Takeover bids, the free-rider problem, and the theory of the corporation'. *Bell Journal of Economics*, 11:42–64.

Grossman, S. and Hart, O. (1986). 'The costs and benefits of ownership: A theory of vertical and lateral integration'. *Journal of Political Economy*, 94:691–719.

Grossman, S. and Miller, M. (1988). 'Liquidity and market structure'. *Journal of Finance*, 43:617–33.

Grossman, S. and Stiglitz, J. (1980). 'On the impossibility of informationally efficient markets'. *American Economic Review*, 70:393–408.

Hardouvelis, G., La Porta, R., and Wizman, T. (1994). 'What moves the discount on country equity funds?' In Jeffrey Frankel (Ed.), *The Internationalization of Equity Markets*. Chicago: University Press of Chicago.

Harris, L. and Gurel, E. (1986). 'Price and volume effects associated with changes in the S&P 500: New evidence for the existence of price pressure'. *Journal of Finance*, 41:851–60.

Haugen, R. A. and Baker, N. (1996). 'Commonality in the determinants of expected stock returns'. *Journal of Financial Economics*, 41:401–39.

Herzfeld, T. J. (1980). *The Investor's Guide to Closed-end Funds*. New York: McGraw-Hill.

Hong, H. and Stein, J. (1999). 'A unified theory of underreaction, momentum trading and overreaction in asset markets'. *Journal of Finance*, 54:2143–84.

Ibbotson, R., Sindelar, J., and Ritter, J. (1988). 'Initial public offerings'. *Journal of Applied Corporate Finance*, 1:37–45.

Ikenberry, D., Lakonishok, J., and Vermaelen, T. (1995). 'Market underreaction to open market share repurchases'. *Journal of Financial Economics*, 39:181–208.

Ikenberry, D., Rankine, G., and Stice, E. (1996). 'What do stock splits really signal?' *Journal of Financial and Quantitative Analysis*, 31:357–75.

Ippolito, R. (1989). 'Efficiency with costly information: A study of mutual fund performance'. *Quarterly Journal of Economics*, 104:1–23.

Jegadeesh, N. and Titman, S. (1993). 'Returns to buying winners and selling losers: implications for stock market efficiency'. *Journal of Finance*, 48:65–91.

Jeng, L., Metrick, A., and Zeckhauser, R. (1999). 'The profits to insider trading: A performance-evaluation perspective'. NBER Working Paper #6913. Cambridge, MA: NBER.

Jensen, M. (1968). 'The performance of mutual funds in the period 1945–1964'. *Journal of Finance*, 23:389–416.

Jensen, M. (1978). 'Some anomalous evidence regarding market efficiency'. *Journal of Financial Economics*, 6:95–101.

Johnson, S., Boone, P., Breach, A., and Friedman, E. (1999).

'Corporate governance in the Asian financial crisis, 1997–98'. Mimeo, MIT.

Kahneman, D. and Riepe, M. (1998). 'Aspects of investor psychology'. *Journal of Portfolio Management*, 24:52–65.

Kahneman, D. and Tversky, A. (1973). 'On the Psychology of Prediction'. *Psychological Review*, 80:237–51.

Kahneman, D. and Tversky, A. (1979). 'Prospect theory: An analysis of decision under risk'. *Econometrica*, 47:263–91.

Keown, A. and Pinkerton, J. (1981). 'Merger announcements and insider trading activity: An empirical investigation'. *Journal of Finance*, 36:855–69.

Keynes, J. (1931). 'An economic analysis of unemployment'. In *Collected Writings, Volume XII*. London: Macmillan.

Keynes, J. (1936). *The General Theory of Employment, Interest, and Money*. London: Macmillan.

Kindleberger, C. (1978). *Manias, Panics, and Crashes*. New York: Basic Books.

Kothari, S. and Shanken, J. (1997). 'Book-to-market, dividend yield, and expected market returns: A time series analysis'. *Journal of Financial Economics*, 46:169–203.

Kyle, A. (1985). 'Continuous auctions and insider trading'. *Econometrica*, 47:1315–36.

La Porta, R. (1996). 'Expectations and the cross-section of stock returns'. *Journal of Finance*, 51:1715–42.

La Porta, R., Lakonishok, J., Shleifer, A., and Vishny, R. (1997) 'Good news for value stocks: further evidence on market efficiency'. *Journal of Finance*, 52:859–74.

La Porta, R., Lopez-de-Silanes, F., and Shleifer, A. (1999). 'Corporate ownership around the world'. *Journal of Finance*, 54:471–517.

La Porta, R., Lopez-de-Silanes, F., Shleifer, A., and Vishny, R. (1997). 'Legal determinants of external finance'. *Journal of Finance*, 52:1131–50.

La Porta, R., Lopez-de-Silanes, F., Shleifer, A., and Vishny, R. (1998). 'Law and finance'. *Journal of Political Economy*, 106:1113–55.

Lakonishok, J., Shleifer, A., Thaler, R., and Vishny, R. (1991). 'Window dressing by pension fund managers'. *American Economic Review Papers and Proceedings*, 81:227–31.

Lakonishok, J., Shleifer, A., and Vishny, R. (1992). 'The structure and performance of the money management industry'. *Brookings Papers on Economic Activity Microeconomics*, 339–91.

Lakonishok, J., Shleifer, A., and Vishny, R. (1994). 'Contrarian investment, extrapolation, and risk'. *Journal of Finance*, 49:1541–78.

Lee, C. M., Shleifer, A., and Thaler, R. (1991). 'Investor sentiment and the closed-end fund puzzle'. *Journal of Finance*, 46:75–110.

Lehmann, B. (1990). 'Fads, martingales, and market efficiency'. *Quarterly Journal of Economics*, 105:1–28.

Leland, H., and Rubinstein, M. (1988). 'Comments on the market crash: Six months after'. *Journal of Economic Perspectives*, 2:45–50.

Lerner, J. (1994). 'Venture capitalists and the decision to go public'. *Journal of Financial Economics*, 35:293–316.

Levine, R. and Zervos, S. (1998). 'Stock markets, banks, and economic growth'. *The American Economic Review*, 88:537–58.

Lintner, J. (1956). 'Distribution of incomes of corporations among dividends, retained earnings, and taxes'. *American Economic Review*, 46:97–113.

Loughran, T. and Ritter, J. (1995) 'The new issues puzzle'. *Journal of Finance*, 50:23–51.

Loughran, T. and Ritter, J. (1997). 'The operating performance of firms conducting seasoned equity offerings,' *Journal of Finance*, 52:1823–50.

Malkiel, B. (1977). 'The valuation of closed-end investment company shares'. *Journal of Finance*, 32:847–59.

Mandelbrot, B. (1966). 'Forecasts of future prices, unbiased markets, and martingale models'. *Journal of Business*, 39:242–55.

Mehra, R. and Prescott, E. (1985). 'The equity premium: A puzzle'. *Journal of Monetary Economics*, 15:145–61.

Merton, R. (1987a). 'A simple model of capital market equilibrium with incomplete information'. *Journal of Finance*, 42:483–510.

Merton, R. (1987b). 'On the current state of the stock market rationality hypothesis'. In R. Dornbusch, S. Fischer, and J. Bossons (eds) *Macroeconomics and Finance: Essays in Honor of Franco Modigliani*. Cambridge, MA: MIT Press.

Merton, R. and Samuelson, P. (1974). 'Fallacy of the log-normal approximation to optimal portfolio decision-making over many periods'. *Journal of Financial Economics*, 1:67–94.

Michaely, R., Thaler, R., and Womack, K. (1995) 'Price reactions to dividend initiations and omissions: Overreaction or drift?' *Journal of Finance*, 50:573–608.

Miller, M. (1997). *Merton Miller on Derivatives*. New York: John Wiley & Sons.

Miller, M. and Modigliani, F. (1961). 'Dividend policy, growth, and the valuation of shares,' *Journal of Business*, 34:411–33.

Modigliani, F. and Miller, M. (1958). 'The cost of capital, corporation finance, and the theory of investment'. *American Economic Review*, 48:655–69.

Morck, R., Shleifer, A., and Vishny, R. (1990). 'The stock market and investment: Is the stock market a sideshow', *Brookings Papers on Economic Activity*, 2:157–215.

Morck, R., Yeung, B., and Yu, W. (2000) 'The information content of stock markets: Why do emerging markets have synchronous stock price movements?' *Journal of Financial Economics*, forthcoming.

Odean, T. (1998). 'Are investors reluctant to realize their losses?' *Journal of Finance*, 53:1775–98.

Peavy, J. (1990). 'Returns on initial public offerings of closed-end funds'. *Review of Financial Studies*, 3:695–708.

Pontiff, J. (1996). 'Costly arbitrage: Evidence from closed-end funds'. *Quarterly Journal of Economics*, 111:1135–52.

Pontiff, J. and Schall, J. (1998). 'Book-to-market ratios as predictors of market returns'. *Journal of Financial Economics*, 49:141–60.

Poterba, J. and Summers, L. (1988). 'Mean reversion in stock returns: Evidence and implications'. *Journal of Financial Economics*, 22:27–59.

Pulvino, T. (1998) 'Do asset fire sales exist: An empirical investigation of commercial aircraft transactions'. *Journal of Finance*, 53:939–78.

Rabin, M. (1998). 'Psychology and economics'. *Journal of Economic Literature*, 36:11–46.

Rajan, R. and Servaes, H. (1996). 'Analyst following of initial public offerings'. Mimeo, University of Chicago.

Rajan, R. and Zingales, L. (1998). 'Financial dependence and growth'. *American Economic Review*, 88:559–86.

Rashes, M. (1998*a*). 'Optimal hedging of noise trader risk'. Mimeo, Harvard University.

Rashes, M. (1998*b*). 'Massively confused investors making conspicuously ignorant choices (MCI-MCIC)'. Mimeo, Harvard University.

Richards, R. M., Fraser, D., and Groth, J. (1980). 'Winning strategies for closed-end funds'. *Journal of Portfolio Management*, 7(1):50–5.

Ritter, J. (1988). 'The buying and selling behavior of individual investors at the turn of the year'. *Journal of Finance*, 43:701–17.

Ritter, J. (1991). 'The long-run performance of initial public offerings'. *Journal of Finance*, 42:365–94.

Roenfeldt, R. and Tuttle, D. (1973). 'An examination of the discounts and premiums of closed-end investment companies'. *Journal of Business Research*, 1:129–40.

Roll, R. (1984). 'Orange juice and weather'. *American Economic Review*, 74:861–80.

Roll, R. (1988). 'R^2'. *Journal of Finance*, 43:541–66.

Roll, R. (1989). 'The international crash of 1987'. In R. Kamphuis, R. Kormendi, and J. W. Watson (eds), *Black Monday and the Future of Financial Markets*. Homewood, IL:Dow Jones-Irwin, Inc.

Rosenthal, L. and Young, C. (1990). 'The seemingly anomalous price behavior of Royal Dutch Shell and Unilever nv/plc'. *Journal of Financial Economics*, 26:123–41.

Ross, S. (1976). 'The arbitrage theory of capital asset pricing'. *Journal of Economic Theory*, 13:341–60.

Ross, S., Jaffe, J., and Westerfield, R. (1992). *Corporate Finance*, 3rd edition. Burr Ridge, IL: Irwin.

Rouwenhorst, G. (1997). 'International momentum strategies'. *Journal of Finance*, 53:267–84.

Russell, T. and Thaler, R. (1985). 'The relevance of quasi rationality in competitive markets'. *American Economic Review*, 75:1071–82.

Samuelson, P. (1958). 'An exact consumption loan model of interest with or without the social contrivance of money'. *Journal of Political Economy*, 66:467–82.

Samuelson, P. (1965). 'Proof that properly anticipated prices fluctuate randomly'. *Industrial Management Review*, 6:41–49.

Scharfstein, D. and Stein, J. (1990). 'Herd behavior and investment'. *American Economic Review*, 80:465–89.

Scholes, M. (1972). 'The market for securities: Substitution versus price pressure and effects of information on share prices'. *Journal of Business*, 45:179–211.

Seyhun, H. N. (1998). *Investment Intelligence From Insider Trading*. Cambridge: MIT Press.

Sharpe, W. (1964). 'Capital asset prices: A theory of market equilibrium under conditions of risk'. *Journal of Finance*, 19:425–42.

Sharpe, W. and Alexander, G. (1990). *Investments*, 4th edition. Englewood, NJ: Prentice Hall.

Sharpe, W. and Sosin, H. (1975). 'Closed-end investment companies in the United States: Risk and return'. In B. Jacquillat (ed.), *European Finance Association 1974 Proceedings*. Amsterdam: North-Holland, 37–63.

Shiller, R. (1981). 'Do stock prices move too much to be justified by subsequent changes in dividends'. *American Economic Review*, 71:421–36.

Shiller, R. (1984). 'Stock prices and social dynamics'. *Brookings Papers on Economic Activity*, 2:457–98.

Shiller, R. (1988). 'Portfolio insurance and other investor fashions as factors in the 1987 stock market crash'. *NBER Macroeconomics Annual 1988*, 287–96.

Shiller, R. (1989). *Market Volatility*. Cambridge, MA:MIT Press.

Shleifer, A. (1986). 'Do demand curves for stocks slope down?' *Journal of Finance*, 41:579–90.

Shleifer, A. and Summers, L. (1990). 'The noise trader approach to finance'. *Journal of Economic Perspectives*, 4:19–33.

Shleifer, A. and Vishny, R. (1990). 'Equilibrium short horizons of investors and firms'. *American Economic Review Papers and Proceedings*, 80:148–53.

Shleifer, A. and Vishny, R. (1992). 'Liquidation values and debt capacity—a market equilibrium approach'. *Journal of Finance*, 47:1343–66.

Shleifer, A. and Vishny, R. (1997). 'The limits of arbitrage'. *Journal of Finance*, 52:35–55.

Shleifer, A. and Vishny, R. (1998). *The Grabbing Hand: Government Pathologies and their Cures*. Cambridge:Harvard University Press.

Siegel, J. (1998). *Stocks for the Long Run*. New York: McGraw Hill.

Smith, V., Suchanek, G., and Williams, A. (1998). 'Bubbles, crashes, and endogenous expectations in experimental spot asset markets'. *Econometrica*, 56:1119–53.

Soros, G. (1987). *The Alchemy of Finance*. New York: Simon and Schuster.

Soros, G. (1998). *The Crisis of Global Capitalism*. New York: Public Affairs.

Spiess, D. K. and Affleck-Graves, J. (1995). 'Underperformance in long-run stock returns following seasoned equity offerings'. *Journal of Financial Economics*, 38:243–67.

Stein, J. (1987). 'Informational externalities and welfare-reducing speculation'. *Journal of Political Economy*, 95:1123–45.

Stein, J. (1995). 'Prices and trading volume in the housing market: A model with downpayment effects'. *Quarterly Journal of Economics*, 110:379–406.

Stein, J. (1996). 'Rational capital budgeting in an irrational world'. *Journal of Business*, 69:429–55.

Stigler, G. (1964). 'Public regulation of the securities market'. *Journal of Business*, 37:117–42.

Summers, L. (1985). 'On economics and finance'. *Journal of Finance*, 40:633–35.

Summers, L. (1986). 'Does the stock market rationally reflect fundamental values?' *Journal of Finance*, 41:591–601.

Summers, L. and Summers, V. (1989). 'When financial markets work too well: A cautious case for a securities transactions tax'. *Journal of Financial Services Research*, 3:261–86.

Teoh, S. W., Welch, I., and Wong, T . J. (1998*a*). Earnings management and the long–run market performance of initial public offerings'. *Journal of Finance*, 53:1935–74.

Teoh, S. W., Welch, I., and Wong, T . J. (1998*b*). 'Earnings management and the post-issue under performance in seasoned equity offerings', *Journal of Financial Economics*, 50:63–99.

Thaler, R. and Johnson, E. (1990) 'Gambling with the house money and trying to break even: The effect of prior outcomes on risky choice'. *Management Science*, 36:643–60.

Thompson, R. (1978). 'The information content of discounts and premiums on closed-end fund shares'. *Journal of Financial Economics*, 6:151–86.

Tirole, J. (1982). 'On the possibility of speculation under rational expectations'. *Econometrica* 50:1163–82.

Tobias, A. (1971). *The Funny Money Game*. Chicago, IL: Playboy Press.

Train, J. (1979). 'Pumping up the tulips'. *Forbes* (October 1). Reprinted and expanded in Train, 1987.

Train, J. (1987). *The Money Masters*. New York: Harper and Row.

Tversky, A. and Kahneman, D. (1974). 'Judgement under uncertainty: Heuristics and biases'. *Science*, 185:1124–31.

Warther, V. (1995). 'Aggregate mutual fund flows and security returns'. *Journal of Financial Economics*, 39:209–36.

Weiss, K. (1989). 'The post-offering price performance of closed-end funds'. *Financial Management*, 57–67.

Wiesenberger, A. (1960–1986), *Investment Companies Services, annual surveys*. New York, NY: Warren, Gorham, and Lamont.

Williams, J. B. (1938). *The Theory of Investment Value*. Cambridge: Harvard University Press.

Wurgler, J. (2000). 'Financial markets and the allocation of capital'. *Journal of Financial Economics*, forthcoming.

Wurgler, J. and Zhuravskaya, E. (1999). 'Does arbitrage flatten demand curves for stocks?'. Mimeo, Harvard University.

Zarowin, P. (1989). 'Does the stock market overreact to corporate earnings information?' *Journal of Finance*, 44:1385–400.

Zweig, M. (1973). 'An investor expectations stock price predictive model using closed-end fund premiums'. *Journal of Finance*, 28:67–87.

Index